SHARED WISDOM

BEST PRACTICES IN DEVELOPMENT & SUCCESSION PLANNING

Severance/Security
Contributions

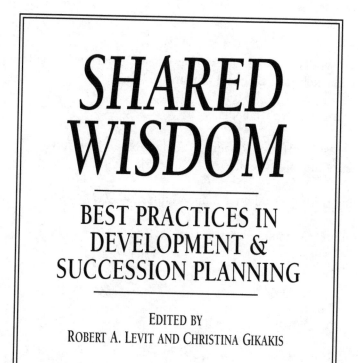

SHARED WISDOM

BEST PRACTICES IN DEVELOPMENT & SUCCESSION PLANNING

EDITED BY
ROBERT A. LEVIT AND CHRISTINA GIKAKIS

THE
HUMAN
RESOURCE
PLANNING
SOCIETY

Shared Wisdom: Best Practices in Development and Succession Planning
Edited by Robert A. Levit and Christina Gikakis

Cover Design: Stephen Bodkin

©1994 by The Human Resource Planning Society, New York
41 East 42nd Street—Suite 1509, New York, NY 10017

For information on additional publications call (212) 490-6387.

Director of Communications: Beverly A. Bachtle

Printed in U.S.A. by Princeton Academic Press

LIBRARY OF CONGRESS CATALOGING-IN-PUBLICATION DATA

Shared wisdom: best practices in development and succession planning /
Edited by Robert A. Levit and Christina Gikakis.

— CIP information applied for —
ISBN 1-881115-05-4

HRPS 1994 BOARD OF DIRECTORS

President
Michael G. Takla   *Towers Perrin*

Treasurer
Duncan F. Tilly   *Canada Trust*

Secretary
Kay Henry   *The Equitable*

Executive Director
Noel Innocenti

Board Members

Thomas P. Bechet	*The Walker Group*
Walter J. Cleaver	*Strawbridge & Clothier*
William J. Colucci	*Fingerhut Corporation*
Pam Farr	*Marriott International, Inc.*
Charles H. Fay	*Rutgers University*
Fred K. Foulkes	*Boston University*
Linda A. Hill	*Harvard Business School*
Robert J. Lee	*Lee Hecht Harrison*
Barbara Lehman	*Sears, Roebuck & Company*
Robert A. Levit	*MCI Communications, Inc.*
William R. Maki	*Weyerhaeuser Company*
Leslie A. Mardenborough	*The New York Times Company*
Robert J.W. Mommers	*ABN AMRO Bank*
Nancy Reardon	*Duracell International, Inc.*
Robert B. Reichelt	*Exxon Chemical International, Inc.*
Carol T. Schreiber	*Schreiber Associates*
J. Alan Stopko	*Stopko & Associates*
James W. Walker	*The Walker Group*
Lorena Warren-Clark	*Gencorp*
John Waterson	*The World Bank*
Calhoun W. Wick	*Wick and Company*

THE HUMAN RESOURCE PLANNING SOCIETY

Mission

The Human Resource Planning Society, a not-for-profit membership organization, is committed to improving organizational performance by creating a global network of individuals who function as business partners in the application of strategic human resource management practices.

Membership

The Society has more than 2,400 individual members and 150 Corporate and Research Sponsors representing a unique mix of leading organizations in business, industry and academia. Members are located throughout North America and in many countries overseas.

HRPS members are a distinctive group and represent organizations of all sizes and types—small entrepreneurial businesses, universities and business schools and large multinationals. HRPS has also established a relationship with a sister organization in Europe, the European Human Resource Forum (EHRF), wherein members of either group can participate in events sponsored by either organization.

Over 60% of our members have a graduate level education, and 60% have held non-human resource assignments. Most hold key management and policy-making positions.

The vast majority have direct or indirect responsibility for key human resource management issues such as organizational effectiveness and executive continuity and development.

Above all, HRPS members are partners with their organizations' leadership in driving their organizations toward superior performance through the effective utilization of human resources.

The Human Resource Planning Society offers a variety of professional development workshops, and an Annual Conference, a biennial Research Symposium, and the annual Corporate Sponsor Forum.

The Society also publishes a quarterly journal containing the most current theory, research, and practice in strategic HR management, and a comprehensive index to the journal. Other publications include research symposia proceedings, conference and workshop binders, Best Practices Book series, an annual membership directory, and a quarterly newsletter.

For further information on membership, programs, or publications, please contact the Society at (212) 490-6387.

PREFACE

The Human Resource Planning Society is an educational association. Since its establishment in 1978, HRPS has published the quarterly journal, *Human Resource Planning*, biennial research symposium proceedings, special research reports, and conference proceedings. The wealth of information developed and shared by HRPS members and contributors is significant.

As a service to its members and the wider HR community, HRPS now offers a special series of books providing selected reference materials on "best practices" in strategic human resource management. The purpose of the series is to provide a review and assessment of concepts, approaches, methods and applications in subject areas of interest and value to HRPS members, and to highlight important articles previously published by HRPS.

This series also serves as a new means for members to contribute to the substantive work of the Society. Each book is developed by a team of HRPS-member editors. The team determines the focus and scope of the book, criteria and selection of articles, and inclusion of new material. As a result, each book takes a somewhat different approach and emphasis.

Each book presents what the editorial team considers best practices. Some best practices are leading edge innovations or experimentations. Others are tried and tested practices that are not particularly new. Accordingly, the articles span the history of HRPS. We discovered that much of the excellent original research, ideas, and writing of years ago is highly relevant and useful when examined in a current context.

These books are recommended for personal learning. They will also be valuable references for HRPS workshops, university courses and programs, professional development activities within companies, and the future assessment of human resource management practices, including new best practices as they are developed.

DEVELOPMENT AND SUCCESSION PLANNING

Shared Wisdom: Best Practices In Development and Succession Planning, is the second book in the Best Practices Series. The editors, Robert Levit and Christina Gikakis, engaged a panel of experts in selecting articles and also took the unusual approach of soliciting follow-up comments from the authors of those articles.

The capacity of an organization to adapt to changing conditions and therefore survive, prosper, and grow is dependent on learning. This requires communication of shared experience, termed by the editors as "shared wisdom." Over the years, members of HRPS have sought to strengthen career management, management development, and management succession planning practices to this end. As we approach the 21st century, the effective development and application of practices in these areas are vital. Development of the capabilities of individuals and teams in an organization is a critical lever for gaining and sustaining a competitive advantage.

This book presents fourteen significant articles describing "best practices" in development and succession planning. They define concepts and approaches that will challenge any organization to achieve a higher level of "shared wisdom." In many ways, organizations are not taking full advantage of the technology that has been developed through research and practice over the past decade or more. This book provides a synthesis of this available resource. Additionally, and perhaps most valuable, the "Afterwards Comments" by the authors puts each article's contributions into a contemporary context.

The editors' perspective is based on hands-on experience in major companies, yielding a highly practical book. They have provided a valuable service to HRPS members in this project by focusing on what is most relevant and useful. Their approach for selecting articles, including the use of an executive panel, their successful solicitation of comments from authors, and their diligent work in editing this fine book, have resulted in a unique expression of best practices in development and succession planning.

OTHER BOOKS IN THE SERIES

The first book in the Best Practices Series is on the subject of human resource forecasting and modeling. Since the early days of HRPS, a primary focus of interest has been on staffing issues and, to address these, human resource forecasting and modeling. The collection of articles and research papers edited by Dan Ward (Texaco), Tom Bechet (The Walker Group), and Bob Tripp (General Motors) provide a valuable resource and reference on this subject.

Subsequent books in the series address organizational change, human resource strategy, and the human resource function. As these are published, new topics will be defined and addressed in further books, in response to member interests.

James W. Walker
Series Editor
Best Practices in Strategic Human Resource Management

ABOUT THE EDITORS

R.A. Levit, Ph.D.

Bob Levit is an explorer, who takes others along on his adventures. Levit's forte is the exploration of ideas and how those ideas can lead to creative and innovative action in a new business world still be "mapped". He is a leader and developer of leaders who gets others to expand their definitions and to go beyond what is reasonably expected to chart a new territory of solutions. He has taught leadership development programs at MCI and Honeywell, as well as the Universities of Maryland and Phoenix. He has pioneered the use of historical metaphors such as Lincoln and Churchill in a new kind of leadership program focusing on arete, the Greek concept of individual excellence. Trained as a psychologist, but fascinated by business, Bob earned his Ph.D. at Columbia by combining interests in clinical and organizational work, with the practical issues facing business decision makers. Before returning to private practice in Washington D.C., he was the director of Human Resource Development for MCI Telecommunications Corporation. He is a member of the Board of Directors of the Human Resource Planning Society and serves as an Adjunct Professor at the University of Maryland, University of Phoenix, and the Union Institute.

Christina Grikakis

Christina Grikakis is a consultant specializing in strategic human resource development. She was previously a Human Resource Development Consultant for MCI Communications Corporation, where she designed methods to evaluate the impact of various Human Resource Development initiatives on organizational goals. In addition, she introduced several alternative learning systems throughout MCI. She holds a B.S. in Mechanical Engineering from George Washington University. Currently her interests include introduction of advanced technologies to organizations, and managing technological change through the Human Resouce function.

CONTENTS

INTRODUCTION

One might consider *Shared Wisdom* a funny title for a book of selected Human Resource articles. What does wisdom have to do with HR? As it turns out everything. Sternberg (1990) defines wisdom as: A cognitive process for understanding the world, a compelling guide to action, and a personal good whose implementation leads to satisfaction. To this definition we would add: A sharing of knowledge and experience among an interested community of seekers.

Many good minds, conference and journal papers, and late night debates have been dedicated to just this kind of activity within the Human Resource community. Questions we have attempted to answer include:

- How does HR lead change?
- Are there any core practices that guide our actions?
- How can these practices be applied in changing business conditions?
- How can we share what we have learned with others?

The objective of this book of selected articles is to answer some of these questions within the context of the definition of wisdom. We wanted to take the best of what has been written in *Human Resource Planning* and reassess its meaning for a new generation of practitioners in the next century. We wanted to create a sort of written dialogue between those who have created HR technology and those who will use it in the future.

The emphasis on wisdom as the communication of shared experience is not the only unusual feature of this book. We have adopted a new format to guide the selection and analysis of this material.

- Articles have been selected and analyzed using the quantitative power of content analysis (Holsti, 1969 and Weber, 1990). Rather than passively presenting previously published journal articles, we have actively analyzed the material for its underlying themes to identify enduring practices that might be useful to those who apply this knowledge in the future. Our approach is discussed in next section of this Overview.

- After each of the articles we provide follow-up comments from the authors reflecting on the utility and robustness of the concepts in their original work. This also adds some currency to the authors' original ideas.

- We have added our own reactions, comments, and experiences to the authors' reflections though the section introductions and our own Afterward.

Our overall approach has been to present you with cogent human resource practices derived from fourteen past articles, present interpretations, and thematic analyses of underlying trends. We wanted to both identify the underlying wisdom in our profession and share it with you, the practitioner. Consider, debate, and question what is presented. Above all, let's work together to add to the wisdom shared here.

ARTICLE SELECTION

We used a combination of expert opinion, qualitative analysis, and personal discretion to identify fourteen articles from which our core practices were derived.

- First, a Q-Methodology (McKeown and Thomas, 1988) was used to sort the titles of articles in Volumes 1-15 of *Human Resource Planning* into subject categories which would eventually became our section headings (Career Management, Management Development, and Succession Planning). Outliers not sorted into these categories were eliminated.

- Articles in each category were reviewed by a panel of subject matter experts. The panel was asked to identify those articles illustrating practices key to human resource management in the twenty-first century. Articles not meeting this criteria were eliminated.

- Fifteen candidate articles were computer-scanned and analyzed via a KWIC (key word in context) content analysis (Weber, 1990). The editors' review of the resulting concordances lead to the derivation of the three underlying themes or practices present in the articles selected by the panel.

- One article was eliminated because of our inability to contact the authors to write a retrospective afterward, leaving us with fourteen.

Qualitative Content Analysis

A unique feature of this book is the use of qualitative analysis techniques such as Q-Methods and Content Analysis. Frankly, we applied these methods for two reasons: (1) We wanted to bring some rigor to the selection process and to the derivation of practices on which practitioners could act. (2) We were consciously under the influence of postmodern approaches to the study of organizations (Clegg, 1990; Berquist, 1993; and Boje and Dennehy, 1993).

We are aware that our organizations, and our writings about them, represent a particular viewpoint and philosophy. We wanted to go beyond this to summarize the practices generally applicable to a diverse and global business environment. We are aware that those practices could, however, be a "symptom" of modernity, and may not be totally appropriate to emerging postmodern organizations. More of this in the Afterward.

Underlying themes

Hopefully, you will find many examples of good tactical practices throughout the selected articles. Three strategic practices summarize their overall content. These practices are:

- Human Resource practices are best managed as *systems integrated with other business activities* and with the overall purpose of the organization. Basically, this practice indicates that Human Resources cannot "stand alone as a functional entity," but must actively be part of a bigger system closely linked with the business of the organization. Human Resource practices should be the backbone of a continuing process of alignment among people, ideas, strategy and markets held in a dynamic balance in an environment of accelerating and irreversible change.

- Human Resource practices should emphasize *experiential learning*, that is, acquisition of new knowledge and skills thought confronting real issues in real environments. As continuous learning becomes the norm in organization life, we must move to embed learning into our work.

- Human Resource practices should be managed to *increase the commitment* of the human resource to the overall purpose of the organization. Human Resources is the steward of the organizational environment, one of the key organizational resources responsible for engaging people in the spirit of the enterprise through personal accountability, direction, and efficacy.

Each of these summary practices is found in at least one of this book's articles. Most of the articles contain all of them. These three strategic practices are the backbones of human resources over the decade. Are they really wisdom? That is left to the reader to assess.

HOW TO USE THIS BOOK

Frankly, books of selected papers can be deadly dull without the active participation of the reader. We therefore ask you not to read the book so much as to work with it. Use it as a tool, engage it in a dialogue, test the content in the context of your biggest challenges. We recommend the following approach:

1. Use the Section Introductions to get a feeling for the contents in each of the three practice areas.
2. Browse through the articles keeping the three strategic practices in mind. Look for applications or problems similar to your own.
3. Where you find possible applications, read the author's follow-up comments to determine how what you have identified has weathered the test of time.
4. Conduct a "mental experiment" to see how the practice might work in your situation.
5. Review the potential results and decide on a course of action.

Best practices mean that others have found these approaches useful. Consider this book a way of "sharing wisdom," and please do not hesitate to share what you learn with others.

Bob and Christina

REFERENCES

Berquist, W. *The Postmodern Organization.* San Francisco, California: Jossey-Bass, 1993.

Boje, D. and Dennehy, R. *Managing In a Postmodern World.* Dubuque, Iowa: Kendall-Hunt, 1993.

Clegg, S. *Modern Organizations.* Newbury Park, California: Sage Publications, 1990.

Holsti, O. *Content Analysis for the Social Sciences and Humanities.* Reading, Massachusetts: Addison-Wesley, 1969.

McKeown, B. and Thomas, D. *Q Methodology.* Newbury Park, California: Sage Publications, 1988.

Sternberg, Robert J. *Wisdom: Its Nature, Origins, and Development.* New York, Cambridge University Press, 1990.

Weber, R. *Basic Content Analysis.* (2nd Edition) Newbury Park, California: Sage Publications, 1990.

ACKNOWLEDGMENTS

We talked to many Human Resource Planning Society members about this project and our methods. We wish to thank these colleagues for their help and support.

Specifically, Jim Walker, the editor of this series, was always there with his help, guidance, and yes, indeed, his own brand of wisdom. Audrey Holder and Rochelle Smith helped with word processing and research.

Much thanks to our executive panel, Pam Farr of the Marriott Corporation, Steven Steckler of TRW, and Gordon Silcox of Manchester, for putting up with the demands of our content analysis method.

Lastly, we recognize our colleagues and friends for their valuable input.

CAREER MANAGEMENT

The HR field is faced with a difficult, and at times seemingly paradoxical, challenge in the development of new systems of career management. No longer can companies promise stability or security to win employee loyalty. Moreover, the need for flexible, adaptive organizations often make it impossible for companies to predict future human resource needs confidently. However, dynamic changes in the modern business environment make it all the more imperative for companies to maintain a highly committed, qualified workforce. The articles in this section shed light on why traditional approaches to career management are inappropriate in many of today's companies, and suggest new tactics to maintain an adequate flow of committed human resources through a modern, flexible organization.

DeLuca discusses how traditional career systems are ineffective in today's volatile business climate. Organizations face the challenge of establishing career systems that can maintain both high organizational adaptability and high workforce commitment. DeLuca proposes a concept called the stable core flexible ring organization as a new approach to career management. This system moves away from a culture based on employee loyalty towards one based on mutual commitment, flexibility, and risk-taking. According to DeLuca, successful organizations will need to move towards a synergistic fit between short-term objectives (revenue goal) and long-term career systems (motivation systems).

Yet as organizations adapt to increasing change and complexity in their business environment, effective management of a company's human resources becomes increasingly difficult. Portwood suggests a systematic approach to career management and notes problems organizations encounter in implementing such a system. His original article was premised on the idea that future human resource needs were predictable, and that career management systems were required only to fulfill these needs. Clearly, the experience of the last decade has altered this assumption. As Portwood later explains, the best organizations can do today is develop a general sense of direction and develop systems that are flexible and responsive to changing business needs. Employees can no longer expect (or be led to believe in) sustained upward mobility as part of a career path, but must be given the authority to seek information and opportunities within the company. Twelve years after his original article, Portwood believes that an integrated approach to career management is even more critical today. Quality, committed, high performance employees may be the only clear strategically competitive advantage an organization can maintain.

DeMeuse and Tornow discuss the evolving employer-employee relationship and its implications for human resource management and business practices. Because organizations can no longer guarantee the type of stability formerly inherent in employer-employee relationships, they must instead generate employer loyalty and commitment through means other than job security and promised promotability. DeMeuse and Tornow point out that companies are realizing that shared accountability and increased decision-making autonomy are ways to recapture and maintain employee commitment. Functions traditionally considered management's role are thus being turned over to the employees, who by necessity receive greater training, information, tools, and decision-making authority. This progressive culture, for which Human Resource is responsible, maximizes organizational impact in the context of these changing work roles. The authors emphasize the importance of Human Resources in ensuring that systems and practices are aligned with, and in support of, the business.

Leibowitz explores general principles for design and management of organizationally sponsored career development systems. Through the use of case studies of successful corporate programs, several key practices and principles emerge. The case studies highlight the need for such practices to be linked to other HR systems. In their afterward, Gutteridge, Leibowitz, and Shore document and highlight some of the growth that has occurred in organizational career development, and the resulting consequences to organizations' practices.

STRATEGIC CAREER MANAGEMENT IN NON-GROWING VOLATILE BUSINESS ENVIRONMENTS[1]

Joel M. DeLuca, Ph.D., Sun Company, Inc.

Low-growth, volatile business environments play havoc with traditional career systems. Promotability slows and the 30-year career diminishes as a valid planning anchor. Career paths must be consciously created rather than managed. Vertical paths become more spiral, with a greater mix of horizontal, professional ladder, and exiting moves. Building "back doors" to move people out of jobs takes on greater importance. A central dilemma is to maintain both high organizational adaptability and high work force commitment; the constant restructurings and downsizings required for the former undermines the employee security needed for the latter. A concept called the stable core/flexible ring organization is being explored as a possible response.

As one of the traditional industries, the energy business has been on quite a ride in the last decade. After nearly a century of stable energy prices (inflation-adjusted), the rise of OPEC's control in the 1970s spurred meteoric price increases, only to be followed several years later by OPEC's dramatic collapse, which then sent prices plunging. These unprecedented and unpredicted events have put the energy industry through great turmoil, from which it is still reeling.

The basic outlook for the industry has shifted from one of a predicted energy shortage to one of a sizable oil surplus. This shift affects all parts of the business and puts particular stress on organizational processes geared for another age. Being successful and competitive in the years ahead will mean a re-examination of the way business is conducted on every front, including how careers are viewed. As environmental uncertainty serves to equalize companies in some respects, competitive edges will evolve around

Reprinted from *Human Resource Planning*, Vol. II, No. 1 (1988), 49-61.

1   The author wished to acknowledge Michael J. Kitson who contributed greatly to a number of the ideas expressed in this paper

controllable aspects related to effectively adapting to volatility. Becoming more strategic about career management has the potential for getting a step ahead of the competition. This paper describes some of the initial directions being explored by one member of the energy industry.

The firm is a mid-sized energy company that has been in the Fortune Top 25 for the last several years. It is a century-old company that employs about 20,000 people, and its annual revenues exceed $10 billion. In its early days, the company was conservative and known for its paternalistic style. In the 1960s and '70s, when many forecasts predicted that oil was going to dry up, the company went through a conglomerate phase. Since then, like most energy companies, it has returned to what it knows best, the energy business. For the last few years the company has been trying to come to grips with the industry's capricious dynamics. Many of the forces impacting the firm can be classified into three arenas: business, organization, and people.

Long-Term Trends in the Business Arena

In all likelihood, the petroleum industry is finished with its growth stage and has entered a period of intense competition, with both traditional and new competitors challenging every facet of the business. Emphasis is moving from a primarily domestic outlook to a more international one, especially regarding energy prices. Prices are likely to remain uncertain, unstable, and volatile for the foreseeable future. As a result, successful businesses in this industry will need to be low cost, efficient, and financially astute.

Pressures exist to reduce fixed assets and inventories, and to apply high technology wherever possible. Companies will need to be very selective in making investments, continually increase productivity, and develop niches of distinctive quality. The energy business is cyclical, and companies must be prepared to manage in both the highs and the lows. There will still be innovations in finding crude oil and refining that crude into market products, but there will be little growth. The current and future environment will be characterized by increasing complexity.

Long-Term Trends in the Organization Arena

The company has been expanding for so long that growth tends to be taken for granted. Being able to integrate vertically and continually enlarge has been a part of the firm's history for nearly a century. It is difficult to picture the years ahead without it.

Another significant trend in the organization arena is the increasing pressure on the traditional hierarchy. The standard authority-based hierarchy has always had its problems, but it worked well in the days of relatively stable environments when classical management practices flourished.

In future environments, the hierarchy may be a less useful device for carrying the whole load of organizing the way the business operates. Some of the old rules will probably have to be rewritten. A key organizational thrust will be towards flexibility—not a strong point of the traditional hierarchy. It may require learning to operate in more network-like structures. The general organizational dictum is that structure follows strategy. In extremely turbulent environments, however, fast-adapting structures may become so strategically advantageous that in some cases structure *is* strategy.

In addition, there will be continual movement toward more decentralized operations and delegated decision-making, which will put added stress on traditional lines of communication. These increasingly decentralized units will need even more to dialogue with each other and with the top of the organization for everyone to keep in step.

On the softer side, increasing attention is being given to ways in which the organization's culture needs to change. The long-term trend is to move from a culture based on loyalty—"keep your nose clean, do what you're told, and we'll take care of you"—to one based on commitment, flexibility, risk-taking, and "going that extra mile."

Long-Term Trends in the People Arena

Perhaps the most evident trend in the work force is its increasing diversity. Many of the past compensation and benefit systems were based on a 30-year career, the man working and the wife and kids at home. That scenario now characterizes less than 17% of the employee population.

The diversity within the work force takes several forms. A growing number of employees want more out of work than just "making a living." More people are looking for jobs that will provide them with a reasonable sense of "making a life," one that has meaning and where they can see their contribution. As a consequence, employees seek active involvement in the issues that affect them. They do not loyally sit back waiting for management to act. At the same time, because of the uncertainty of the energy industry, more people are also worried about their security.

Add to the baby boom bulge (which has yielded too many people in certain age groups) the rise of the dual-career family, and the range of diversified needs and wants expands far beyond what we had to cope with in the past.

Implications for Strategic Career Management: Changes in the Flow

A flow of human resources through the corporation is pictured in Exhibit 1. Traditionally, most people entered through the bottom and experienced their careers as decades of movement up through the hierarchy until retirement. Keeping a healthy flow of the right human resources moving through the organization in a timely manner is one way to view the overall task of career management. The long-term trends in the business, organization, and people arenas indicate some significant shifts in the pattern of this traditional flow.

EXHIBIT 1
Traditional Career Flow Pattern

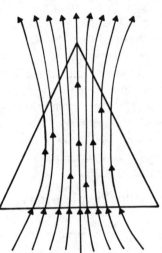

Probably the single greatest impact will come from the lack of growth in the foreseeable future. Without company growth, a major force in the natural flow of careers is lost. Growth opened up new positions, and people could move and advance at rather rapid rates. A primary effect of no growth is slowed promotability. Typically, the company sought ambitious employees who believed that if they performed well they would rise to the top. With diminished promotability, there is a reduction in the prime motivator that drives the system. Add the trend toward leaner, flatter organizations and there are even fewer positions to go to. To make matters worse, the baby boom bulge hits at a particular time when there are already too few slots and too little turnover. Together, these trends portend a major 'people jam' in the flow, with nothing in sight to unblock the system. How to deal with the consequences of no growth and greatly slowed promotability will be a fundamental question of the 1990s.

The second major implication is the loss of the 30-year career. In unpredictable business environments, the company can no longer imply a "career for life" as it did in the past. When the business shifts to stay in sync with its environment, the necessary skills may shift faster than retraining can respond. With the uni-dimensional 30-year career shattered as the centerpiece of the career process, multi-dimensional processes have to be emphasized and developed.

A third implication stems directly from the previous two. Without the engine of growth pulling the process forward naturally, and with the insufficiency of the 30-year career concept, the flow must become strategically managed. A mature organization living in a volatile environment enters into a situation where it not only must manage the flow, but it must *create the flow consciously*. Otherwise, career processes grind to a halt.

To carve out career paths consciously, it is necessary to re-examine the basic set of movements. The first is vertical. At a given career choice point, a person can move upward in the hierarchy through promotion. People can also move upward professionally, via professional ladders, as they develop depth in their specialties. Then there are horizontal moves, choices for people via job rotation and lateral assignments, to develop breadth rather than depth. More frequently now is movement outward to a new firm. Lastly, though rarely emphasized, there is downward movement in most corporations.

Given the forces impacting the company, one might see a different mix of career moves in the future as shown in Exhibit 2. A primary difference will be the significant decrease in upward hierarchical moves. There will be an increase of lateral moves, upward professional moves, and moves outside the corporation. Combining these options into overall career patterns, the path to the top departs from a linear straight line. It changes toward spirals, involving perhaps a similar number of job moves, but with more lateral and special assignments than ever before. Integrating the environmental pressures with options available to the organization can result in a consciously created flow pattern looking more like Exhibit 3 than the traditional flow illustrated in Exhibit 1.

SOME CAREER ISSUES IN A LOW-GROWTH, VOLATILE ENVIRONMENT

Succession Planning

In an environment of unpredictable twists and turns, the company needs increased depth and diversity of "bench strength" to have the right person available when the future reveals itself. Succession planning has always had the difficult task of ensuring that the best talent is developed and ready when needed. This task becomes more difficult when future needs are harder to predict.

But perhaps even greater than getting the right people into key executive positions will be the difficulty of easing executives out of those positions in a timely manner. The more quickly business demands change, the more likely it is that different talents will be needed in top jobs. For example, the value of a financially oriented CEO may decline rapidly if business conditions shift to marketing-based needs. Fast shifting business

EXHIBIT 2
Potential Shift In Mix Of Career Moves

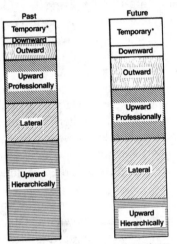

* Open positions filled with non-permanent employees

EXHIBIT 3
Future Career Flow Pattern

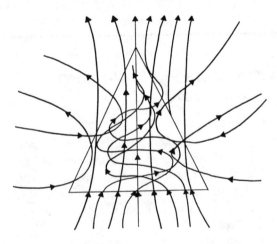

environments may be one of the reasons why the average tenure of American CEOs is decreasing. However, once in a top position, executives seldom become eager to leave, even when business needs change. A growing issue for succession planning in turbulent environments will be finding better ways to get people out of top jobs more readily without relying on the expensive buy-out approaches of the past.

High-Potential Identification

An emerging issue, with slowed promotability, revolves around the notion of the psychological sense of movement. Can high potential people really be satisfied without rapidly moving them upward in the hierarchy? Will spiral career paths be enough to satisfy their sense of progress so that they will stay with the company?

Lateral Movement

Increased horizontal movement, while providing opportunities in some ways, also generates its own career issues. People may not be motivated by "breadth" careers if they sense little recognition for such paths. When only upward movement is viewed as "making it," lateral moves may be considered hollow substitutes. A cultural change in direction, valuing the breadth and versatility of generalists, would need to be pursued. Compensation systems emphasizing some form of skill or knowledge pay may likely need development. Can such systems be made workable in managerial environments?

Professional Ladders

There is a general sense that professional ladders which reward depth of expertise exist more in form than in substance. In managing the upward professional dimension, there is likely to be an increase in the number and height of professional ladders. Two basic issues in this area are: How high should the ladders go? And would they ever be comparable with managerial ladders? Additional considerations include asking: Do we really want long-term professionals in the organization, or would we rather have more planned turnover in order to bring in new employees with fresh ideas?

Downward Movement

Traditionally, downward movements are seen as unsavory demotions. With diminished upward movement, downward moves might become an acceptable alternative to long-term stagnation. As people alter the priorities in their lives, jobs lower in the hierarchy but demanding less responsibility may fit in better with their overall employment desires. The future value of such moves depends on whether the negative stigma can be removed.

Outward Movement

At present, and for some time to come, leaving the organization will be perceived as something more than just another job move. It's a major trauma and is often viewed as a sign of failure. In a low-growth era, this perception would have to change. Leaving the company would need to be treated as a natural possibility, and this view would have to be backed up with high-quality transition programs. In the past, people were often reluctant to depart the company because of benefits emphasizing long-term careers. Individuals took a financial penalty for leaving early. A prime direction in opening up this path is towards "portable pensions," and the company has initiated such a program starting in 1987.

"Back Doors"

Much of what has been said about vertical, horizontal, and other career moves implies the existence of open positions. Previously, company growth opened many jobs, allowing paths for careers to be *managed*. This prevalence of growth-induced openings focused human resource attention on getting the right person through the "front door" into the job. A major issue in *creating* paths involves a stronger emphasis on "back doors"; that is, on processes for getting people out of jobs. While the company has always faced this difficulty, the future will likely move it from a secondary issue to a primary one. Developing less disruptive mechanisms for getting people out of jobs will become more essential in preventing stagnation of the career flow process.

Selection

The inability to provide 30-year careers for everyone makes it necessary to re-think the selection process. In the future, there will be more emphasis on filling specific job needs rather than hiring people for long-term careers. Selecting for the long term will necessitate a more in-depth process and clearer probationary periods. A quandary in this area will be to develop ways of attracting highly qualified applicants without the lure of a promising career.

Internal Job Posting

In the past, many open positions were publicly posted. Individuals anywhere in the organization could bid on them. It was a formal system encouraging self-directed careers. During growth eras, the posting system worked well as hundreds of jobs were constantly opening up. In a non-growth environment, however, open positions become a scarce resource and require more conscious management. With the right planning, one open position can be leveraged to create a chain of openings along which multiple career moves can be made.

An era is now beginning in which management will have to take a stronger role in directing careers, in order to ensure a flow of talent for key positions. The company will need to find a new balance between organizationally managed and individually managed careers without frustrating employees' desires to shape their own fates.

Managed Turnover

Faced with the continuing need to trim itself down, the organization may need to further reduce employment. In a shrinking company, conflict arises when new people are hired while current employees are being laid off. In practice, this conflict often results in a relatively low emphasis on recruiting new talent. The organizational bind has two sides. New people with fresh ideas can be brought in, but at the risk of offending current employees. Alternatively, hiring can be stopped while the company is reducing, which risks stagnation just when innovation is the key to survival. Either way, it is becoming a significant issue to address.

Even after streamlining, there will be movement toward a managed turnover with regular review and exiting of poorer performers. These open slots could be filled with new personnel from outside the corporation. The added difficulty here is that such turnover could threaten the stability of those remaining, since they may never know when they might be the next person to be "managed out" of the organization.

Job Design

Job satisfaction comes from a mix of extrinsic and intrinsic rewards. When promotability is slowed, a prime extrinsic motivator is diminished. An employee is unlikely to remain motivated in an unsatisfying job if it does not lead to promotion. To maintain desired performance, the company may have to make up some of the loss in extrinsic job satisfaction with increases in intrinsic satisfaction. Job redesign to raise intrinsic satisfaction is a likely response.

Job design is fairly well understood in theory. However, the actual practice of re-design to increase intrinsic satisfaction, particularly in white-collar arenas, has not been widespread. Too often, increasing a job's challenge has translated into merely doubling the workload, leading more to overload and burnout than to satisfaction. Increasing job challenge in ways that truly provide greater intrinsic rewards becomes a heightened priority in low-growth environments.

The issues mentioned here, from succession planning to job design, are but a sampling of those needing attention in an era of volatility without predictable growth. The companies that identify and address these issues before they become major problems will have a tangible jump on the competition in attracting and retaining top-notch talent in the maturing energy industry.

A STRATEGIC ORGANIZATION PLANNING APPROACH

Traditionally, human resource issues are addressed segmentally, broken down into their component pieces, and then a particular response is tailored for each piece. Similarly, in the previous section, separate career issues resulting from the company's business, organization, and people trends were distinguished and discussed independently. The basic approach the organization will likely take is to analyze each issue on its own merits and develop a specific program to deal with it.

At the same time, a parallel approach is being explored that involves a shift from human resource planning to a strategic organization planning framework. The term "strategic" in this regard means stepping back to consider the whole set of issues together with their interrelationships. The intent is to discover an overall response that handles several issues simultaneously. The term "organization planning" refers to raising the level of focus to organization structure and design.

The business forces mentioned previously can be summarized as uncertain, volatile environments with increasing change and complexity. A major impact of competitiveness stems from the natural reaction of people to uncertainty. As business conditions alter, the company must change, and in a volatile environment, change can mean cycles of increasing and decreasing employment. When downsizing is needed, everyone in the organization can feel threatened and uncertain about their fate. Consequently, there is often resistance to such change. The resistance lowers productivity and hampers the company's ability to get up and running again in the new environment. The more change, the more people feel uncertain and threatened, with resulting decreases in their commitment.

Many of the issues can be boiled down to a central dilemma. For the company to be competitive in the foreseeable future, two things are essential: (1) a highly adaptable organization and (2) a highly committed work force. Every living system needs to maintain a critical balance between stability and change in order to survive. Organizations, like other living systems, can survive unprecedented change to the extent they can establish new anchors of stability from which to manage the change. Otherwise, chaos or apathy dominates. By restructuring frequently, the organization can better stay in fit with the business environment, but it risks losing the commitment possible with a stable and secure work force. By holding the structure and employment levels steady, the company can help keep a committed work force but risks going out of fit with the ever-changing environment. An organizational-level response to this dilemma might provide a more strategic look at career management. What follows is one controversial attempt being examined in this direction. It involves rethinking the structure and nature of the organization.

THE STABLE CORE/FLEXIBLE RING CONCEPT

In its oversimplified form, the organization would establish a stable core of personnel whose long-term careers would be in the company and a flexible ring of personnel whose overall careers would include time in the company but extend to include other companies as well. The stable core would have some form of employment stability. Their employment would not be threatened by the constantly changing structure and fluctuating size of the corporation. The flexible ring would be professionals and others in jobs with designated time spans, say two to five years, who would predictably and knowingly leave the organization at the end of that period. In good times, as roughly pictured in Exhibit 4, the corporation would grow mainly through expanding the flexible ring. In bad times it would shrink mainly through planned attrition of the flexible ring. The exact structure of the stable core would be determined by the organization and could take on a variety of shapes, as illustrated in Exhibit 5.

EXHIBIT 4
Stable Core/Flexible Ring Design

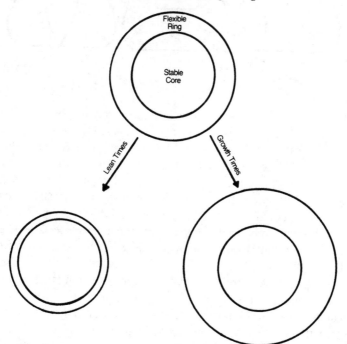

EXHIBIT 5
A Few Options For Stable Core/Flexible Ring Concept

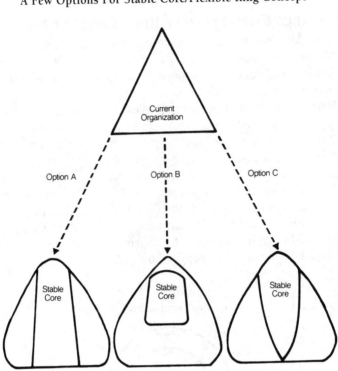

In terms of their careers, those in the stable core would generally be oriented toward a long-term *career in the company;* those in the flexible ring, towards a *career in their particular profession.* In terms of selection, a candidate for the stable core would be reviewed for potential value as a long-term employee, capable of handling many jobs in the company over time. A flexible ring candidate would be hired primarily for a particular job and not for a career. In the mix of generalists and specialists, those in the stable core could become mostly generalists. Flexible ring individuals could be brought in basically for their depth in a given specialty. The flexible ring professionals would be distinguished from most contractors in that they would be fulltime employees. They would be with the company long enough to make a solid contribution but not so long that they would become co-opted by the organization's current mindset.

The primary role of those in the stable core would be to bring a sense of integration. They would represent the continuity essential for stable progress. The task of those in the flexible ring would be to promote the latest concepts and tools, keeping the company on the leading edge in their fields. By bringing new ideas and fresh approaches to old problems, the specific role of the flexible ring would be to prevent organizational obsolescence and stagnation. As a counterbalance, a key role of those in the stable core would be to prevent organizational recklessness, a possibility when too many new ideas flood the system. The flexible ring individuals would be looked to for their *content expertise* in their given specialties, whereas the stable core would provide much of the organizational *context expertise*. With the proper mix of each role's contribution, a balance could be maintained between continuity and innovation.

Potential Advantages of the Stable Core/Flexible Ring Concept

The stable core/flexible ring organization attempts to establish a vehicle for change that does not require job-threatening employment reductions at every turn. Having a core of personnel with security and stability down through the organization increases the probability of adaptive change. Rather than resisting change, this stable core can actually promote it and make change happen because it is not threatening their own employment.

Knowing when each of the flexible ring positions expire and having the expiration dates staggered, the organization can shrink by planned attrition. Moreover, each person has some degree of stability from knowing their length of tenure with the organization. This knowledge may alleviate some of the crippling effects on motivation and productivity that come from continually "living under the shoe" when key people feel they can be laid off without much warning.

The stable core/flexible ring concept can provide an additional form of stability in volatile environments. It allows an increase or decrease in employment with less shock and disruption than other organizational forms. By facilitating a more evolutionary approach to organizational change, the design can reduce the inefficiency caused by constant reorganizations. It also allows managed career paths for both those in the stable core and for those in the flexible ring. Every person in the organization is given the ability and the foresight to manage their careers under conditions that otherwise would mean uncertainty for all.

The stable core/flexible ring approach also addressed a chief concern of a nongrowing company. It provides a planned method for ensuring a continuous influx of new ideas, via the arriving and leaving of professionals in the flexible ring. In the past, the organization would hire people for jobs, but they wanted to stay for careers. As long as the company was growing, this was not a major issue, but in a volatile, low-growth situation it creates a dilemma. The flexible ring allows the company to resolve the dilemma by hiring for specific job needs without implying long-term careers.

The stable core/flexible ring approach, while different from current practice in some respects, is not a radical departure from existing trends. Many organizations have been moving towards establishing buffers in their organizations. The clearest sign in this regard is the increasing number of contractors and temporary workers in all types of corporations, particularly in the traditional industries. Also, in tracking the careers of professionals inside the corporation, one finds that many leave within a five-year period. However, the exit is generally unplanned and incurs a loss of the benefits and pensions associated with long-term stays. Flexible ring individuals would be backed with portable pensions, allowing the possibility of building a pension through a professional career spanning several organizations.

Challenges

Movement towards a notion like the stable core/flexible ring structure handles some problems but introduces many others. In the past, a person was either with the company or not with the company. It was an either/or situation of employment. To have an organization in which there are long-term employees who know they are long-term and short-term employees who know they are short-term creates a very different sense in terms of managing the corporation. Cultural changes necessary to make such a design work need to be identified and addressed. New management methods are required.

The optimal way to manage the ring/core relationship is different from traditional managing. For example, it has historically been difficult for managers who are not professionals to supervise professionals. Managers frequently believe their subordinates should have one loyalty—to the company. Professionals frequently believe they have two loyalties, one to the company and one to their profession. This difference in employment orientation can create problems. When a rift occurs regarding where the professional's loyalty should be, a standoff may develop causing the professional to leave prematurely. For this and other reasons, there are growing needs to find better ways of managing professionals altogether.

Another side-effect can evolve if the ring/core relationship is not managed well: an elitist orientation can develop around those in the core. Individuals in the ring may then become second-class citizens trying to get into the core. Preventing such a two-class system from developing would be a major priority in implementing the core/ring concept. One approach might be to ensure that those in the ring, or at least about 90% of them, would indeed leave the organization when their time was up. If it became common practice for those in the ring to end up in the core, the ring would be seen as just the staging ground for permanent employment. In that case a strong sense of elitism could occur. For the strength of the concept, both the professionals and the long-term employees would have to feel on a par with each other in terms of what they contribute to the organization. They should see themselves as different from but not better than the other, each performing a valuable role for the corporation. Compensation systems to reflect this philosophy would need to be developed.

It is not apparent whether such a concept could be managed in practice. It requires sophisticated manpower planning which may or may not be possible in various parts of the company. Methods for designating flexible ring positions would have to be devised. Staggering the job periods, so that a relatively smooth flow could be maintained, would have to be planned and designed.

Running a stable core/flexible ring organization would be difficult enough in itself. Transitioning to a core/ring structure also creates a host of its own difficulties. It is clear that in getting from here to there, many problems would arise, only a few of which have been touched upon here. Yet, they may be the better class of problems to be addressing. They are problems that result from truly trying to take the company into the future, rather than from relying on piecemealing, patching, and re-patching of past career systems.

THE STABLE CORE/FLEXIBLE RING CONCEPT IN PERSPECTIVE

From a broader view, the stable core/flexible ring approach is a bit arbitrary and simplistic. It represents a way of trying to address the multiple trends and issues the corporation faces. The stable core/flexible ring organization may be more valuable as a working concept than as organizational reality. Any company that will be expanding and contracting will need some way to handle the fact that growth is not driving the career movement of people. It will also need some approach to manage the fact that unpredictable employment reductions play havoc with everybody's motivation and commitment.

Perhaps the actual value of a stable core/flexible ring concept is that it directly challenges the either/or dichotomy of employment with the company. Management would have the greatest flexibility if it could create any type of employment arrangement based upon how business needs develop. Ideally, the direction strategically would be toward the broader concept of flexible employment.

Flexible employment represents a continuum of possibilities, where any form or continuation of employment arrangements would be possible and efficient to construct. It could mean positions like those in the flexible ring that have automatic "back doors" built in. It could mean varying work weeks, ranging from part time to full time and including any distinction in between. People could work 30-hour weeks, but scheduled at 10 for three days followed by four days off. Flexible employment could mean "renting" a substantial part of the work force from employment firms. It could also mean gradual retirement rather than going directly from full time to zero employment. Retiring employees could move initially from 40-hour weeks to 30-hour weeks, then to 20-hour weeks, then to 10, and finally to full retirement, depending upon their desires and the company's needs.

Flexible employment can benefit individuals as well as the company. Spouses who want more flexibility in raising their families may want to negotiate different employment arrangements better suited to their individual lifestyles. Moreover, today's professionals show more signs of wanting non-binding career paths. Thus, there is a growing possibility of synergy between company business needs and individual personal needs. Companies that find efficient ways to actually capitalize on the increasing diversity of employee needs to become more organizationally flexible will have a head start in inheriting the future.

In sum, the problems that a low-growth, volatile environment can cause for traditional industries are many. In one sense it has never been more difficult to stay competitive. On the other hand, there has never been a greater opportunity for the HR function to move into a strategic position in terms of helping the business. New concepts, new approaches, new possibilities of contributing to the business make it a tough but exciting time for HR in the traditional industries. By becoming more strategic and focusing on broad organizational approaches, the human resources function can further evolve beyond a service function into a true business partner.

AFTERWARD COMMENTS

Joel M. DeLuca

Since the original publication of the article in 1988, a lot has happened. Within that time, the concept of the changing career landscape was gaining wider credibility with management, and more lateral and less upward career moves were starting occur. I wish the concepts in the original article could be given some of the credit for the changes, but these changes were more forced on the organization by its volatile environment than by a systematic conscious thought process.

It seems that the greatest barrier to more flexible career strategies is not the ideas themselves but management's tenacious holding on to the model of careers that they were raised with. The concept of the stable core flexible ring generated a lot of excitement and since publication I have seen the concept being explored by a number of corporations. However, even in academia the social scientists who focus on careers tend to assume organization design as a given, while social scientists who address organization designs seem to pay scant attention to career path implications. This fragmentation between organizational structure concerns and career path considerations seems to have spilled over into organization practice and to have created specialists with entirely different backgrounds, research models, and methodologies, making serious dialogue difficult.

Given the increasing nature of change in the environment, there would seem, however, to be some inherent synergy between organization design concepts and career system concepts. One of my hopes in writing the article was to help stimulate joint thinking about external environmental fit issues—organization design—with the primary long-term motivational system of the organization—its career system. I have seen some progress in this direction but not much. My strong belief is that any organization that can find synergistic fit between its short-term economic system (how it makes money) and its long-term career system (how it motivates people) will come out a clear winner in dynamically changing environments.

In 1989 I was recruited to join Coopers & Lybrand as its national director of human resource planning. I felt that in joining a 17,000 person professional services organization the link between people and business would be a lot clearer. That is not quite what I found. The annual turnover rate in the industry approximates 25% at every staff level.

The primary career system is up-or-out, with some managers viewing people merely as commodities. As one said, "after all, most of them are going to just leave anyway, so why invest in them." The up-or-out system is industry-wide and has been working well enough for a hundred years that it was just taken for granted. I could sense, however, that the industry was about to enter a more volatile and competitive environment and found myself looking forward to the challenge of introducing new career and organizational design concepts to such an organization.

At first, this was quite difficult. The one-track career system of up-or-out was so deeply embedded that some people found it inconceivable that there could be any other way to run the business. However, as historical growth slowed and competition rose to new levels more an more managers became interested in alternative views. Surveys of those who voluntarily left the Firm showed that out of the 16 classical retention factors "time for a personal life" and "time to keep commitments in one's personal life" were the only two factors given by most as primary factors for leaving. With this and other kinds of data we become empowered to move away from the "one size fits all" mentality. As a consequence, the Firm is increasingly moving from the simple diagram shown in Exhibit 3. We now have a human resource planning goal to move away from a one-track career system to a multi-track system.

In moving forward toward a multi-track career system we still faced such embedded resistance that we developed a different type of change methodology called a "Strategic Grass Roots" approach to introducing different career tracks into the organization.[1] It is based upon a pull-through from the field versus the traditional push-through approach from headquarters. This more organizational learning-based design has led to pilot efforts for eight simultaneous tracks: an MBA track, a liberal arts, a career manager (vs. up-or-out) track, a high potential track (basis for creating a stable core), a paraprofessional career track, two-year analyst term position, part-time partner career track, and an international career track. Headquarters is involved in each of these pilot efforts but the major work and responsibility for success lies with the parts of the field with a local vested interest. As a result we are currently in a period of confidence about actually moving to a multi-track career system that will alter the design of the organization.

---

[1] Chapter 10 in Susan E. Jackson's (Ed). *Diversity in the Workplace*: Human Resource Initiatives, New York. The Guilford Press 1992.

As a final observation, those HR professionals in my prior company and those in my current organization after much thought have arrived at what we consider the root cause of the resistance to more diverse career concepts. Most large organizations of today were implicitly founded under principles of employee homogeneity and one-size-fits-all career notions. Tomorrow's organizations need to be founded on employee heterogeneity and multiple sizes based on need. With the former view came great benefits: only one model is needed; equity is a small problem; administration is easier; and efficiency is great. New career concepts alter this fundamental view, moving from homogenous assumptions to heterogeneous ones. In other words, managers have to learn how to manage diversity. For any new view to succeed, HR professionals need to help managers address the value of multiple models, fear of an equity flood brought about by diverse treatment of people, more complex administrative mechanisms with less efficiency but greater overall effectiveness. This may not be easy but it puts human resources in the forefront of creating competitive organizations of the future.

THE TIE THAT BINDS—HAS BECOME VERY, VERY FRAYED!

Kenneth P. De Meuse, University of Wisconsin-Eau Claire
Walter W. Tornow, University of Minnesota

The relationship between employer and employee has gone through a metamorphosis during the past two decades. It has changed from one of mutual dependence and relative permanence to one of self-reliance and temporariness, from high commitment and strong loyalty to "what have you done for me lately?" Today the emotional bond (corporate knot) has become severely strained. Executives in the 1990s must recognize this transformation and manage employees accordingly. In this article we present reasons for this evolution and address how its effect on organizational life. Specific implications for executive policies and management practices during the 1990s are described.

"I don't trust them. They have lied to me too many times."

A disgruntled employee

"My staff schedules Friday lunches together just like this will be the last Friday we'll be together. We do this every Friday —waiting to be terminated!"

A frustrated manager

I n 1956, William H. Whyte wrote the book, *The Organization Man*. It described a phenomenon in Corporate America in which an employee completely invested himself in *his* company—working 60- to 70-hour weeks, being on the road whenever and wherever needed, relocating on a dime's notice. In other words, he did whatever the company asked. In return, *his* employer would provide a "good job" with "good pay," offer plenty of advancement opportunities, and grant annual merit increases. In other words, the company offered financial security! It was a womb-to-tomb mentality.

Reprented from *Human Resource Planning*, Vol. 13, No. 3 (1990), 203-213.

Such an employer-employee relationship gave order, predictability, accountability. It reassured employees who had 30-year mortgages, monthly car payments, and plans for their children's education and retirement. On the other hand, it also permitted employers to develop 5- and 10-year strategic plans, because it guaranteed a stable work force for managerial succession and business continuity. It was a tidy, neatly wrapped, little world. The corporate knot between employer and employee was well-tied.

During the 1990s, Whyte's book no longer applies. Obviously, now the book would be titled, *The Organization Person* because more than half of the employees in America are women. But much more importantly, the phenomenon of such an "organization man" no longer exists. Nowadays, a new corporation-person bond is emerging, one that assumes each party is much less dependent on the other, one in which mutual loyalty is rapidly disappearing, and one in which mutual trust may be at an all time low.

Public opinion polls clearly show employees are becoming less committed to their employers. For example, a 1986 *Business Week* poll of 600 mid-level managers indicated that 65% believed salaried employees were less loyal to their employers now than they were 10 years ago. A 1987 *Industry Week* readership poll revealed that 70% felt loyalty between employees and their companies was rapidly disappearing. Fully 60% admitted they were less loyal than they were five years ago.

Evidence reveals that, likewise, employers are less committed to their employees. In many companies, "RIFs" (reductions in force) have become a way of life. Approximately two million managers have lost their jobs since 1980 due to corporate takeovers. The *Wall Street Journal* estimated that in 1985 alone, 600,000 mid-level managers were squeezed out in corporate belt-tightening. Many of the pillars of American business have cut staffs in recent years: AT&T, Apple Computer, General Motors, Du Pont, CBS, Eastman Kodak, Dow Chemical, Control Data, Ford Motor Company, Kraft, Westinghouse, Honeywell—the list goes on and on.

Further, more and more top executives appear to be taking care of themselves via the "golden parachute." For instance, when CBS was taken over by Sony, Thomas Wyman was booted out as CEO. He did not leave empty-handed, however. He received $4.3 million up front plus $400,000 a year for the rest of his life; he was only 57 years old (Bell, 1988). When Brunswick Corporation bought Bayliner Boats, the Bayliner CEO retired. He retired with $400 million! We live in a time of golden parachutes, silver parachutes, tin parachutes, and no parachutes. What message do these executive cash bonanzas communicate to the average employee? PROTECT THYSELF FIRST—WE ARE!

Perhaps, the most disconcerting evidence that the "tie is fraying" can be found in a 1989 Louis Harris poll of 1,041 office workers. Only 39% of these employees felt their company's management was honest and ethical when dealing with employees. Harris concluded, "office workers plain just don't trust management to deal fairly with them" ("Office Workers Less Satisfied," 1989, p. 12A).

THE PSYCHOLOGICAL CONTRACT

Academic scholars frequently refer to the emotional bond between employer and employee as the "psychological contract" (Schein, 1980; Schermerhorn, Hunt, & Osborn, 1985; Tornow, 1988). It represents an implicit agreement that each party will treat the other fairly. It is unwritten and unofficial and therefore not legally binding. Assumptions and expectations about each other are only vaguely communicated. The motivation for compliance is based entirely on presumably shared beliefs and mutual trust. Consequently, if the "contract" is broken, deep, long-lasting feelings of betrayal and resentment result.

The psychological contract differs greatly from other employment contracts. Employment contracts (e.g., offer of employment letters, policies in employee handbook, specific employee agreements) are explicit, written, and legally binding. These documents clearly spell out each party's responsibilities and duties. If the contract is broken, sanctions occur. Whereas the motivation for compliance in the psychological contract is based on mutual trust, the motivation in the employment contract is based on fear of legal reprisal. Thus, with employment contracts one's vulnerability is lower and the rule enforcement is not dependent upon each party's sense of fair play.

As we begin the 1990s, the tie that binds in the case of employment contracts is a legal one that remains very strong. In contrast, the emotional tie (psychological contract) appears to be very frayed.

The Psychological Contract of Yesterday

Exhibit 1 depicts the employer-employee relationship during the 1950s and 1960s. It shows that the fundamental premise was a fair day's work for a fair day's pay. When that agreement was intact, the tie was strong. The company had an employee who was dependable, who would work hard, and who (above all) would be *loyal*. In turn, the employee had employment with a company who he/she could count on, who paid fairly, and who offered continuing fringe benefits. In short, a company who provided *job security*. Each party benefitted.

EXHIBIT 1
The Psychological Contract of Yesterday

Employee's Responsibility	Employer's Responsibility
• Fair day's work	• Fair day's pay
• Sustained good work	• Continued employment
• Sustained good work	• Merit pay increases
• Extra hard work	• Advancement
• Quality work	• Recognition & acknowledgement
• LOYALTY	• JOB SECURITY

EXHIBIT 2
The Psychological Contract of Today

Employee's Responsibility	Employer's Responsibility
• Focus on personal needs	• Focus on corporate goals
• Career/self development	• Corporate growth
• Legal protection	• Legal protection
• SELF-RELIANCE	• SELF-RELIANCE

The Psychological Contract of Today

The situation is vastly different today (see Exhibit 2). Today both parties are much more self-reliant. An "I will take care of myself" orientation pervades the relationship. The employee plays a much more active role in monitoring job duties, supervisory practices, merit raises, and career development. The employer uses a more performance-based, impersonal, cost-conscious perspective when managing employees. Because of the need to be flexible and adaptive to change in the organizational environment, the employer-employee relationship frequently assumes a short-term posture and immediate results are emphasized.

WHY THE CHANGE?

Paul Hirsch, in his book *Pack Your Own Parachute* (1987), refers to an employment strategy in sports called "free agency." In such a strategy, professional athletes attempt to maximize their position by peddling their services to the ball club who offers the biggest paycheck. Their exclusive focus is their own welfare. Their sense of loyalty to teammates, ball club, community, and owner is deferred. Hirsch suggests American managers might want to adopt a similar strategy.

This employment orientation is a far cry from the "organization man" phenomenon of the 1950s. What could have caused such a drastic shift? The answer lies in two areas. First, tremendous changes have occurred in society in general. Second, significant changes have occurred in the work environment in particular.

The Changing American Landscape

America has changed greatly and continues to change. In many respects, we are becoming a society of individuals. Our sense of identity is to self, rather than to a group. There appears to be an eroding attachment to national heritages, religions, communities, families, and *corporations*.

A sense of permanence and continuity is being replaced in our relationships with temporariness. Even our marriage vows have transformed from "love, honor, and obey till death due us part" to "love, honor, and obey till love due us part." The average American moves every five years.

Moreover, there appears to be a growing need for instant gratification. Rather than expecting to work long and hard for things we value (new car, new house, college degree, job advancement), we want it immediately. If we do not have the money, we borrow it. If we do not have the patience or tenacity for earning a college degree, we purchase it. If our employer won't grant us an advancement, we go elsewhere.

Social controls are giving way to legal controls. The so-called "man-of-his-word" and "handshake" rituals are going the way of the dinosaur. Two-thirds of the world's lawyers practice in America. As a society, unwritten agreements are being replaced by written contracts. Should we expect our workplace to be anything different?

Perhaps related to this point is the apparent loss of mutual trust in our society. Burglar alarm systems, locked cars, and walking your child to school are some manifestations of a non-trusting world. Employment contracts, legal documents, and binding agreements are manifestations of a non-trusting workplace. Along with an erosion in mutual trust, there also appears to be a weakening of the norm of reciprocity. Returning favors and helping out friends is as uncommon today as quilting bees and barn-raisings.

Finally, two societal factors directly tied to the work world are (a) the increasing number of highly educated professionals working in companies and (b) the plethora of corporate mergers and takeovers. In the case of professional employees, their allegiance most frequently is to their profession rather than the company. For example, she is an engineer first, an employee of IBM second; he is an accountant first, an employee of General Motors second.

The onslaught of mergers and acquisitions has precipitated an unprecedented number of corporate restructurings and concomitant employee layoffs. This is the first time in the history of business that employee termination may be completely independent of poor performance or incompetence—terminations frequently occur because the acquiring firm needs to reduce the debt load. A terminated engineer from a high tech firm in California put it this way: "It took me nine months to realize they laid off the position, not me!"

The Changing Work Environment

The above societal changes have had a direct affect on the workplace in America. During the 1950s and 1960s, employees had stability, permanence, and predictability. During the 1970s and 1980s, employees experienced constant change, temporariness, and uncertainty. During the 1950s and 1960s, there was a relatively stable, full-time workforce. Today, there is "just-in-time" manufacturing and a "just-in-time" workforce. In 1980, there were 28 million part-time employees; six years later there were 34 million. Fully 85-95% of American corporations presently use temporary workers (Kanter, 1989). In some respects, Corporate America has moved from using employment agencies to secure employees to using outplacement firms to remove employees. Exhibit 3 displays some of the major trends that illustrate just how significantly the work environment has been changing (also see Marks, 1988).

In short, there is a new reality today. The implicit, psychological contract between employer and employee has been profoundly altered. The conditions of the 1950s and 1960s fostered:

1. reciprocal dependence,
2. within-company growth,
3. linear career development,
4. prescribed retirement at age 65,
5. corporate identity,
6. commitment to company, and
7. strong corporate loyalty.

Nowadays, the focus is on:

1. self-reliance and taking responsibility,
2. across-company growth,
3. multiple careers,
4. extended employment,
5. self (professional) identity,
6. commitment to self, and
7. weak corporate loyalty.

THE PSYCHOLOGICAL CONTRACT—A PERIOD OF TRANSITION

Although these changes may leave one with a sense of disillusionment and frustration, they were necessary and adaptive. Such changes in the business environment have permitted companies to reduce cost and to become more market-oriented, competitive, and flexible. They have provided American corporations and employees alike opportunities to become more mature, independent, and successful.

EXHIBIT 3
The Changing Work Environment

1950s and 1960s	vs.	1970s and 1980s
Stability		Constant change
Permanence		Temporariness
Predictability		Uncertainty
Stable workforce		Shifting workforce
Full-time employees		Part-time employees
Internal employees		External employees
Fixed work patterns		Flexible work patterns
Employment...Retirement		Gradual retirement
Employee Retention		Targeted turnover (RIFs)
Develop employees		Buy employees
Value loyalty and tenure		Value performance & skills
Company-defined benefits		Company-defined contributions
Job security		Job tentativeness
Advancement opportunities		Limited opportunities (plateauing)
Creating value through slow growth		Buying value through rapid acquisition (M&As)

Under the traditional (paternalistic) mode of management, where company loyalty was rewarded with lifetime employment, mutual complacency tended to creep in. Today, neither employer nor employee guarantees lifetime security. This situation does not mean that loyalty and commitment must die. Rather, it means they must be generated through different avenues.

To recapture employee loyalty and commitment, companies are realizing the need to share more with their employees when it comes to power. They must share risks as well as gains. This approach of Total Employee Involvement (TEI) includes providing important information about the business, delegating responsibility for performance management, sharing decision-making authority, and allocating rewards based on corporate success (Lawler & Mohrman, 1989).

Knowledge—a key source of power—gets shared. Employees throughout the company are informed of the organization's mission, goals, and strategy (vision), as well as the business conditions that represent threats and opportunities to the company's continued well-being. Greater self-management of performance is encouraged by providing employees with clear objectives and standards of performance, as well as the necessary feedback systems that allow employees to adjust performance accordingly. In addition, organizations gain employee commitment by creating more opportunities for employee involvement in decision-making regarding their work and by linking rewards to employee contributions to the success of the business. Employers act "to make everyone an owner in the organization" (Hallett, 1988, p. 36).

In return for sharing more power and control with employees, organizations expect their employees to be more self-reliant and to take greater responsibility for their performance and career management. The result is that loyalty and commitment become more focused on the employment relationship and what employer and employee must do to keep the relationship mutually beneficial .

IMPLICATIONS FOR MANAGING IN THE 1990S

The changing psychological contract has significant implications for effective human resource management (HRM) practices during the 1990s. The creation of a progressive organizational culture to capitalize on this newly evolving employer-employee relationship is needed. Issues pertaining to both these areas are presented in this section.

Initiating Effective HRM Practices

Staffing

Successful organizations will develop a more flexible workforce through part-time and contract arrangements. Such an approach benefits both employers and employees. Employers (a) can hire for fluctuating needs, short-term projects, or crisis situations, (b) save money on medical and other employee benefits, and (c) retain valuable employees who cannot or choose not to work full-time (Bergsman, 1989). Also, such a staffing strategy helps maintain an up-to-date skills mix and balance of experience to meet the needs of the business in a cost-effective way.

Employees, in turn, benefit from greater flexibility in work schedules and place. Further, the organization's core employees experience greater employment security by being buffered form the up-and-down vagaries of the typical business fluctuations.

Other staffing practices to consider include greater use of job rotation, job sharing, lateral transfers, and job enrichment as ways to counterbalance decreased opportunities for the traditional upward mobility track. Finally, more emphasis should be placed at the entry-level hiring stage to assure that applicants get realistic job previews and understand the expectations and responsibilities of working in this changing kind of environment.

Performance Management

Drawing on the Total Quality Management (TQM) precepts from Japanese management practices, employers need to redesign their performance appraisal systems so they act more as total and continuous performance management processes (Ishikawa, 1985). Such an approach allows employees to become more autonomous and take more responsibility for managing their performance. As a first step, performance "contracting" should take place with the employee's key customers/clients. This step assures a clear understanding of what products and services are expected and the standards for evaluating performance effectiveness. Secondly, performance feedback should be put into place that permit employees to monitor their own performance and make the needed adjustments when necessary. For this purpose, soliciting inputs from multiple sources can frequently be valuable to capture the multiple needs and perspectives of an employee's multiple clients.

In short, the emphasis needs to shift from managers *doing* performance appraisals—which all too frequently turn out to be treated as one-shot, once-a-year events that are not well liked by either manager or employee—to a continuous process of work-oriented communication that focuses on managing performance. In this approach, both manager and employee take responsibility.

Compensation

Traditional systems of compensation have the effect of heavily rewarding tenure and position, rather than contribution and ability. Such compensation packages promulgate the "fair day's pay for fair day's work" and entitlement mentality. Successful employers of the 1990s will require employees to have a stake in departmental (company) profits and losses. Whereas job security once denoted life-long employment and retirement plans, today it means having a shared destiny in the success and failure of the business (Santora, 1989).

A key compensation strategy for getting there is for employers to begin switching from fixed to more variable forms of pay (Brown, 1989). The latter can better reflect the need for more risk sharing and incentive motivation. To assure that incentive compensation maintains its motivational effects, compensation designers need to differentiate when it is more appropriate to link rewards to the individual, team, or organizational level of performance (Sundstrom, De Meuse, & Futrell, 1990).

Finally, employers will need to take a more strategic look at their reward system by looking at *total* compensation. How does the design of the total system link to the overall business strategy of the organization?

Training

In training and developing employees, the focus must shift to activities that favor life and career planning, as well as continuing education and retraining. These activities reduce the chance for skills obsolescence and organizational dependency on the part of the employee. They also tend to increase the employee's sense of autonomy and self-confidence. As a result, the employer is able to maintain a more up-to-date workforce. In addition to recognizing its value to the current employer, it also serves to enhance the perceived marketability of the employees outside the company. Marketability provides insurance in case of drastic action taken by the employer to reduce the workforce.

Termination.

Shorter product cycles, increased competition, globalization, and the merger environment are causing more and more companies to implement RIFs. How one manages the downsizing process greatly influences employee morale, productivity, and the likelihood of "wrongful discharge" suits (Robino & De Meuse, 1985). As a rule, companies should (a) inform affected employees as soon as possible, (b) provide job search and placement assistance (e.g., conducting resume writing and interview skills workshops; notifying other firms of impending layoff with listing of position titles), and (c) dispense equitable severance pay. Such practices communicate an openness and sensitivity that fosters trust. Mutual trust is an imperative for successful companies during the 1990s (De Pree, 1989).

Many companies are developing innovative programs that decrease the likelihood of massive layoffs and other drastic forms of employment swings. For example, Motorola weathered an economic slump in the semiconductor business without significant layoffs during the mid-1980s. Rather than laying off 10% of their workforce to match the weakened demand, employees began working a four-day week every other week. This strategy permitted Motorola to keep thousands of employees on the payroll who otherwise would have been laid off. Consequently, Motorola employees felt a sense of corporate commitment and unity (shared destiny). In contrast, Texas Instruments dealt with the semiconductor slump by instituting layoffs. These layoffs were accompanied by a loss of skilled employees, a reduction in morale among those who stayed on, a difficult transition back to full production, and problems of quality control while new employees learned their jobs (O'Toole, 1985).

Creating a Progressive Organizational Culture

HR as a Strategic Partner

In the past, personnel departments all too frequently were administrative in scope and reactionary in nature. Their primary purpose appeared to be processing insurance forms, moving paper from one line manager to another, and establishing the bowling league. Personnel lacked clout, true corporate identity, and real purpose.

Today, there is tremendous complexity, diversity, and sophistication confronting human resources management. Society has changed; employees have changed; companies have changed. So must the recruiting, training, motivating, leading, communicating, and retaining of people change. It is critical that human resources become a strategic partner in the corporate hierarchy. The days when "everyone knows that anyone can do HR" are past.

To be a strategic partner, the HR function must be staffed by competent, professionally trained managers and representatives. The head of HR must have a fundamental understanding of other areas in the company, such as marketing, manufacturing, engineering (Coates, Jarratt, & Mahaffie, 1989). The senior HR manager must help other executives view the workforce as a valuable asset to be nurtured, rather than labor costs to be reduced. This individual will be able to document the HR function's value by establishing measurement systems that clearly show the financial impact HR contributes to the bottom line.

The HR function must be a role model and champion the way in facilitating the needed changes in the employment relationship. Human Resources must assure that the organization's HR systems and practices are aligned with and in support of the needs and strategies of the business. Also, the function should foster a climate that values growth and development and help define strategies for regaining employee commitment and loyalty.

Line Managers as Effective HRM Practitioners

Line managers need to change their role from one of planning, organizing, and controlling to one of leading, facilitating, and supporting. They must lead through visioning and gaining commitment, and emphasize the management of processes rather than people, since people now are more self-managing. Toward this end, managers need to assure that employees can and will do their jobs effectively. This requires giving them training, information, tools, and decision-making authority. Performance management must be a continuous process, as should be the search for opportunities to recognize employee contributions.

Employees Empowered to be Self-Managing

Employees working under the new psychological contract must actively communicate and validate their expectations and assumptions about the employment relationship. They need to stay informed of organizational directions and business challenges and assume responsibility for managing their performance and development planning. In addition, employees must keep their skills updated and maintain a network that links them with others for support and coaching. Employers, in turn, need to recognize and accept these changes. Management must empower employees to have more influence and control over their performance and work careers.

CONCLUSION

Is the work place worse than before? Is it better than before? It depends on one's expectations and values. We can state with certainty that it is different! Management must recognize these differences and lead, communicate, motivate, select, train, and pay accordingly. What worked before will not necessarily work now! These are new times; they demand new management and new organizational practices. The psychological contract between employer and employee is just as important as it was 30 years ago. However, today's "contract" is one of shared destiny and mutual benefit rather than one of job security and corporate loyalty.

REFERENCES

Bell, R. *Surviving the 10 Ordeals of the Takeover.* (New York: AMACOM. 1988).

Bergsman, S. "Part-time Professionals Make the Choice." *Personnel Administrator,* 1989, 34(9), pp. 49-52; 105.

Brown, D. "The Corporate Times They are a' Changing." *Management Review,* 1989, 78(9), pp. 7-9.

Coates, J.F., Jarratt, J., and Mahaffie, J. "Workplace Management 2000: Seven Themes Shaping the U.S. Work Force and its Structure." *Personnel Administrator,* 1989, 34(12), pp. 51-55.

De Pree, M. *Leadership is an Art.* (New York: Doubleday, 1989).

Hallett, J. "New Patterns in Working." *Personnel Administrator,* 1988, 33(12), pp. 32-37.

Hirsch, P. *Pack Your Own Parachute.* (Reading, MA: Addison-Wesley, 1987).

Ishikawa, K. *What is Total Quality Control? The Japanese Way.* (Englewood Cliffs, NJ: Prentice-Hall, 1985).

Kanter, R.M. "From Climbing to Hopping: The Contingent Job and the Post-Entrepreneurial Career." *Management Review,* 1989, 78(4), pp. 22-27.

Lawler, E.E., III., and Mohrman, S.A. "High-Involvement Management." *Personnel,* 1989, 66(4), pp. 26-31.

Marks, M.L. "The Disappearing Company Man." *Psychology Today,* 1988, 22(9), pp. 34-39

"Office Workers Less Satisfied–Survey Reports." *Huntsville Times,* June 1, 1989, p. 12A.

O'Toole, J. "Employee Practices at the Best Managed Companies." *California Management Review,* 1985, 28(1), 35-66.

Robino, D.J., and De Meuse, K.P. "Corporate Mergers and Acquisitions: Their Impact on Human Resource Management." *Personnel Administrator,* 1985, 30(11), pp. 33-44.

Santora, J.E. "Compensation: Du Pont Builds Stakeholders." *Personnel Administrator,* 1989, 34(9), pp. 72-76.

Schein, E.H. *Organizational Psychology* 3rd Ed. (Englewood Cliffs, NJ: Prentice-Hall, 1980).

Schermerhorn, J.R., Jr., Hunt, J.G., and Osborn, R.N. *Managing Organizational Behavior* 2nd Ed. (New York: John Wiley & Sons, 1985).

Sundstrom, E., De Meuse, K.P., and Futrell, D. "Work Teams: Applications and Effectiveness." *American Psychologist,* 1990, 45, pp. 120-133.

Tornow, W.W. "Contract Redesign." *Personnel Administrator,* 1988, 33(10), pp. 97-101.

Whyte, W.H. *The Organization Man.* (New York: Simon & Schuster, 1956).

AFTERWARD COMMENTS

Kenneth P. De Meuse, University of Wisconsin-Eau Claire
Walter W. Tornow, Center for Creative Leadership

The 1990s continue to be a challenging period for American Companies and employees alike. Almost daily headlines announce another plant closing, a factory relocating overseas, or a major corporate layoff. Downsizing and streamlining have become a way of life as U.S. firms transform their operations in order to remain competitive in the world marketplace.

A recent example is General Motors and the removal of Robert Stempel as C.E.O. According to a recent *Time* magazine article, the company will embark on a sweeping new round of layoffs to restructure. Impatient with Stempel's slowness in carrying out plans to close American plants and cut 74,000 of its 370,000 employees over three years, the directors now want to eliminate a total of 120,000 jobs during the decade.

As companies try to make ends meet, HR strategies have been implemented that further cut the tie between employer and employee. For example, many companies have redesigned their health benefit programs, capping yearly expenses per individual employee. This belt-tightening measure places an additional burden on employees during times of soaring health care costs. Companies also are revamping pension funds, as well as replacing full-time employees with part-time ones to save money on employee benefits.

Many companies have, however, instituted other types of change American firms have implemented such strategies as total quality management (TQM), self-managed work teams (SMWTs), and total employee involvement (TEI) in an attempt to become globally competitive. In addition, vision statements, team building, succession planning, and a wide variety of Japanese management practices and activities have been incorporated into the American workplace during the past few years. All these measures attempt to enhance product quality and nurture employee commitment.

Paradoxically, many of the same companies that are trying to build employee commitment (and attachment) are also the ones downsizing, streamlining operations, and relocating plants outside the United States. Such opposing strategies (from an employee perspective) send mixed signals to the workforce. On the other hand, management is asserting that employees are a valuable human resource; on the other hand, employees are being let go.

It may be that simultaneously incorporating both belt-tightening measures and activities to enhance employee involvement is not possible. The literature suggests that when words (verbal content) and actions (nonverbal content) are in conflict, it is the nonverbal communication to which people respond (Stewart, Hecker, & Graham, 1987). When senior management implements strategies that both foster employee commitment and employer-employee unity and cut costs and downsize wherever possible, employees might not support either one. The credibility of management is undermined since the characteristics of each strategy are diametrically opposed (see Table 1).

TABLE 1

Management Strategies

Characteristics	Belt-Tightening	E.E.I.
Motive	Survival	Growth
Focus	Cutting Costs	Improving Product Service
Time Frame	Immediate	Long-term
Managerial Style	Autocratic	Participative
Communication	Top Down	All Ways
Fosters	Self-centeredness	Mutual Commitment
Builds	Individuality	Employer-Employee Unity

Note: E.E.I. denotes "Enhanced Employee Involvement."

Recent research suggests the benefits of corporate downsizing may be illusory (De Meuse, Vanderheiden, & Bergmann, in press). An article appearing in The Economist ("Pink-slip productivity," 1992) reported that

75% of those companies downsizing believed financial performance did not increase and 67% found no improvement in productivity. Likewise, a recent study conducted by McKinsey and Company found that two-thirds of the 30 TQM programs examined had stalled or fallen short of yielding meaningful improvements (Fuchsberg, 1992).

The environment organizations are facing today is characterized by constant and rapid change, ambiguity, diversity, and complexity. The challenge to management and employees becomes how to create and maintain an employment relationship that promotes both the values of continuity and commitment while also emphasizing the need for flexibility and responsiveness.

We believe the new psychological contract for the organization of tomorrow (or, today) requires four fundamental ingredients, relating to leadership, structure, employees, and human resource policies.

First, the organization needs leadership for a quality corporate culture; one that promotes learning, simplification, and innovation (Tragedain, 1992). Second, the organization needs structures and processes that permit, indeed promote, quick and flexible responses to changing market environments. Third, employees need to have "meta skills" that allow them to adapt or adjust rapidly to changing business and skill requirements—skills for learning how to learn and exercising judgment in situations of uncertainty (Stamp, 1992). And, finally, HR policies and practices must link business strategies with leadership and HR strategies. The latter should empower employees as much as possible to be self-managing, to have a realistic understanding of expectations and assumptions about the employment relationship as well as influence over their work performance and career.

REFERENCES

De Meuse, K. P., Vanderheiden, P. A., & Bergmann, T. J. (in press). Is lean and mean really better than fat and happy? To be presented at the Human Resource Planning Society Research Symposium. Cornell University, NY.

Fuchsberg, G. (1992). Quality programs show shoddy results. *The Wall Street Journal*, pp. B1; B7.

"Pink-slip productivity." (1992). *The Economist, 322,* 79.

Stamp, G. (1992). *Personal Communication.*

Stewart, D. W., Hecker, S. & Graham, J. L. (1987). It's more than what you say: Assessing the influence of nonverbal communication in marketing. *Psychology and Marketing, 4,* 303-322.

Tragedian, H. (1992). *Personal Communication.*

DESIGNING CAREER DEVELOPMENT SYSTEMS: PRINCIPLES AND PRACTICES

Zandy B. Leibowitz

Recent trends have forced many organizations to begin recognizing people as a strategically important resource. At the same time, employees in many key areas are becoming more assertive in demanding the organization recognize their needs for personal growth and career opportunity. The paper discusses some of the steps organizations might take in aiding their employees toward these personal goals.

Specifically, the paper outlines some general principles for design and management of organizationally sponsored career development systems, and provides several case examples of successful corporate programs.

Organizational career development is a relatively new field. It's one that's evolved very quickly in the last 10 years and now has a whole body of research to support it. What I'm going to cover in this paper will provide an overview of some of the key issues in the area and also discuss some practical models that organizations have put in place in career development. Specifically, the objectives of this paper are to:

- Define and provide an overview of organizational career development systems.
- Describe twelve key principles that can be used in designing a career development system.
- Provide case examples of organizations who have designed systems.
- Provide a framework for applying the principles in participant organizations.

Reprinted from *Human Resource Planning*, Vol. 10, No.4 (1987), 195-207.

Let me start with defining a career development system. This is a field that is fraught with definitional problems. A number of terms are used that range from career planning to career development to career management to career development systems and the problem with all those terms is nobody's clearly defined them and, in most cases, they all inherit the legacy of meaning promotional systems in organizations. The term I'm going to be working with today is a broad term. It balances individual needs with the organizational requirements and is called a career development system. These are the characteristics of a career development system:

- An organized formalized, planned effort. It's not just an ad hoc series of activities. There's some plan associated with it. It's not just taking people off for a one day career planning seminar.
- Attempts to achieve a balance between individual and organizational needs. It's a way to blend individual characteristics, skills, desires, interest, with what the organizational requirements are and combine those two data points together.
- Ongoing vs. one time.
- Builds on a refinement and development of existing human resource structures.

The beginnings of organizational career development evolved around life career planning workshops where employees go off and create their career plans and they'd get all excited and they'd come back to their organization and there weren't any supports or structures or any reality for them to implement any of those plans. There's a need to tie back individual plans to organization structures. Organizations who have been very effective in this area have leveraged other human resource activities. They have tied career development to succession planning, they've tied it to performance appraisals, they've tied it to some of their training and development. They've tied it to some of their compensation systems. In summary, those are the four characteristics that, I believe, describe an organizational career development system.

Let me now give you a little bit of background on how we conducted the research for the recent book that was mentioned in the introduction to today's session, *Designing Career Development Systems*, Jossey-Bass, 1986. We identified 50 companies across the country who were doing so-called good career development. We were able, through a network of colleagues, to identify who those organizations were and what we wanted to know from them was what contributed to their success. Why were they successful? And so we designed a series of interview questions to find out what were some of the principles or practices that they had in place. What we used as framework for those interview questions was an interesting approach. We decided from our work with organizations that what you are doing when you're putting an organizational career development system in place is you're really creating organizational change. It is no different than implementing any other kind of change effort; again, it's much broader than a one-time event. And so it is fraught with all those issues that any other change effort is fraught with: Primarily the fact that organizations don't like to change. They are no different than you and I. They are creatures of habit. They tend to move to homeostasis. It's much easier to do business as usual. What we were looking for and what we used as an underpinning of our interview questions was a change model. The model, illustrated below, is based on some of Dick Beckhardt's work, dealing with organizational transitions.

CHANGE ≯ NEED X VISION X FIRST STEP

This formula illustrates that in order for an organization to change, the cost of that change has to be offset by several elements that need to be in place. The first element states that there needs to be a clear statement of what are the needs or problems or opportunities driving that change? Why change? The second piece is that there needs to be a clear picture of where you're going. What's going to be different as a result of changing? What's the vision, so to speak. Finally, you need to know how to get there. You need an action plan or some first steps.

Let me ask you, those of you who are mathematically inclined, to take a look at this formula. If there is a zero in any one of these, what do you have? Zero. You have no change, and that's the whole point. All three parts of the formula need to be in place. Interestingly enough though, organizations have patterns around this formula. They are like you and me. Some of us are much better at one of the three of these than others. There are some organizations which we found in our interviews were very good at identifying problems or needs or opportunities. They are the organizations that do a climate survey every year and have piles of them. And they have them in somebody's desk drawer. They never do anything with them, and yet every year career development comes out as the major issue. But they're afraid to share it and they continue to collect data to surface the problems and needs. Then there are those organizations who are very good at the second step. They're very visionary. They're very exciting places to work. They're always creating these integrated, conceptual systems. You walk in and they've got pictures all over the wall. They never quite move from that picture though. And then, thirdly, you've got those organizations who take action and then figure out what they did.

What we were looking for in our interviews was what organizations were doing in each of these three steps. We wanted to see what were some of the practices and principles that related to the three. We did, in fact, find that there were some of the practices and principles around the three steps. We also found something else. We found that those organizations who were successful had taken on a fourth category, which was maintaining the change. They were not only identifying needs and creating a vision and putting in place an implementation strategy, they had some structures in place to maintain the change. So we added a fourth category (Exhibit 1). I'm not going to go over these principles in detail; however, I will highlight several of them in this paper.

EXHIBIT I

Leibowitz, Farren, Kaye, Designing Career Development Systems

I. Needs: Defining the Present System
   Principles:
   - Address specific needs and target groups
   - Assess current human resource structures
   - Investigate organization culture

II. Vision: Determining New Directions and Possibilities
   Principles:
   - Build from a conceptual base or model
   - Design multiple interventions for employees and the organization
   - Involve managers

III. Action Plan—Deciding on Practical First Steps
   Principles:
   - Assure top management support
   - Codesign and manage project with an advisory group.
   - Create a pilot and establish a budget and staffing plan

IV. Results: Maintaining the Change
   Principles:
   - Create long-term, formalized approaches
   - Publicize the program
   - Evaluate and redesign

The first principle that I really want to spend a few minutes on is one we identified across the board from every organization that we interviewed. That is, the one thing that made a clear difference in whether organizations were successful in career development was that first category, defining the present system and identifying the needs or the problems or the opportunity. Organizations we interviewed told us that career development was successful in their organization because it was tied to some need or problem or opportunity. It emanated from a statement of what it is they were trying to address, not coming in with workshops or microcomputer systems, which were solutions in search of problems. Instead, they started with an articulation of what was the problem or need they wanted to address and then designed their programs to respond to that problem or need. Let me share with you a list of some of the problems or needs that we surfaced in organization:

- Shortage of promotional employees
- Numerous plateaued employees
- Rapid turnover of non-exempt population
- Loss of high potential employees
- Shrinking middle management cadre
- Need to adapt to rapidly changing technology
- Blending talent due to merger/acquisition
- Lack of "bench strength" in managerial ranks
- Slow growth or shrinking organization
- Lack of compliance with EEO standards
- New employees leaving soon after starting their jobs

Some of these may look familiar to you. It's interesting, that some of these are recent drivers for career development, such as mergers, acquisitions, succession planning, lack of bench strength and management pools. These needs in particular over the last two or three years have become the first step to initiate career development in many organizations. Most importantly we found that what was really critical was being very clear about why you were initiating career development in your organization. Which of these you were trying to address, and then creating your approaches in response to these needs.

Let me now share with you a visual depiction of a career development system that covers many of the twelve principles (Exhibit 2). If you look at the core of the model, what we're trying to support, bottom line, is an employee-supervisor discussion. If you take that a little farther, it's particular employees with particular needs such as new employees who are leaving quickly, or new supervisors, or target groups. Those are the particular employees you're trying to strengthen having a career discussion with their supervisor. If you now take a look at the top of the model, there are many career development technologies described, e.g., career resource centers, workshops. That's an area that's grown very rapidly. I think too rapidly because again sometimes they're not used in the context of what the needs or issues are the organization is trying to address. These are the pieces many of us know about. We know about workshops, we know about workbooks, we know about microcomputer systems, but we're often not sure what to do with them. In the model those interventions are tools to support the employee and that supervisor talking to one another. If you move down to the bottom of the model, what I see them talking to one another about are several data points. The first is: What do I do as an employee that makes me unique? What are my skills, my strengths, my interests? What's my work experience been like? What do I do well? What do I need to strengthen? The traditional self-assessment piece. Another data point I see them talking about is do you see me, you, my supervisor, in the same way I see myself? And that's a step that's often left out of career development, the so-called reality check. All of us have a clear picture of ourselves and we tend to hold on to it for dear life. It's very important for employees to check that picture out.

EXHIBIT 2
A "Systems" Model

- Philosophy of Career Development
- Roles and Responsibilities

- Career Resource Centers
- Workshops
- Workbooks
- Rotation Programs
- Individual Counseling
- Mentor Programs
- Microcomputer Programs

- Accountability
- Skills

Manager-Employee Discussion

- Performance Appraisal

- Self Assessment
- Reality Check
- Goal Identification
- Development Planning

- Strategic Planning
- Human Resource Planning

- Institutionalization of Process

- Training and Development
- Tuition Reimbursement

Another discussion point is around goals and options. If I, as an employee have a certain concept of what I do well and you agree with me, what are the possibilities in this company? Where can I fit? Where does my self-assessment, in fact, connect with the reality in this organization? Where can I go? And, finally, putting in place some action plan or development plan. What are the steps I need to take to realize those goals and objectives? Those are the four discussion points between an employee and a supervisor.

Now let's move out to the perimeter of the model because the perimeter for me illustrates the system's pieces that really make a difference. The discussion between an employee and supervisor can go on but in order for that discussion to be supported and to be successful, some of these systems' pieces must be in place. If you take a look from the top, some of them include an articulation by an organization of what is the organization's career development philosophy? Who's responsible for what in career development? Roles and responsibilities should translate to what organizations have in place to support those roles and responsibilities. If organizations believe that it's the responsibility of their employees to engage in self-assessment activities, what's in place for them to play out that responsibility?

Let's move down the left-hand side. Another key piece is, if organizations want their supervisors to hold career discussion with their employees, what are they doing to both make them accountable and how are they providing them with training or giving them some skills to hold those discussions? Those are key supports; managers coaching employees doesn't happen automatically. There are probably 10% of managers in any one company who do a good job in this arena. The other 90% have to have some additional accountabilities and some skills. Other systems and pieces illustrated in the model include linking those other human resource structures such as performance appraisal. There needs to be some interface between how employees are doing right now in their current job and what the implications are for next steps. There has to be a tie there. We use this adage that says career development without performance appraisal is hope without reality. Performance appraisal without career development is reality without hope. What is needed are hope and reality; the two need to be tied together.

Some of the other system pieces include: How do you link development plans to what you already have in place in training and development? How do you link it to tuition reimbursement? What's the tie between supervisors and employees having some concept of the organizational realities with strategic planning activities, with some of your human resource planning activities. What's the supply and demand question? What's going to be needed? Do employee goals fit that picture of what's going to be needed? And, finally, the last bullet on the model, is institutionalization of the process. How do you keep career development as an on-going way of doing business rather than just simply a once a year, let's sit down and get this over with discussion?

With that as a general systems model, what I want to share with you now are some examples of how organizations have taken this picture and individualized it to meet their needs and requirements.

First is a model of a career management program in a large telecommunications company. Let me start with a little bit of background about this company and why they chose to get involved in career management. This was an organization that, predivestiture, was charged with some of the systems engineering issues in the organization. There were a lot of electrical engineers, a lot of systems' engineers doing troubleshooting for the organization. After divestiture they became the marketing arm of the organization. From a career development perspective that's switching, at least 360 degrees, between the skills required for a good systems engineer versus what's required for a good marketing person. The organization viewed this shift as a career development problem, so the first thing they did was identify the profile of a good marketing rep. What, in fact, were good marketing reps doing or not doing, and they used a number of data sources to do that. They, of course, looked to their competitors. They also had some assessment center data around skills and attributes that they used. They also had a core of marketing reps whom they had hired and some of them had been in place for about 6 months to a year. They interviewed a lot of the successful reps in terms of what they were doing to make them successful. They took all that data and they came out with a template of skills and competencies required by a good marketing rep. As a first step, what they then did is create a process around that data (Exhibit 3). If you look down the left-hand column, they designed a series of planning booklets for their employees. In those booklets employees completed some self-assessment activities around the competencies—what do I do well, what am I good at, what do I need to strengthen? They also did some looking at what was important to them in their work: what was being satisfied, what was missing? After completing that first booklet, they then sat down and had a discussion with their supervisors to reality check their assessments. Supervisors were trained in coaching skills to hold these discussions. Some of the training included viewing video tapes. As a second step, employees completed the second booklet. The objective of the second booklet was to create an interface between their skills and competencies and the various positions on the career path. So that, in fact, if I wanted to be a senior marketing rep, I had a clear picture of what was required in that particular position and I could take a look at my assessment data to see where I fit, where I fell down. The output of that second activity was to articulate three career targets. Finally, the last piece was, "If I want to reach one of these targets, what do I need to do to get ready?" Or, in some cases, it was a clear determination that there was no way that some employees were ever going to fit those jobs. As a result one of the development actions that came out was a rotational program where they were able to move into some of the other parts of the company such as market planning and product planning that were more amenable and more consistent with some of their engineering backgrounds and skills.

EXHIBIT 3
Career Management Program Telecommunications Company
Objective: To help identify "best fits" to a marketing role
First Step: Identification of Key Marketing Skills/Attributes

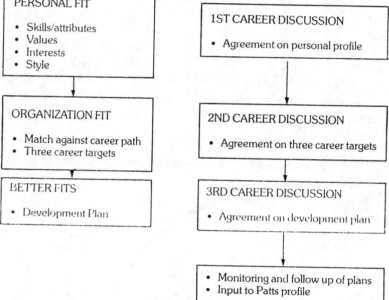

EMPLOYEE STEPS

SUPERVISOR-EMPLOYEE
DISCUSSIONS

PERSONAL FIT
- Skills/attributes
- Values
- Interests
- Style

1ST CAREER DISCUSSION
- Agreement on personal profile

ORGANIZATION FIT
- Match against career path
- Three career targets

2ND CAREER DISCUSSION
- Agreement on three career targets

BETTER FITS
- Development Plan

3RD CAREER DISCUSSION
- Agreement on development plan

- Monitoring and follow up of plans
- Input to Patts profile

The name of this program was "Creating Better Fit." The objective was how the organization could better align the employees that they had with the positions that were available. And if they didn't fit, to be able to help them to access other places in the organization to which they could go. Let me just quickly review this model. Again, it's needs driven. The need was to change and to move this organization from a system engineering organization to a marketing organization. Part of the whole effort was to strengthen the employee-supervisor career discussion process. As a matter of fact, there was absolutely no connection here between the human resource department and the employees. This was all manager-driven, the human resource people never talked to the employees. They, in fact, supported the supervisors in talking with their employees. And, finally, the result of what came out of these discussions were development plans or plans to move people throughout the system. The path profile in the model is an automatic skills inventory where some of the data that came out of the last discussion was, in fact, housed in that system for future retrieval for looking at particular positions and people in the system.

Next, is a model (Exhibit 4) that many organizations are facing as a challenge right now. This is a little less need-driven. You can't clearly define a particular employee group, but it is a career development challenge that organizations are facing. That is, how do you, in some integrated way, tie career development to your performance appraisal? Let me start by giving you a little bit of background on this organization. They have a really excellent performance appraisal system and that's one key. If you' re going to, in fact, tie career development to performance appraisal, make sure what you already have can support that fit. Don't build a castle on a weak foundation. So make sure what's already there is good. They started with a good system, called Performance Development and Review System (PD&R). As they described it, the "D" in the PD&R was a lower case "d"

EXHIBIT 4
Career Development Performance Appraisal System

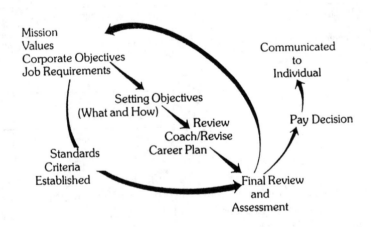

and their objective was to make it an upper case "D." They wanted to add some attention to the development aspect. What they had in the past was a form containing a paragraph that said "what do you think you'd like to do, what are your career steps?" And, they'd get responses like "I don't know," or "nobody would pay attention to it." It wouldn't be filled out and there wasn't a lot of quality there. They wanted to really amplify that development paragraph and make it much more a substantive statement around what people wanted to do and what kinds of things they needed to do to get ready. So what they did is they set up a calendar-driven, institutionalized system, so that some of the context and background were an articulation against the mission and the organization's values. They have a very strong corporate statement about values. Based on that information, an employee would sit down with their boss in January and they would define some clear result statements and some behaviors—how they were going to accomplish those results. What are you going to be held accountable for and how are you going to do it. Midyear, in June, they would sit down and they would review those actions to see what needs to be changed, what needs to be revised, why employees might be off track. But, this is where they added the career development piece. There is at least, an hour long discussion at this point around career options. What they've trained their supervisors to do is to have that discussion again with in the context of how their employees are doing in their current job. In order for the employees to get ready for that discussion, they went through a microcomputer system that helps them to look at their skills, their values, their interests, and set some goals within the organization. The system is able to search a data base of options based on their self-assessment profile. They then come prepared to the discussion with that information and use it as the basis of an exchange with their supervisor. Finally, there's another session where there's a performance review looking back on results and behaviors and also taking a look at the career development plan and updating and changing it and using that as a continual discussion tool to keep career development issues alive and well. One key that made this system successful was separating out the career development discussion from the settling of objectives and the appraisal piece. It's a separate time but it's tied. As such it gets around the issue of how can a supervisor be a judge, jury, and helper at the same time. It doesn't require them to do all of that at one session. It separates them.

The third model was a utilities organization, and the objective was to develop the skills of their mid-career managers and to help them put in place a career development plan. What might be their next career steps? (Exhibit 5) But, there was a dual purpose. The other purpose was to provide managers with some skills in coaching and counseling their employee. They tried to combine two tracks. Let me just touch on what are some of the interesting pieces of this model. They started with a template of the key competencies for good managers. From a career development perspective, these competencies provided an articulation of what counted for success in a mid-manager job in this organization. They served as a reference point for manager and employees to measure up against.

EXHIBIT 5
Mid-Career Managers Program Model

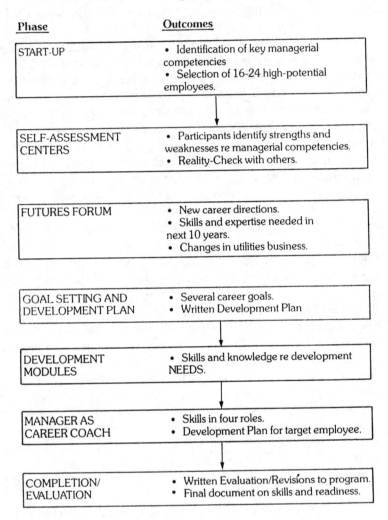

Phase	Outcomes
START-UP	• Identification of key managerial competencies • Selection of 16-24 high-potential employees.
SELF-ASSESSMENT CENTERS	• Participants identify strengths and weaknesses re managerial competencies. • Reality-Check with others.
FUTURES FORUM	• New career directions. • Skills and expertise needed in next 10 years. • Changes in utilities business.
GOAL SETTING AND DEVELOPMENT PLAN	• Several career goals. • Written Development Plan
DEVELOPMENT MODULES	• Skills and knowledge re development NEEDS.
MANAGER AS CAREER COACH	• Skills in four roles. • Development Plan for target employee.
COMPLETION/ EVALUATION	• Written Evaluation/Revisions to program. • Final document on skills and readiness.

The second step was to identify a group of select high potential employees by management nomination. The next interesting step was to set up what they called a Self-Assessment Center and they designed a number of activities where employees were able to experience some simulations and some "in-basket" activities and use this data to identify development needs vis-a-vis the competencies. They also provided the participants with information about where the utilities industry was going, e.g., deregulation, so that these managers would have a perspective to set their career goals within the broader industry. They then created development plans vis-a-vis their strength and development needs. Finally, they created development modules that participants could use and participate in to strengthen the competencies in which they were weakest. Many of these modules emphasized non-training activities such as on-the job learning and readings. Lastly, they received training in career coaching skills to work with their employees. Again, the objective of this program was two-fold: to provide mid-managers an approach to develop themselves but, also, to provide them some skills to work with their employees.

The next case study (Exhibit 6) is an organization that is a brokerage house. What initiated career development was a Class Action Suit. The recommendation, however, was that they not only design a career development program for women and minorities because such an effort might preclude the isolated groups from moving into midstream activities. The intent of this program was, in fact, to open up the potential pool of all employees who could move into management. Traditionally, what happens is that there is a funnel created of people who are considered for management. The objective of this program was to flip that funnel and to try to identify people who traditionally don't even get into that funnel. They did that in some interesting ways. They sent out a general call to supervisors and managers to begin to identify people who traditionally they might not have thought about who might have management potential, then they got them involved in a number of development activities. They also set up a formal mentor program. They chose mentoring because women and minorities don't often have access to the political chain and to people who are above their particular management level. This was a way to, in fact, formalize some of that access by pairing them with mentors. Each mentor had about three or four mentees. Also, many of the participants had never had the opportunity to work on project teams. They set up what they called development quartets where four people worked on particular projects that were of interest to the organization, e.g., looking at a way to streamline a procedure in part of the organization. As a result they put together some recommendations and made a presentation. The presentation provided a high degree of visibility for participants.

The final output of this whole effort was what I call a living, breathing resume or a profile. What they did is create a profile that is much richer than what you'd find in a skills inventory. It was a handwritten profile, had four pages to it and it was like a living resume. It included questions like: "If you had to design one particular project that you think would impact your division, what would you do?" It provided a lot of data to people looking at that profile. Those profiles were what were circulated for future staffing decision of management candidates. This program has been able to document, in fact, in the first year that it was in place they increased their numbers of women and minorities moving into management by about 34%.

EXHIBIT 6
Management Readiness

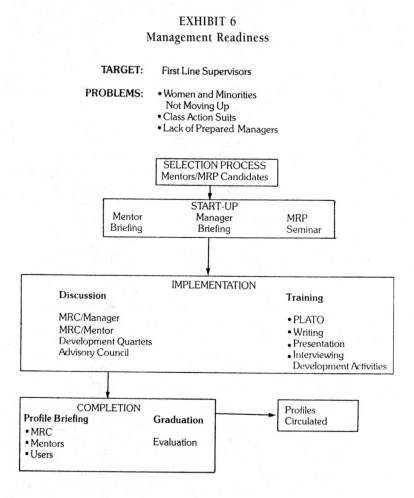

TARGET: First Line Supervisors

PROBLEMS: • Women and Minorities
               Not Moving Up
             • Class Action Suits
             • Lack of Prepared Managers

SELECTION PROCESS
Mentors/MRP Candidates

START-UP
Mentor   Manager   MRP
Briefing   Briefing   Seminar

IMPLEMENTATION
Discussion   Training

MRC/Manager   • PLATO
MRC/Mentor   • Writing
Development Quartets   • Presentation
Advisory Council   • Interviewing
                                Development Activities

COMPLETION
Profile Briefing   Graduation   Profiles
• MRC   Circulated
• Mentors   Evaluation
• Users

The final model I want to cover is Succession Planning model (Exhibit 7). This is another challenge that many organizations are facing, which is how do you link career development to succession planning? And, in fact, they are very much related. What's happened in the past, is that many organization have done succession planning and simply dealt with the replacement issues. They have not, in fact, developed people to move into those positions. They've ignored the development piece. So this is an attempt to develop people, to get them ready for particular positions. What this model starts with is putting the whole concept of supply and demand within the context of strategic planning. Where's the organization going, and then some articulation on what positions and what skills and requirements are going to be needed in the future? That's the demand side of the formula, that's traditionally what gets done in most places. Now where this model moves from what's traditional is on the development piece. And what they've done here is the same as what we talked about before. They've flipped that funnel. So what you've got is not a selection initially of your high potential or your potential replacement candidates. Instead, it's an opportunity for pools of people to, in fact, participate in development activities and then the selection decision is made. This model also very much opens up succession planning. That is, what you've got in these development activities is a clear statement of participation by the employees as to what their strengths are, and what they're interested in. That data, in fact, is surfaced to the Selection Committee. Candidates have a real say in their development and future movement. Also, what they used here, similarly to some of the other models, is defined competencies, and they then used a number of self-assessment procedures. Participants completed what was called a written assessment and they included in that written assessment a number of multiple data points. They assessed themselves, their boss assessed them, subordinates assessed them, and their peers assessed them. All that data was summarized. The other thing they did was a variation of a Self Assessment Center. Participants completed activities and simulations to also judge their strengths and development needs. All of that was combined again into a development plan. They then sat with their supervisor to talk about that plan. Finally, they participated in development activities that were again tied to the competencies. So if things needed strengthening, that's what was being worked on, not simply development for development sake. Then at the end, there was a reassessment and the profile and skills and readiness statement was sent to a Management Committee.

In summary, let me cite some of the commonalities of these models. What was presented was that most of these models addressed a particular need or target group. The program that emanated was designed to address that need or problem. There were several key commonalities to some of these programs. One was that, of course, there was an employee-supervisor discussion. Another was that there was an opportunity for employees to articulate and identify their skills, strengths and development needs. And in many cases, what we saw was a multiple assessment model. The third element was that there was an opportunity to connect a participant's picture of what's agreed upon that they're good at and what they need to strengthen with some potential goals and targets in the organization. And finally, there is a pulling together of all this into a development plan this ties back to the previous self assessment. All of these pieces tied together translate into a career development system.

EXHIBIT 7
Succession Planning a Development Approach

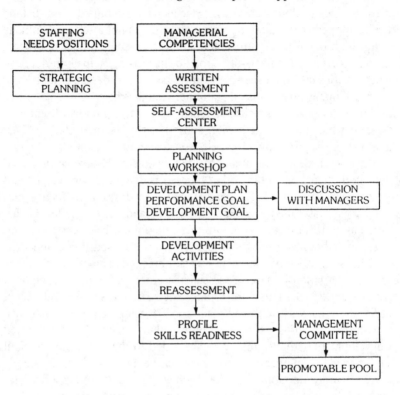

Afterward Comments

Thomas Gutteriedge, Zandy Leibowitz, and Jane Shore

Organizational career development (OCD) has evolved over the last several decades as a key business strategy for improving workforce effectiveness. Yet there have been only a few systematic attempts to document this growth, to examine its implications or highlight best practices. *Organizational Career Development: Benchmarks for Building a World-Class Workforce* builds upon the survey methodology of a 1978 AMA sponsored study (Walker and Gutteridge, 1979) and the case study approach of a 1983 research project. While our comments focus exclusively on the U.S. study, parallel research was also conducted in Australia, Europe, and Singapore. The book examines the results from these international surveys and compares the findings with our U.S. results.

The 1990-91 U.S. survey included a random sample of 1,000 U.S. corporations and 96 governmental agencies. A mailed questionnaire, together with a targeted telephone follow-up, produced a 26% corporate response rate and 27 governmental responses (28%). This preview will deal only with the corporate sample.

Our "typical" respondent organization was a large multinational manufacturing organization, headquartered in the Midwest, with an annual budget of over $1 billion. Among our key findings were:

- Over two-thirds (68%) of our respondents either had (47%) or were establishing (21%) a career development system. The top three drivers cited by organizations for establishing a career development system were: desire to develop/promote from within (23%), shortage of promotable talent (14%), and organizational commitment to career development (13%). Twelve percent cited the development of an organizational strategic plan. This emphasis on upward mobility is somewhat surprising given the prominence of such issues as plateauing, delayering, and low growth organizational career structures.

- Among the reasons cited by those firms who either did not have a system (31%) or had discontinued their system (2%) were: insufficient support by top management (54%), insufficient budgetary resources (37%), and lack of HR capability (27%).

- Respondents viewed the responsibility for OCD to be 51% employees', 25% managers, and 24% organizations' (top management and HR staff).
- A majority of OCD programs (74%) are targeted to fast track management candidates; half are targeted to minorities and women. Fifty-nine percent included non-exempt salaried employees but only 36 percent included hourly workers.
- Usage of various career development practices included (in rank order):

Tuition reimbursement	95%
In-house training and development programs	92%
External serminars/workshops	91%
Employee orientation programs	86%
Job posting	83%
Personnel career counseling	83%
Supervisor career discussions	83%
Job rotation	54%
Supervisor training in holding career discussions	44%
Job enrichment	41%
Career planning workshops	34%
Career planning software	13%

It seems that OCD practices still focus heavily on traditional training and development activities and upward mobility.

In terms of organizational attitudes, organizations, managers, and employees all view career development as an important undertaking. Career development is seen as bringing important returns to the organization, through, for example, improved utilization of employee talents, enhanced job performance, implementation of the organization's strategic plan, and assistance in helping employees deal with a low growth environment.

Career development does not usually create such feared negative consequences as increased turnover, heightened employee anxiety, and organizational disruption; however, career development means an increased burden for supervisors that few are equipped to handle.

Other findings include:

- Nearly half of respondents used a task force or advisory group to help design or implement their career development system and rated their effectiveness as above average (3.6 or 5 point scale).

- Nearly one-quarter of the respondents do not evaluate the impact of their career systems and, of those that do, nearly two-thirds rely heavily on informal verbal feedback. Less than thirty percent of the respondents perceive their OCD systems to be somewhat or very effective.
- Many organizations plan to expand and refine their current programs with greater systemization and integration.
- Among the perceived impact of OCD efforts are:
  Enhanced employee retention
  Enhanced employee skills and morale
  Enhanced empowerment
  Demonstration of organizational commitment
  Improved HR planning
  Better strategic advantage
- Among the things respondents said they would have done differently were more training and buy-in of managers, better funding and commitment of resources, and more systemized implementation, evaluation, and accountability.
- Respondents believe OCD has changed in the last decade by shifting toward:
  Greater employee responsibility
  Becoming a results-oriented part of a strategic business plan
  Increased formality and systemization
  Greater efficiency and range of available tools

While the current survey results were surprisingly similar to the 1978 ones, the best practice investigation showed how innovative tools and techniques have grown increasingly sophisticated.

Some examples of best practices are as follows:

- Corning Incorporated has a system for developing its workforce that has moved beyond its initial career information and planning activities. Development options are directly linked to business needs and strategies, and the process is tied to other company HR initiatives. Conditions of success for development systems are established, as a means of benchmarking and measurement. Also, a process is being designed to hold managers accountable for employee development and training.
- Internal placement and development is facilitated through 3M's Job Information System. All jobs up through the Director level are posted electronically, and the system is linked to a human resource review process. Feedback to applicants is emphasized and among the ben-

efits of the program are improved employee skill identification and expanded career information.

- An insurance company's Technical Excellence Program is a way of retaining and rewarding talented technical contributors. The program provides an annual allowance to participants as well as cash awards for educational accomplishments and projects that save the company money. Response to the program has been positive and plans are underway for its expansion.

- A telecommunications company has a development initiative designed to enhance the role of managers as people developers. The initiative combines accountability and skill-building through three features: a required development discussion between employees and managers, manager documentation of direct reports' development activity, and a survey for 360 degree feedback.

- Ford instituted the Leadership Education and Development Program to meet the need for middle manager training in response to a changing environment. The program, developed in partnership with the University of Michigan, emphasizes adult learning principles and on-the-job application. Ongoing evaluation has documented the program's success.

In summary, our examination of organizational best practices has uncovered a number of features of success, including tying development to business strategy, building systems linkages, providing evaluation and continuous improvement, line manager involvement and accountability, offering multiple tools and interventions, and emphasizing publicity and high visibility.

REFERENCES

Walker, J. W., Gutteridge, T. G. *Career Planning Practices*. AMA Survey Report. New York: AMACOM, 1979.

Gutteridge, T. G., Leibowitz, Z. B., Shore, J. E. *Organizational Career Development: Benchmarks for Building a World-Class Workforce*. San Francisco: Jossey-Bass, 1993.

ORGANIZATIONAL CAREER MANAGEMENT: THE NEED FOR A SYSTEMS APPROACH

James D. Portwood

In the rush to institute career-oriented programs, many organizations may be ignoring the considerable complexity of the career development process. Career programs cannot be effective unless they are closely integrated with a comprehensive human resource management system from which information and support may be drawn. The necessary prerequisites for an effective career management effort are discussed, as well as some of the problems often encountered in mounting such programs. The author is an Assistant Professor of Industrial Relations and Organizational Behavior at Temple University in Philadelphia.

Effective management and utilization of people in organizations has never been an easy task. That task, however, is becoming increasingly difficult (and important) as companies attempt to cope with a rising tide of uncertainty and change in today's business environment. Organizations have experienced mounting pressure in the human resource area from such diverse factors as spreading government regulations, escalating employee aspirations, and stiffening labor market competition for critical skills. Such problems have forced management to search for new and innovative means to encourage maximum development and productivity from employees.

For many organizations, the response has been to institute some sort of career management program. The attractiveness of this option is based on evidence that improved development and promotion possibilities afforded by such programs can aid in recruiting efforts, while increasing the commitment and tenure of current employees (Hall and Hall, 1976). Career management efforts also provide informa-

Reprinted from *Human Resource Planning*, Vol. 1, No. 4 (1981), 47-59.

tion that is helpful in identifying and speeding the development of high potential management talent as well as in tracking minorities to insure compliance with EEO/AA requirements (Morgan, et al. 1979).

What is less often discussed, but equally significant, are the risks and problems involved in implementing a career management program. Such programs can be extremely costly in terms of management and employee time, training expenses. and information processing requirements (Walker, 1978). The organization also risks raising employee expectations which may later go unmet. Failure to fulfill aspirations encouraged by career programs can lead to a backlash of employee frustration and alienation. Fears such as these have often caused managerial resistance to career management efforts, thus reducing significantly the probability of program success.

In view of these facts, it is important for organizations to give serious consideration to the consequences before deciding to institute any career management program. The potential advantages are attractive, but once begun it is difficult to back away from this commitment. Since the cost of failure is relatively high, organizations should be aware of and willing to commit the time and resources necessary to insure an effective program. This article will identify some of the prerequisites for successful career development and discuss implications for the design and operation of career management programs.

ACCOMMODATING EMPLOYEE ASPIRATIONS AND ORGANIZATIONAL REQUIREMENTS

Careers have been described as the most fundamental transaction to take place between individuals and organizations (Leach, 1977). This view suggests a process of two actors pursuing personal needs or goals through mutual exchange or accommodation. Such an adjustment process would ideally continue until both sides perceived equity in the exchange. This model of career management is not always adhered to, however. Career development efforts are sometime seen as primarily a management tool, with the focus directed toward what the program can do for the organization. This strategy ignores the need to involve individuals in the planning of their own future. A one-sided approach of this type often leads to employee apathy or frustration, and failure of the program.

Management should deal with employees as co-equal partners in career planning and decision making. This, however, will require a significant shifting of emphasis in some organizations. Preparatory education of management, emphasizing the necessity of this cooperative approach, can be an important preliminary step in launching career management efforts.

At the opposite extreme, career programs are sometimes focused wholly on the desires of the individual employee. Elaborate systems and procedures may be developed in isolation from the actual reality of the organizational setting. Here the problem is a failure to link individual career plans to organizational manpower planning (Wellbank, 1978). Employees encouraged to express personal needs and elaborate career plans without reference to organizational constraints as well as opportunities, are likely to develop unrealistic (and unattainable) expectations concerning future career possibilities. Later, faced with a mismatch between individual aspirations and employer needs, employees will often reject both the program and the organization.

To insure the coherence and coordination needed for a successful career program, business must link individual and organizational demands both conceptually and procedurally in the career management process. Conceptually, a career may be thought of as a parallel decision-making process, with individuals seeking out and pursuing attractive occupations (internal career), while organizations develop and utilize employees under their control as the external career (Van Maanen and Schein, 1977).

Both individuals and organizations should recognize that they are constrained in their career-related decision making by the action of the other party. Schein (1978) suggests that this recognition comes only when both sides adopt a "career development perspective," focusing on the fact that careers involve individuals growing and maturing within an organizational context.

Procedurally, linking individual and organizational decision making will require extensive two-way communication. Each side must be willing to inform the other of prior actions and decisions, as well as provide information relevant to future career planning. A mutually agreeable mechanism for integrating and recording career-related plans and decisions must also be developed. This "agreement" can then be referred to by both parties as they develop career management strategies.

The integration process involves three specific activities: (1) person-job matching, (2) individual career counseling, and (3) development of an individual career plan. Initially, the organization must assess the degree of fit between each current or prospective employee and projected career opportunities available in the company. This assessment begins with employees' induction into the organization, but it must also be continued as individuals develop and progress. It is important for the organization to be aware of individuals' suitability for future as well as current positions (Ackerman, 1979)

An operational model for integrating individual and organizational career management efforts is outlined in Figure 1:

FIGURE 1
Integrating Individual Needs and Organizational Requirements

A personal assessment of job and career match should also be under-taken periodically by each employee. Research suggests, however, that individuals often do a very poor job of managing their careers (Sarason, et al. 1975). While this may seem to be primarily a problem for the employee, evidence of high turnover and low productivity among mismatched workers indicates that it is a problem management cannot ignore (Porter and Steers, 1973; Schein, 1968).

One way to avoid these problems is to increase employee awareness of the need for personal career assessment. Support and information can then be provided to assist employees in their analysis. This assistance should begin with the initial job orientation and continue, through individual career counseling as the employee progresses in the organization.

Career counseling can take the form of periodic manager-subordinate conferences, or meetings with a human resource department representative. Whatever the format, the goal of this counseling should be to prepare the employee to make intelligent career decisions within the existing organizational context (Kravetz and Derderian, 1980).

Both parties should also be working toward the development of a formal career plan. This plan should specify career parameters established through the merging of individual and organizational requirements. The plan can be used as a "road map" identifying alternative career options, as a mechanism for directing employee development efforts, and as a statement against which to judge career progress.

If carefully developed and adhered to, individual career plans can form the basis for a solid, successful career management effort. Recognizing the need to formalize career plans, most organizations have made written documentation of this contractual agreement part of the overall career management process. Even when extra care is taken to specify career plans, however, problems can still arise. These problems generally stem from one of two deficiencies. First it is often the case that neither individuals nor organizations are fully aware of the scope of their needs, or the constraints they impose on the career planning process. This lack of understanding results in career plans that may be unrealistic, overly optimistic, or incomplete.

The second problem arises when career programs are instituted and plans drawn up without attention to the adequacy of support systems necessary for implementation of the career program. Support systems in areas such as employee appraisal, development, and information processing are often nonexistent or inappropriate to meet requirements of the career management program. The next sections will consider what specific individual and organizational factors should be considered, and what type of support systems should be in place prior to any career program being initiated.

ORGANIZATIONAL ANALYSIS

It was noted earlier that success in career management efforts depends on organizations and individuals making realistic and compatible career/job decisions. Effective career decision making, in turn, depends on accurate, comprehensive information concerning demands, conditions, and constraints likely to impact career outcomes. In this relationship, the organization must take responsibility for providing information on company context and expectations. Organizations, however, often fail to meet this obligation.

Such failures can easily be explained; you can't deliver what you don't have. Many organizations concentrate almost exclusively on job task requirements in selecting and developing employees, while ignoring other factors relevant to person/organization matching. Schneider (1976) concludes that these neglected factors are critical enough in manpower management efforts to warrant including a formal "organizational analysis" as part of the human resources management system. The analysis would focus on such issues as organizational goals, reward systems, and climate, as well as general job requirements. A factor model of the intraorganizational milieu is presented in Figure 2.

It has been suggested that individuals evaluate their relationship with an employing organization in terms of the balance between inducements and contributions associated with that relationship (March and Simon, 1958). When making career decisions, individuals must assess the status of this balance for positions they may be asked to accept. Organizations may assist the decision process by providing specific information on job demands and rewards available in positions for which these employees may be considered.

As a first step, the organization must itself be aware of all demands and rewards associated with these positions. Many times organizations restrict their discussions with employees to issues of task performance vs. extrinsic rewards. Figure 2 indicates some other significant dimensions that should be analyzed and discussed.

FIGURE 2
Organizational Analysis
Defining the Job Content/Context

Organizations certainly require individual task performance as one contribution, but output usually results from the efforts of many employees working together in predictable patterns (Liddell and Slocum, 1976; Alderfer, 1977). Companies, therefore, must consider how employees behave, as well as what they produce. This suggests that information should be made available to employees concerning rules and policies to be followed (conformance requirements), expected relations with others in the work group (compatibility requirements), and required commitment and tenure on the job (attachment requirements).

On the opposite side of the inducements contribution equation, extrinsic rewards represent only a portion of the inducements employees now demand and expect from their careers. Increasingly, employees are focusing on the availability of intrinsic rewards such as challenge, autonomy, and personal growth in evaluating career opportunities (Hackman and Lawler, 1971; Hackman, 1977). If organizations are interested in presenting an accurate picture of job-related inducements, they will need to assess and describe career options in terms of both intrinsic and extrinsic reward possibilities.

Since jobs do not exist in isolation, the inducement contribution balance is affected by the general physical and psychological context within which the jobs are embedded. Organizations have particular modes of operation based on the type of structures, leadership styles, and social climates they develop. Current research findings emphasize the need for individuals to understand and accept the existing job environment, since both job satisfaction and motivation have been shown to be influenced by the degree of fit (Pritchard and Karasick, 1973; Downey, et al. 1975).

Organizations must be ready to identify and communicate to career track employees all critical aspects of the intraorganizational environment. Relevant information of this type, coupled with a detailed job description, should prepare the individual to evaluate available career opportunities in terms of his or her own career plans. This assumes of course, that the individual has developed career aspirations that are stable, comprehensive, and realistic.

INDIVIDUAL ANALYSIS

Organizations accepting the above assumption concerning employees' personal career preparation may be rudely surprised, however. Douglas Hall (1976) has characterized managers planning their careers as having much in common with Alice in Wonderland. That is, they get lost in the woods and have a hard time finding their way out. This problem often begins with some confusion over career goals and leads managers to adopt a passive or reactive strategy in the career development process (Roe and Baruch, 1967).

Organizations may benefit both the employee and themselves by encouraging and facilitating individual self-analysis. As a starting point, it will be important for the organization to assess each employee's degree of career maturity. Schein (1978) discusses maturity in terms of career stages, suggesting that individuals progress through a series of such stages from early exploration through final disengagement. At each stage, individuals face new problems, but also become successively more focused and directed in their career efforts. Knowledge of individuals' career stages or levels of maturity will provide the organization with some understanding of the likely stability and scope of career aspirations. From this they should be better able to assist employees in identifying and coping with personal barriers to career fulfillment. As an example, in early career stages employees may need help in articulating career aspirations. At later stages, more emphasis may be placed on meshing personal aspirations with organizational needs, or redefining aspirations to meet personal and organizational constraints.

In assessing the status of employees' career aspirations, the organization should remember that each individual's career potential is influenced by a unique combination of personal needs, abilities, and life characteristics (see Figure 3):

FIGURE 3
Individual Analysis
Identifying Employee Expectations/Constraints

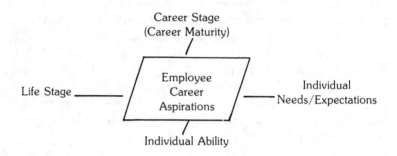

It is critical for both organizations and individuals to recognize the characteristics and accompanying implications associated with each of these factor sets.

An individual's career aspirations generally reflect some aspects of that person's needs and self-perceptions (Super, 1957; Holland, 1966). Specifically, people tend to seek out career opportunities they feel will meet their needs and match their self-identity. As the search process progresses, individuals develop expectations concerning rewards and demands associated with various jobs and organizations. They also generate aspirations relative to their own future. People, however, are often unsure of their needs and/or the nature of jobs they are considering. This can lead, in turn, to unrealistic expectations, and aspirations.

In this case, the organization may assist individuals by providing realistic information concerning job and career opportunities, while encouraging them to consider and express personal needs, expectations and aspirations. Evidence suggests that organizations may be especially effective in influencing employee expectations if the effort is begun early in their tenure with the firm (Wanous, 1975; Portwood and Miller, 1976).

The organization may also help by identifying for the individual potential barriers to personal career goal attainment. In addition to organizational constraints discussed earlier, the individual may be subject to self-imposed barriers due to deficiencies in personal ability or interference from nonwork commitments. The organization should help the individual to see and deal with these conflicts. Some conflicts can be alleviated. However, if this fails, the organization will need to assist the individual in making some difficult decisions concerning his/her future in the firm.

Personal ability sets an upper limit on attainable career aspirations. Effective career management programs would not project individuals past their level of competence. Training may serve to increase skill up to a point, but this, too, has its limits. Many managers will "top out" in their careers somewhere in the middle management ranks. Such an occurrence could have a significant negative impact on many aspiring managers. Carnazza (1981) has found, however, that organizations can work constructively with these managers to continue their personal growth even though career progression has ceased. This suggests the need to include all managers in career programs, not just high potential "movers."

Employees today are increasingly burdened with off-job commitments that complicate career management efforts. As with limits imposed by personal ability, the organization must be sure that the individual is aware of impending conflicts and is given the opportunity to (as much as possible) accommodate these commitments. Such constraints take on added significance because they may also block organizational plans for utilizing individuals.

With the increasing incidence of dual-career families, and the increasing reluctance of employees to give up family, community and leisure pursuits, organizations are finding it more difficult to plan effectively (in manpower and succession planning) without considering these constraints (Greenhaus and Kopelman, 1981). To give themselves as much flexibility as possible and to aid individuals in their career decision-making, organizations may need to collect additional data on employees' existing and anticipated nonwork roles. The organization can then work with employees to reduce potential conflict arising from work and nonwork commitments.

Once the organization has a firm grip on its own situation and is assured that its employees are prepared to participate knowledgeably, it is possible to implement a career management program. Integration of the individual and organizational perspectives, however, only provides a conducive environment for career management. Success depends on a well-organized, comprehensive system for carrying out the process.

SYSTEM DEVELOPMENT

The specific structure and sequence of activities in career management programs varies widely across organizations. The variation is often dictated by the unique characteristics of the organizational setting and environmental forces present as the career program evolved. All programs, however, require certain basic support systems regardless of exact implementation strategies.

Logical promotional progressions (career paths) must be established to provide career program participants with alternative career opportunities from which to choose. Such choices would be of little value if programs were not available to train and develop participants so that they are prepared to take advantage of these promotional opportunities. The effectiveness of training and development is, in turn, dependent on the availability of information concerning employee needs and current status (monitoring system), and on the degree of line management commitment to follow up this training on the job.

These functions are generally recognized as important to career management efforts and are incorporated into most programs to some extent. What is less often recognized is that the effectiveness of these primary support systems is significantly influenced by the availability and compatibility of numerous secondary support systems. The critical primary and related secondary support systems are shown in Figure 4.

FIGURE 4
System Development
Implementing Necessary Activities/Technologies

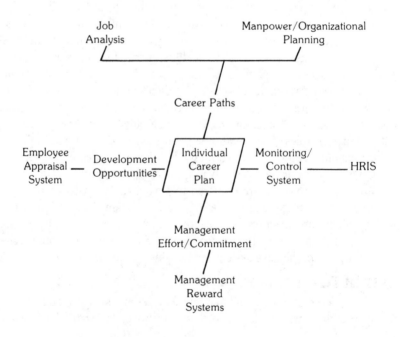

At the heart of any career program is the individual career plan. As noted earlier, this plan should be developed and updated through open negotiations between the organization and the program participant, and should reflect an accommodation between individual aspirations and organizational requirements. If this plan is to be a living, useful document, it must reflect current organizational reality, and mechanisms must be available to implement stated provisions.

To provide an organizationally based framework for mapping out individual careers, many organizations are developing career pathing structures. Ideally, career paths should identify career options for the employee, noting logical job progressions and possible developmental opportunities (Walker, 1976). The path structure must reflect the reality of what the organization is willing and able to deliver, and must provide meaningful experience for the participant. To insure that these requirements are met, career pathing must be linked to other systems that can furnish necessary information related to these issues.

The first goal of career pathing is to expose the individual to a range of experiences beneficial to his or her development. This requires that the organization know what experiences would be beneficial and what positions are likely to provide such experiences. Wellbank (1978) has suggested that one way to obtain such information is by tapping into the standard job evaluation process. Since this system assesses skills and responsibilities for a wide range of jobs in the organization, information should be available on both the requirements of the position to which the individual aspires, and potential experiences to be found in a number of lower level jobs.

The organization must also be aware that not all potential career paths may be viable given decisions being made concerning overall organizational operations. Career planners must have information on expected levels of operation, possible shifts in organizational emphasis, etc. This means having access to strategic and manpower plans. The problem with this is that these plans may not be developed with the career management function in mind. This can often make the data meaningless or difficult to assess in the career management context. Job evaluation and planning systems may have to be modified if they are to provide effective support for the career management programs. (See J. Houk, 1981, for an example of HR planning-career management integration.)

Analysis of jobs included in the employee's chosen career path should suggest areas where skills training and development might be beneficial. It is important that organizations have a range of training and development opportunities available to supplement and enhance on-the-job learning. Such programs may include formal in-house training, planned attendance at outside seminars, or tuition rebate programs. The primary concern with all of these options should be that the training meets the needs of the individual and enhances the probability of career goal attainment.

Simply having these opportunities available, however, is not enough. To maximize the effectiveness of the training effort, development programs should be tailored to the specific requirements of each program participant. This can only be done by assessing an individual's current skills and experiences in relation to the particular career path he or she has chosen. Some useful information can be obtained from the performance evaluation data that is generally available in organizations. But most performance appraisal systems are designed to assess only behavior on the current job. Several theorists (Huse, 1967; Cummings and Schwab, 1973; Leach, 1980) have noted the difficulty of attempting to use traditional performance appraisal data as a basis for evaluating developmental needs or future potential. Appraisal systems may need to be modified to meet such demands, usually by conducting separate developmental and potential appraisals that reflect shifts in relevant criteria.

Both career pathing and employee development are long-term projects requiring considerable management effort and time. The importance of these activities to career management success, coupled with the time and substantial investment necessary to develop and coordinate such efforts, suggests the advisability of installing some sort of monitoring control system to insure adequate program direction.[1]

The major problem for systems with the scope and complexity usually associated with career management programs is that over time they tend to become fragmented and disorganized. This may result in individuals being blocked or forgotten as control deteriorates. At the same time, loss of coordination across subfunctions such as training and development career counseling and manpower planning, can mean lost time, duplication of effort, and interfunction conflict.

The role of the monitoring/control system should be to develop and maintain adequate levels of integration among the various subsystems and to track individual progress in the program. This system would involve such responsibilities as: (1) reviewing the viability of career paths in view of current strategic and manpower plans; (2) assessing the adequacy and applicability of development experiences available to employees: and (3) seeing that training and job rotation schedules are logical, given the specifics of each employee's individual career plan.

---

[1] Responsibility for formal monitoring and administration of career programs is often housed in the human resource department. However, line management must also be involved since they have much closer contact with employees and their immediate work environments. See Ackerman (1979) for an example of one HR control system utilizing management oversight committees.

SHARED WISDOM

One characteristic common to all of these responsibilities is that large amounts of information must be available on request. The monitoring control system must be able to determine the status of specific programs and individuals at any point in time and on short notice. A continuous stream of decisions are required concerning such things as transfers, promotions, and training schedules.

The sheer volume of data relevant to career management efforts (career plans, counseling reports, performance evaluations, training and job history records) suggests that the most effective way to meet information management needs may be through computer-based information systems. Many companies now have such systems (Hennessey, 1979). The main advantages of these systems are immediate access and virtually unlimited capacity. These factors are especially important as organizations grow larger and decision-makers are removed farther in time and space from sources of information (Lavin, 1981).

No system, no matter how sophisticated can operate without accurate, representative data. The system must be linked with manpower planning, performance appraisal, and training systems, so that data may be funneled to the monitoring/control function through the HRIS. While much of the general organizational and oversight activities may be carried out by a centralized staff organization, Schein (1978) suggests that actual implementation of the career management program will depend on the effort and commitment of the line management group. Line managers must be active in such areas as providing information, offering counseling, and giving support and encouragement to subordinates. Perhaps the most important role is as a teacher or "mentor" for subordinates participating in the career development program (Levinson 1980). Managers, through their control of employees daily activities, dictate the type and range of experiences available. It is these on-the-job experiences which most influence employees' job/career development. Managers who are committed to, and take responsibility for, subordinates' career development can encourage employee confidence aggressiveness, and positive expectations (Anderson, 1973).

Without this attention and positive reinforcement on a daily basis, the probability of career program success is greatly reduced. It is naive to assume, however, that all managers will be able or willing to support the organization's career management efforts. Many managers may have little understanding of, or interest in this process. Hall (1976) has noted that managers may be reluctant to counsel and instruct subordinates for fear of showing their own ignorance of effective career management strategies. Training and development may be needed for both career program participants and their managers.

Hall (1971) suggests that managers be given some reason to accept what can be a difficult responsibility. Formal organizational recognition of the career development function as part of the manager's job is essential to managerial cooperation and commitment. Recognition could include making this activity part of managers' performance appraisal criteria. Specific rewards, both extrinsic and intrinsic, could be tied to managerial success in developing subordinates. Perhaps the most powerful motivator would be to make the manager part of the career management program. These managers would then see their own success as linked to the effectiveness of the system.

CONCLUSION

As this article demonstrates, a fully-developed career management program involves considerable complexity and is linked to almost every aspect of the human resource management system. It can also be an expensive operation requiring commitment of substantial amounts of human resource and line management time for counseling, development and assessment. Finally, it requires considerable knowledge and expertise on the part of participants so they can effectively carry out their responsibilities to the program.

Organizations that make the necessary commitment of time and resources will generally be rewarded with a more productive, stable, and satisfied work team. But companies should not assume that, like the bread loaf, half a career management program is better than none. Career management requires an integrated systems approach: the supporting framework is essential to achieve any of the goals normally associated with career management programs. Failure of the program after employee expectations have been raised and time has been invested may result in a backlash of alienation which leaves things much worse than if the program never existed.

This result suggests that career management programs may not always be advisable in all organizations, at least not without considerable preparation. Companies should begin by recognizing that career management is not just another procedure to be added on as desired. It must be thought of as a logical culmination to the development of a comprehensive, integrated human resource management system. Hall (1978) summarizes the problem when he notes:

The current interest is at once satisfying for someone with a long interest in the area and yet vaguely unsettling for fear careers may become the latest management fad in a long line ranging from time study analysis through human relations training, MBO, job achievement, and behavior modification.

If organizations are to make career management more than a fad, they must avoid the mistakes made in adopting these earlier programs. To escape this trap Schein (1978) recommends adoption of a career management perspective, focusing on the development of a *long-term* interactive relationship between the employee and the organization. This is a most fundamental kind of change. Organizations, to implement a successful career management program, would have to not only change what they do, but how they think about human resources.

REFERENCES

Ackerman, L., "A Human Resource Management Control System," *Human Resource Planning*, Vol. 2, No. 4 (1979), pp. 197-204.

Alderfer, C. P., "Group and Intergroup Relations," in *Improving Life at Work*, J. R Hackman and J. L. Suttle, eds. (Santa Monica. Calif.: Goodyear, 1977). pp. 227-96.

Anderson, S. D., "Planning for Career Growth," Personnel Journal, Vol. 53, No. 5 (1973).

Carnazza, J., T. Ference. A. Korman. and J. Stone, "Career Prospects, Job Performance, and Manpower Development Programs," *Human Resource Planning,* Vol. 4, No. 1 (1981).

Cummings, L. L. and D. P. Schwab, *Performance in Organizations: Determinants and Appraisal.* (Glenview, Ill.: Scott Foresman and Company, 1973).

Downey, H. K., D. Hellriegel and J. W, Slocum, "Congruence Between Individual Needs, Organizational Climate, Job Satisfaction, and Performance," *Academy of Management Journal.* Vol. 18, No. I (1975) pp. 149-55.

Greenhaus, J. H. and R. E. Kopelman, "Conflict Between Work and Non-Work Roles: Implications for the Career Planning Process," *Human Resource Planning.* Vol. 4, No. I (1981).

Hackman, J. R., "Work Design," in *Improving Life at Work.* J. R. Hackman and J. L. Suttle, eds. (Santa Monica, Calif.: Goodyear, 1977) pp. 96-162.

Hackman, J. R. and E. E. Lawler, "Employee Reactions to Job Characteristics," *Journal of Applied Psychology Monograph*, 55. (1971) pp. 259-86.

Hall, D. T., *Careers in Organizations*, (Pacific Palisades, Calif.: Goodyear Publishing Company, 1976)

Hall, D. T., "Potential for Career Growth," *Personnel Administration*, Vol. 34, No. 3 (1971).

Hall, D. T., and F. S. Hall, "What's New in Career Management," *Organizational Dynamics,* (Summer 1976) pp. 17-33.

Hall, D. T., F. S. Hall and R. W. Hinton, "Research on Organizational

Career Development: Where Are We and Where Do We Go From Here?" *Human Resource Planning,* Vol. 1, No. 4 (1978) pp. 203-33.

Hennessey, H. W., "Computer Applications in Human Resource Information Systems," *Human Resource Planning,* Vol. 2, No. 4 (1979) pp. 205-13.

Holland, J. L., *The Psychology of Vocational Choice,* (Weltham, Mass.: Blaisdell, 1966).

Huse, E. F., "Performance Appraisal – a New Look," *Personnel Administration,* Vol. 30 (1967) p. 3t.

Houk, J., "Human Resources Planning at Crocker National Bank," *Human Resource Planning,* Vol. 4, No. I (1981).

Kravetz, D. J. and S. E. Derderian, "Developing a Career Guidance Program Through the Job Family Concept," *The Personnel Administrator,* Vol. 25, No. 10 (1980) pp. 39-42.

Lavin, M. J., "HRDIS: A Computerized Human Resource Development Information System," *Human Resource Planning.* Vol. 4, No. 1 (1981).

Leach, J. J., "The Notion and Nature of Careers," *The Personnel Administrator,* Vol. 22, No. 7 (1977) pp. 49-55.

Leach, J. J. "The Careers of Individuals and Organizations," in *Management of Human Resources,* E. Miller, E. Burack, and M. Albrecht, eds. (Englewood Cliffs, N.J.: Prentice Hall, 1980) pp. 166-185.

Levinson, D. J., "The Mentor Relationship," in *Managing Career Development,* M. A. Morgan, ed. (New York: D. Van Nostrand Company, 1980) pp. 117-19.

Liddell, W. W. and J. W. Slocum, "The Effects of Individual Role Compatibility Upon Group Performance: An Extension of Schultz's FIRO Theory," *Academy of Management Journal,* Vol. 19, No. 3 (September 1976) pp. 413-26.

March, J. G. and H. H. Simon, *Organizations.* (New York: John Wiley and Sons, 1958).

Morgan, M. A., D. Thall and A. Martier, "Career Development Strategies in Industry: Where Are We and Where Should We Be?" *Personnel,* Vol. 56, No. 2 (March-April 1979).

Porter, L. W., R. M. Steers, "Organizational Work and Personal Factors in Employee Turnover and Absenteeism," *Psychological Bulletin,* Vol. 80 (1973) pp. 151-76.

Portwood, J. D., "Contribution vs. Competency: Analyzing a New Framework for Staffing Decisions," *Human Resource Planning,* Vol. 2, No. 4 (1979) pp. 163-74.

Portwood, J. D., "The Relationship of Individual Differences to Employee Work Experience: Are the Best Always the Best?" Paper presented at the 1977 National Academy of Management Meetings: Kissimee, Florida, August 9-12, 1977.

Portwood, J. D. and E. L. Miller, "Clarifying the Psychological Contract: Using Job Orientation to Improve the Employee-Position Fit," Paper presented at the 1976 National Academy of Management Meetings: Kansas City, Mo., August 1976.

Pritchard, R. and B. Karasick, "The Effect of Organizational Climate and Job Satisfaction," *Organizational Behavior and Human Performance,* Vol. 9 (1973) pp. 110-19.

Roe, A. and R. Baruch, "Occupational Changes in the Adult Years," *Personnel Administration,* Vol. 30 (1967) pp.26-32.

Sarason, S. B., E. K. Sarason and P. Cowden, "Aging and the Nature of Work," *American Psychologist,* Vol. 30, No. 5 (1975).

Schein, E. H., *Career Dynamics: Matching Individual and Organizational Needs,* (Reading, Mass.: Addison-Wesley Publishing Company, 1978).

Schein, E. H., "How Graduates Scare Business," *Careers Today,* Vol. 1, No. 4 (1968).

Schneider, B., *Staffing Organizations,* (Pacific Palisades, Calif.: Goodyear, 1976).

Super, D., J. Crites, R. Hummel, H. Moser, P. Overstreet and C. Warnath. *Vocational Development: A Framework for Research,* (New York: Teachers College Press, 1957).

Tetz, F. F., "Evaluating Computer-Based Human Resource Information Systems: Costs vs. Benefits," *Personnel Journal,* Vol. 53, No. 6 (1973) pp. 451-455.

Van Maanen, J. and E. H. Schein, "Improving the Quality of Work Life: Career Development," J. R. Hachman and J. L. Suttle, (eds.) *Improving Life at Work,* (Los Angeles: Goodyear, 1977).

Walker, J. W., "Does Career Planning Rock the Boat?" *Human Resource Management,* Vol. 17, No. I (Spring 1978) pp. 2-7.

Wanous, J., "Realistic Job Previews for Organizational Recruitment," *Personnel,* Vol. 52 (1975) pp. 50-60.

Wellbank, H. L., D. T. Hall, M. A. Morgan, W. C. Hamner, "Planning Job Progression for Effective Career Development and Human Resources Management," *Personnel,* Vol. 55, No. 2 (March-April 1978).

AFTERWARD COMMENTS

James D. Portwood, Temple University

A lot of things can happen in twelve years—and they have. In the decade or more since I wrote my original article, changes in the business environment have forced a radical transformation in corporate America. Rising global competition has been exerting relentless pressure on organizations to streamline operations and control costs, while technological advances have allowed firms to eliminate or significantly redefine many positions. At the same time, the whole economic landscape has continued to shift, moving away from manufacturing and toward the service and information sectors.

These trends have also dramatically altered career options and prospects for both managerial and non-managerial personnel. As large bureaucratic structures have been downsized or replaced by flatter self-managing "expert systems," typical career ladders have often disappeared as well. In general, employees can no longer expect significant sustained upward mobility as part of their career pattern. The rapid pace of organizational change will, for many, make career transition as likely a prospect as traditional career progression. What, then, do these trends mean for organizational career management efforts; and what is then, the current relevance of suggestions I made for such efforts in 1981?

The overall theme advocating an integrated approach to career management still have value, even if the implementation details require some updating. While career structures have been changing, the need for organizations to adopt a systematic strategically driven framework for managing employees and their careers has, if anything, become even more critical today. With the rise of global financial markets and information networks, and the easy transfer of technology, quality, committed, high performing employees could well represent the only sustainable competitive advantage available to organizations. Attracting and holding key people may, therefore, be an overriding success, and even a survival factor for companies in the future. The difference will be the types of people needed, and what it will take to attract and hold them.

In the original paper I emphasized the need to select individuals with specific career paths in mind, train and develop them in anticipation of future promotion possibilities, work with employees to outline formal career plans, and reward managers for assisting in this process. One assumption underlying these specific suggestions was that organizations could reasonably predict future corporate structures and consequent human resource needs. Another was that an organizationally sponsored career management program could buffer employees from the uncertainties of a changing world. Today I have less confidence in these assumptions.

The level of turbulence in corporate environments has reached a point where the best many organizations can do is develop a general sense of direction, and maintain as much flexibility as possible in structures and systems so they may be able to respond quickly to new realities. Human resource and career management strategies (both organizational and individual) must also become more adaptive.

Earlier I suggested a highly structured career management process, with formal career counseling sessions and considerable documentation to identify organizational options and individual plans. The aim was to create a realistic context for career dialogue and increase employee confidence in their ability to reach career objective within the existing company. In today's highly uncertain environment such a formal system might well give participants a false sense of security and predictability which would be counterproductive. Individuals must be encouraged to confront the reality of career ambiguity and constant organizational change. Management will need to support employees in this effort, but perhaps in a more personal and informal manner.

Where organizations cannot guarantee specific career opportunities or paths, mutual trust and constant two-way communication between employees and management may need to replace (or at least supplement) formal agreements and structured programs. This will put more pressure on organizations and their managers to make every employee a "partner" in analyzing and preparing for the company's future. Individuals must feel empowered to seek information and opportunities within the company, and should expect to have questions answered when the response may affect their career prospects.

It will also be important to shift the emphasis from specific person-position or person-path matching toward more flexible negotiated commitments to value the relationship and invest in developing individual competencies. Employees for their part must be willing to refocus career strategies toward maintaining their contribution potential even as required tasks, and even corporate objectives, change. Individuals will, however, have to accept the need for, and commit to, making changes and engaging in personal development with relatively little prospect of significant vertical mobility, one of the traditional motivating factors for such effort and commitment.

The situation will put extra pressure on HR administrators to coordinate staffing, training, and reward systems to support the revised organizational career management strategy. Specific suggestions for bringing these HR functions into line include the following:

Staffing. The previous paper advised organizations to select employees based not only on their readiness for the current job, but also their potential to move along expected career paths. It is still important to assess employee potential (to the extent possible given uncertainty over future HR needs), but perhaps equally important in the current situation is to look for evidence of personal flexibility and tolerance for ambiguity in job recruits. Since the only guarantee is that things will change, an individual's long term value to the company is directly related to a willingness and ability to adjust to new situations and job demands.

Training. Developing individuals for future positions is also still a good idea, but organizations must take care not to focus on potentially obsolete skills. In a fast changing world, developing basic competencies (e.g. communication, decision making) and teaching employees how to learn may be the best strategy for organizations. Individuals will then be in the best position to adjust and learn necessary skills as the need arises. It will also help if organizations promote and fund a philosophy of lifelong learning and training on demand for employees, so they may take advantage of career options or grow in their current jobs as opportunities present themselves.

Compensation. Increasing pay has always been one of the primary motivations for seeking career advancement. With fewer possibilities for future promotion, organizations will need to restructure reward systems to encourage a career focus and organizational commitment among employees with low probability for movement. The most logical step would be to shift to a competency and/or productivity based system, which rewards individuals on the basis of contribution regardless of level in the hierarchy. This step would, in turn, also require that attention be given to performance appraisals and job designs. Employees must feel they have the opportunity to realize their full potential and be fairly and accurately assessed.

In summary, organizations still need to be concerned with employee career aspirations and career experiences. The rules change, but the "game" goes on. Don't be surprised, however, if some of the new players come around to ask you where you put the ladder.

CHOOSING CAREER MANAGEMENT PRACTICES TO SUPPORT YOUR BUSINESS STRATEGY[1]

Stephen A. Stumpf, New York University

Organizationally supported career management practices are frequently discussed in the human resource literature from the implicit viewpoint that career management efforts will benefit most organizations. This article examines the benefits of thirteen organizational career management (OCM) practices in light of the needs of organizations pursuing different business strategies. Some business strategies, such as trying to hold and maintain a dominant position within an industry, are likely to benefit from many OCM practices. Other business strategies, such as focusing on a product-market niche or trying to overcome a failing position, will benefit from only a few specific practices.

D uring the last two decades there has been substantial interest in the concepts of career management and business strategy. Extensive literature has emerged on the meaning of careers for both individuals and organizations (Hall, 1976; 1986; London & Mone, 1987; London & Stumpf, 1982; Schein, 1978), and on the meaning of strategy for both single product/service businesses and conglomerate organizations (Thompson and Strickland, 1986). These literatures have grown to the point where a systematic examination is needed of the relationship between the ways organizations manage the careers of their employees and their choice of business strategy. The basic concepts of organizational career management (OCM) are identified below. A description of several business strategies follows including recommendations regarding which OCM practices are most likely to satisfy the human resource

Reprinted from *Human Resource Planning*, Vol,. 11, No. 1 (1988), 33-47.

[1] An earlier version of this article entitled "Designing Organizational Career Management Practices to Fit Strategic Management Objectives" by S.A. Stumpf and N. M. Hanrahan appeared in R. Schuler and S. A. Youngblood, *Readings in Personnel and Human Resource Management,* 2nd Ed.), St. Paul, Minn.: West, 1984.

management (HRM) needs and financial resources of organizations with specific strategies.

OCM can be defined as activities and opportunities that organizations sponsor to help ensure they will meet or exceed their future human resource requirements. OCM practices include: career planning, development of career paths, training and development activities, target development programs, promotion from within, formal staffing policies, standard promotion criteria, assessment centers, job posting, job matching, career counseling, outplacement counseling, and mentor-protege relationships. Organizations manage careers by providing such programs, and in some cases, by selectively making them available to specific individuals. Which practices are appropriate and likely to be cost effective for a specific business depends on many factors, including the availability of labor, current and anticipated financial conditions, values of top management, the socio-economic and industry environment, and the firm's current business strategy.

The last factor—the firm's current business strategy—is a primary consideration in selecting career management practices. Strategy involves the matching of organizational skills and resources with constraints and opportunities in the environment. Every firm has a strategy, whether explicit or implicit, good or bad. Business strategy is the method of competing in the selected businesses, and of managing the internal aspects of the business to support the chosen approach.

Most business strategies are related to the size and strength of the business; its market share; and the growth, stability, or decline in the market served. Business strategies may also reflect possible ways to expand or contract a business. For example, an organization may have a strategy of growth through product diversification or growth through vertical integration.

ORGANIZATIONAL CAREER MANAGEMENT

Today's typical employee will change jobs four or five times during his or her career, making training and career development issues an integral part of business and society. In addition, over 30,000 businesses will declare bankruptcy each year, and hundreds of thousands of new ventures will enter or exit various businesses.

Organizations will experience many threats to their productivity that are personnel-related. A few of these threats are: (1) the loss of key personnel in managerial or technical positions; (2) technological or market changes that result in an underdeveloped skill level in part of the work force; (3) dual career family issues and employees who are unwilling to relocate; (4) corporate image changes, which affect the ability of the organization to attract new employees; (5) and external forces that require altering of the composition of the work force (e.g., Equal Employment Opportunity laws).

The effects of such threats can be reduced through effective OCM practices. Although OCM is sometimes used synonymously with the term personnel management or HRM, OCM has a more specific meaning. Human resource functions to which OCM relates, but which are distinguishable from OCM, include: human resource forecasting, job analysis, selection systems, compensation programs, labor and industrial relations issues, and performance appraisal systems. While the contribution of HRM functions may vary based on the organization's strategy, the focus of this article is on OCM.

INTENDED BENEFITS OF OCM

There are many intended benefits of OCM practices. Whether or not a benefit is actually experienced depends on how the particular OCM practice is designed, operationalized, and supported; the magnitude of the need the practice is intended to fill; the needs of the employees; and whether or not a particular practice fits the organization's strategy.

While the benefits of OCM practices are proported to be endless by some and trivial by others, several intended benefits are commonly acknowledged (e.g., Hall, 1987; London & Stumpf, 1982; Storey, 1976). The foremost organizational benefit relates to reducing turnover of valued employees through one of three mechanisms: (1) coaching and guidance via trained career counselors, supervisors, and/or personnel staff; (2) helping employees plan their career actions through an identification of needs, provision for training and development activities, and/or mentor-protege relationships; and (3) identifying promotion and transfer possibilities through promotion from within policies, formal staffing policies, standardized promotion criteria, job posting, and job matching systems. Turnover is likely to be reduced when employee career concerns are considered and, hopefully, dealt with by the organization.

A second intended benefit of some OCM practices is to encourage turnover of less productive employees. Promotion from within policies and clear standards for promotion encourage individuals who do not meet those standards to confront their low promotion potential and take corrective action or withdraw to a more suitable organizational environment. Similarly, career counselors and outplacement counseling can help individuals to establish realistic career expectations and facilitate the departure of surplus or less effective employees.

The evaluation and development of skills for future work-roles is another intended benefit of some OCM practices. Several aspects of career planning programs, training and development opportunities targeted to future work-roles, and assessment centers are generally designed and used for this expressed benefit.

Some OCM practices are designed to inform employees of the organization's policies and procedures. By providing relevant career-related information, the organization hopes its employees will be able to plan their career actions to accommodate organizational goals. Such information sharing is a component or by-product of career planning, career pathing, formalizing staffing policies, standardizing promotion criteria, the posting of job vacancy information, and mentor-protege relationships.

In addition to the four primary intended benefits, there are several other benefits organizations may seek through their OCM practices: (5) development of a common corporate value orientation in middle and upper management ranks, (6) maintenance of internal management continuity in the midst of environmental forces or uncertainty, (7) reduction of the threat of competitors raiding their key employees and obtaining a competent resource and insider information on their strategy, tactics, and technology, (8) public perception that they are a socially responsible and humanistic organization, and (9) maximum managerial discretion in staffing decisions through minimizing formal policies and increasing individual flexibility and judgment.

The evolution of a similar value orientation among middle and upper management is enhanced when individuals experience similar work-roles or career paths, have comparable developmental activities, and are groomed from within with the assistance of mentors or strong role models. Internal management continuity can be maintained through promotion from within, formalizing promotion policies, and the use of mentors to assess and guide lower level managerial actions. Competitive raiding is less likely to be effective if employees feel that their career is being effectively managed in the current work context. Career planning, training and development activities, standardized promotion criteria, job matching systems, and mentor-protege relationships are likely to facilitate such feelings. The corporation's image is most likely to be affected by how the organization treats its employees, particularly the questionable performer. Career counseling and outplacement activities are often targeted to help such employees. Lastly, maintaining managerial discretion implies collecting extensive information on employees (e.g., via assessment centers or mentor-protege relationships), without committing the organization to specific practices, policies, and procedures. The U.S. Civil Service regulations regarding personnel practices are an example of how managerial discretion is reduced by formalized policies and procedures. Managers in such formalized systems must often defer their judgment to policy guidelines that prevent free action.

OCM PRACTICES

The primary intended benefits of 13 OCM practices mentioned above are summarized in Exhibit 1. Relative cost estimates are also indicated and categorized as high (H), medium (M), or low (L) for the development and maintenance of an OCM practice. Descriptions of these OCM practices are not provided here since they are widely discussed in the HRM literature.

Given these 13 OCM practices, their intended benefits, and the relative costs identified in Exhibit 1, we now focus on several business strategies and the OCM practices that support specific strategies. A method of diagnosing strategy is suggested below, followed by the likely HRM needs of various strategies and the likely availability of financial resources to develop and deliver OCM programs.

BUSINESS STRATEGY

The process of developing strategy involves the determination of the basic goals of the organization, and the adoption of courses of action and allocation of resources necessary to accomplish these goals. The approach involves an analysis of both the firm's environment and its internal capabilities. The essence of strategy is relating the company to its environment in a way that enhances efficiency and effectiveness. Development of strategy benefits the organization by aiding in the formulation of goals and objectives, identification of major issues, allocation of resources, integration of administrative and operating activities, and assisting in the training of future managers.

While the field of strategic management has grown many fold over the past decade, it is still relatively uncommon for organizations to explicate specific business strategies. When strategies are made explicit, they are sometimes so general that employees obtain minimal guidance in terms of the organization's goals and objectives. While it would be helpful to the senior management of an organization for its strategy and objectives to be known by key managers, sharing one's strategy with competitors or other outsiders could have negative effects-hence the often vague nature of strategy statements.

STRATEGY DIAGNOSIS

Given a less than clear statement of strategy, it is necessary for one to investigate and diagnose the organization's current strategy before enacting OCM programs. Thompson and Strickland (1986) suggest that you answer as many of the following questions as possible to analyze your current business strategy.

1. What is our breadth and depth of product line in comparison to rival firms?
2. What are our marketing practices and distribution channels?
3. What is the adequacy of our production capacity, quality, and costs?
4. Are we a leader or follower in R&D, engineering, and technology?
5. What are our financial capability and performance objectives?
6. What managerial skills are needed? Available?
7. What is our relationship with the parent company?
8. How have we responded to perceived market opportunities and threats?
9. Which particular customer groups and/or product uses do we focus on?
10. What is our competitive approach to pricing, product differentiation, product quality, and customer service?
11. Do we emphasize what are considered to be the key success factors in the industry?
12. What are our distinctive competencies?
13. What is our current market share and market share relative to the industry leader?
14. What is the market's growth rate?

The answers to the first 12 questions provide the information base for diagnosing and analyzing business strategy. Questions 13 and 14, focusing on the firm's current market position and projected growth rate, allow one to assess the viability of a strategy. By considering both sets of issues, it is possible to define and evaluate the firm's business strategy.

The conceptualization of business strategies depends, in part, on the firm's relative market position in the industry. Firms that have a low market share relative to competitors tend to have different strategic options than firms in a dominant market position, or firms in a failing market position. Low market share firms must continually address issues of short term survival and profitability. Even successful small niche firms must carefully guard their boundaries. Their size makes them vulnerable to acquisition and requires careful management of resources. Firms in a dominant market position typically have the resources to survive in the short run; their concern is with keeping competitive firms weak and maintaining their market superiority. They often consider integrating operations vertically and diversifying into other product lines. Firms that are failing due to competitive forces or industry decline need to minimize their losses and determine whether alternative products or services can facilitate a recovery.

EXHIBIT 1
Intended Benefits and Costs of
Organizational Career Management Practices

Intended Benefits	OCM Practices												
	Career Planning	Career Paths	T & D Activities	Targeted Development	Promotion from Within	Formal Staffing Policies	Standardize Promotion Criteria	Assessment Centers	Job Posting	Job Matching	Career Counseling	Outplacement Counseling	Mentor-Protege Relationships
1. Minimize Turnover of Key People Through:													
a. Coaching and Guidance	X										X		
b. Development	X		X										X
c. Promotion and Transfer					X	X	X		X	X			
2. Encourage Turnover of Less Productive People					X		X				X	X	
3. Evaluate and Develop Skills for Future Roles	X			X				X					
4. Inform Employees; Goal Directed Behavior	X	X				X	X		X				X
5. Develop Common Corporate Value Orientation		X			X	X							X
6. Maintain Continuity					X	X							X
7. Reduce Competitive Raiding	X		X						X		X		X
8. Positive Corporate Image											X	X	
9. Maintain Managerial Discretion									X				X
Relative Costs [a]													
1. Development	M	H	M	H	L	M	M	H	L	H	L	L	L
2. Maintenance/Delivery	M	L	H	H	L	L	L	H	M	L	H	M	L

[a] H = high, M = medium, L = Low

Business and corporate strategy alternatives are defined in general terms below within three general categories: low market share strategies, dominant position strategies, and failing market position strategies. The relative availability of financial resources to invest in OCM practices are noted along with likely HRM needs and OCM practices to satisfy these needs. The human resource management needs identified for each strategy are those most critical to enacting that strategy. The failure to satisfy such needs are viewed as costly and detrimental to the firm's success. Strategies, financial resources available, and human resource needs are summarized in Exhibit 2. Exhibit 3 links these needs to OCM practices that can

EXHIBIT 2

Likely Needs and Financial Resources for
Various Business Strategies

Likely Needs

	Financial Resources Available L = little M = moderate H = high	Minimize Turnover — Coaching & Guidance	Minimize Turnover — Development	Minimize Turnover Promotion & Transfer	Encourage Turnover	Evaluate & Develop Skills for Future Roles	Inform Employees — Goal Directed Behavior	Develop Common Corporate Value Orientation	Maintain Continuity	Reduce Competitive Raiding	Positive Corporate Image	Maintain Managerial Direction
		1a	1b	1c	2	3	4	5	6	7	8	9
Low Market Share Position:												
1. Niche or Specialist	M	X			X				X	X		
2. Superiority or Prestige	M	X			X				X			
3. Growth	L			X			X					
Dominant Position:												
4. Offense or Confrontive	M	X	X	X		X				X		
5. Integrate Vertically	M		X			X		X				
6. Diversify Concentrically	M	X	X	X		X	X					X
7. Hold and Maintain	H	X	X	X	X	X	X		X	X		
Failing Position:												
8. Hold and Maintain	L		X		X				X			
9. Harvest	L	X									X	
10. Diversify	L			X								X

provide suitable benefits. Practices are recommended below on the basis of the number of needs fulfilled and the availability of financial resources.

LOW MARKET SHARE STRATEGIES

Three business strategy alternatives are most viable for firms in a low market share position: targeting the business into a niche or specialty, offering products or services that are superior or of higher prestige than competitors' products, and seeking growth through beating or acquiring smaller firms offering comparable products.

Niche or specialist strategy

The niche or specialist strategy involves searching out and cultivating product-customer segments that dominant firms have neglected or cannot profitably serve. To the extent that niches can be identified or specialty products offered, there is likely to be reasonable profit with a modest need for the financial resources to sustain the strategy. This suggests that a moderate amount of financial resources could be made available for OCM practices. The most salient human resource needs for firms pursuing a niche or specialist strategy, given their relatively small size, are to minimize turnover of key personnel, encourage turnover of non-productive personnel, maintain internal stability with respect to the strategy, and protect themselves from competitor raiding. Since the strategy does not imply substantial growth, a reduction in turnover through developmental means or promotion and transfer opportunities is not likely.

Example: People Express airline had a niche strategy in the early 1980s. In discussing the threat of competitive actions, their CEO viewed the niche they had selected as fairly secure. Personnel policies to support their aggressive niche strategy called for nearly doubling the workforce, and investing more time in training both crews and flight service personnel. All employees were required to purchase stock, and attractive stock options were offered to discourage turnover of valued employees.

Two OCM practices are designed to minimize turnover of valued personnel through coaching and guidance activities: career planning and career counseling (see Exhibit 1). Three OCM practices are designed to facilitate managerial continuity in strategy and operations: promotion from within, formal staffing policies, and mentor-protege relationships. Non-productive personnel can be encouraged to leave through promotion from within, standardized promotion criteria, career counseling, and outplacement counseling. Raiding can be prevented by career planning, training and development activities, promotion criteria, job matching, and mentoring.

Given the relative costs and intended benefits of these practices, five can be recommended based on the likely financial resources available and the number of desirable benefits: career planning, promotion from within, formal staffing policies, standardized promotion criteria, and mentor-protege relationships. These activities satisfy the primary human resource needs associated with the strategy for moderate to low costs. They also provide several additional benefits that are consistent with the strategy, including the development of employee skills for future roles, informing employees of career possibilities, and developing a corporate value orientation. The

OCM practices omitted seem to have unnecessarily high costs for the benefits provided that are germane to a niche or specialist strategy.

Superiority or prestige strategy

Firms pursuing a product superiority or prestige strategy capitalize on opportunities to improve the quality of products offered by dominant firms in order to appeal to the quality or performance oriented consumer. The improvement may take the form of some objectively identifiable difference in the product, or it may be a perceived difference created in the mind of the consumer (through advertising, for example). The pricing of products positioned to be superior or prestigious usually generates sizeable profit margins before administrative and marketing costs are considered. To the extent that the firm is not in a failing position, moderate financial resources are likely to be available for OCM practices.

Example: Bear Stearns & Company, a New York Financial investment firm, follows a strategy of seeking segments of the market that other firms find too specialized. The firm is characterized by a willingness to take risks where others would not. Since the firm is a partnership, most members share in losses and gains. This makes its drive for success a common value system which has become an integral part of the firm's management orientation.

Three HRM needs seem critical to sustaining a superiority or prestige strategy: minimizing turnover of personnel through coaching and guidance, maintaining continuity, and encouraging turnover of less productive personnel. Since superiority and prestige strategies necessitate the identification and implementation of ways of maintaining product eliteness, there is a constant need to remain one step ahead of competitors. However, market growth opportunities and financial resources available for growth are likely to be limited. Turnover of valued employees makes it increasingly difficult to stay ahead of competitors—particularly competitors with dominate market positions who could expand their product lines to eliminate the superiority or prestige attribute of the low market share firm's product. Since quality and status are so important, less effective personnel must be turned over quickly. Given the tenuous survival of low market share firms, it is critical that their strategy be clear and stable. Clarity and stability can be enhanced through OCM practices that maintain managerial continuity over time.

Five of the seven OCM practices identified in Exhibit 1 based on the above three HRM needs are recommended for firms pursuing a superiority or prestige strategy: career planning, promotion from within, formal staffing policies, standardized promotion criteria, and mentor-protege relationships (see Exhibit 3). Career counseling is not recommended because of its high relative cost to sustain. Again, there are secondary benefits to the five practices recommended that are consistent with the superiority or prestige strategy's HRM needs, including developing employee skills for future roles and informing employees of OCM practices.

EXHIBIT 3
OCM Practices That Are Most Likely to
Satisfy Needs or Various Strategies

OCM Practices

Strategies	Career Planning	Career Paths	T & D Activities	Targeted Development	Promotion from Within	Formal Staffing Policies	Standardized Promotion Criteria	Assessment Centers	Job Posting	Job Matching	Career Counseling	Outplacement Counseling	Mentor-Protege Relationships
Low Market Share Position:													
1. Niche or Specialist	A		C		A	A	A			B	B	B	A
2. Superiority or Prestige	A				A	A	A				C	B	A
3. Growth	C	C			A	A	A		A	C			A
Dominant Position:													
4. Offense or Confrontive	A			A	C	A	B	A	C	A	B	A	A
5. Integrate Vertically	A	B	C	B	A			B					A
6. Diversify Concentrically	A	B	A	C				B	B	B	A		A
7. Hold and Maintain	A	B	A	C	A	A	A	C	A	B	B	B	A
Failing Position:													
8. Hold and Maintain	C			B	A	B	B				A	B	A
9. Harvest											A	B	
10. Diversify										A			A

A = meets several human resource management needs and has manageable costs.
B = meets some human resource management needs, but costs could be a deciding factor.
C = meets few needs and costs are probably beyond resources available.

Growth strategy

A growth strategy for low market share firms generally takes the form of focusing the firm's competitive energies on the products and customers of smaller rivals. The goal is to absorb the market share of other firms. This is sometimes done through price cutting, extensive advertising, or acquisition—all of which reduce profits in the short run and leave few financial resources available for OCM activities.

Firms following a growth strategy have one primary HRM need: to ensure a reasonable flow of competent managers to run the expanding business. This is most directly accomplished through promotion and transfer actions that serve to reduce turnover of valued employees, and through informing existing employees of the company's future direction.

Eight OCM practices are intended to yield such benefits: career planning, career paths, promotion from within, formal staffing policies, standardized promotion criteria, job posting, job matching, and mentor-protege relationships. These practices, with the exception of career planning, career paths, and job matching systems, tend to be of low to moderate cost. Although each practice is likely to yield the desired benefits, organizations may choose not to enact all of the practices due to their cumulative cost. In such instances, senior management should consider the additional benefits of each practice and select those yielding the most useful outcomes.

DOMINANT POSITION STRATEGIES

There are four strategies presented in Exhibit 2 for firms in a dominant position in their industry: an offense or confrontive strategy, integrate vertically, diversify, and a hold and maintain strategy. Given a dominant position in the industry, it is likely that the firm will be larger and more profitable in terms of absolute dollars than low market share firms. This should result in greater financial stability and a longer time perspective with respect to human resource issues, with moderate to high resources available for OCM.

Offense or confrontive strategy

Taking or keeping the offense or being confrontive implies a drive to outperform other firms in the industry. Firms with such a strategy often introduce new products, develop lower cost methods, innovate customer services, and establish more efficient means of distribution. There is also a tendency for firms following the offense strategy to confront smaller firms, making it hard for smaller firms to grow. Competitive price cuts are often met with even larger price cuts; competitive promotional campaigns are met with similar or better campaigns, and so on. While financial resources are generally available for OCM practices due to the firm's dominant position, the aggressive stance often requires financial backing. As a result, fewer dollars end up being available for OCM practices than might otherwise be the case.

Dominant firms with an offense or confrontive strategy have three important HRM needs: to minimize turnover of key personnel, to evaluate and develop employee skills for future roles, and to reduce or minimize competitive raiding of technical or managerial talent. Turnover of valued employees and competitive raiding need to be minimized to sustain the dominant position. If new product ideas, lower cost methods, innovative services, and the like are copied by competitors, it becomes increasingly difficult to maintain a competitive edge. Evaluation and development of employee skills for future roles is necessary to ensure a continuous flow of talent to fill the positions that result from a successful offensive that increases sales or market share.

Exhibit 1 suggests that eleven OCM practices are likely to satisfy one or more of these needs. Since the cost of all the OCM practices is likely to be prohibitive, practices should be used that provide the maximum intended benefit for the most reasonable cost. Specifically, the use of a career planning program, a limited number of T&D activities, promotion from within, standardized promotion criteria, job posting, career counseling, and encouraging mentor-protege relationships are low to moderate cost OCM practices that should complement the firm's strategy. Other practices, such as targeted development, assessment centers, and job matching, are excluded because of their high relative cost compared to the incremental benefits likely to be realized.

Integrate vertically

Integrating vertically—by entering the business of the firm's suppliers or distributors—is a strategy that involves the development or acquisition of one or more lines of business not previously part of the firm. Vertical integration is most common when abnormally high profits are being made by suppliers or distributors, leading to a diminishing profit margin associated with further expansion of the main product line or a lack of economies of scale due to further expansion. The roles that suppliers and customers play in the production-distribution process are examined for profitable growth opportunities.

Example: Dow Jones & Company, Inc., a publishing and communications company, has also been in the forest-products business for years. They entered the industry to find secure paper suppliers for their newspapers. Dow Jones also manages a delivery service for its *Wall Street Journal.* The high costs of postage coupled with the U.S. Postal Service's service problems lead Dow Jones to integrate forward—hundreds of employees hand deliver nearly a million copies of the *Wall Street Journal* every morning— before 7:00 a.m.

HRM needs for firms following a vertical integration strategy are to minimize turnover of key personnel, evaluate and develop personnel for future roles, and create a corporate climate that enhances a common value orientation. Given business expansion, it is necessary to have a growing, competent workforce that is developing the requisite skills for the new businesses. A developmental approach is viable due to the well defined nature of the expansion. Turnover can be partially controlled through career planning and mentor-protege relationships. Employee skills can be assessed and developed through career planning, assessment centers, and targeted development. The development of a corporate value system can be facilitated by promotion from within and developing people along specified career paths and targeted development.

Diversify

Diversification involves expanding into businesses that are related to the firm's existing business or business portfolio in some way. The relationship between the businesses can be via technology, production processes, customers served, channels of distribution, and so forth. The benefits of diversification are the maintenance of some common core of business activity while spreading financial, economic, and market risks over a broader corporate base.

Example: Pillsbury Co. acquired Haagen-Dazs, a maker of premium ice-cream, in 1983. Through this diversification, Pillsbury enlarged its presence in both the frozen food and restaurant industries. The company has used its strengths in marketing, distribution, and advertising expertise to promote the rapid growth of Haagen-Dazs. Pillsbury also retained the existing Haagen-Dazs management, providing them with the financial and technical resources to support development and growth.

The HRM needs associated with this growth strategy are to retain effective employees and promote, transfer, or develop employees for increased responsibility and future work roles; inform employees of corporate actions and OCM practices; and, maintain corporate managerial discretion in the career decisions involving senior management. Turnover of valued employees must be minimized and relevant skills developed to ensure a competent technical and managerial talent pool to fill positions resulting from the expected expansion. Employee skills need to be known and used in staffing decisions by corporate management. Further, employees need to be kept informed of OCM activities to facilitate the self-management of their career and minimize turnover due to uncertainty.

The use of career planning, career counseling, T&D activities, and mentor-protege relationships can help to reduce turnover and facilitate employee development. To the extent that turnover is also being addressed through promotion and transfer actions, job posting and job matching systems are desirable.

The evaluation and development of employees can be accomplished through career planning, assessment centers, and targeted development.

However, the benefits of the latter two OCM practices depend on how well management can specify the skills needed to perform effectively at various levels and in various positions. To the extent that substantial diversification has occurred and the firm is beginning to take on a stable form, assessment centers and targeted development are viable; otherwise they may be premature.

Because of the changes and growth that generally follow a diversification strategy, it is generally necessary to keep employees closely informed if goal directed career management behaviors are expected. Career planning activities, establishing career paths, formal staffing policies, standardized promotion criteria, and job posting systems provide employees with information that is helpful in managing their careers. However, the need to maintain corporate managerial flexibility suggests that formal staffing policies and standardized criteria not be established at the corporate level. While such practices provide employees with useful information, the necessary information could be less formally communicated as part of career counseling or mentor-protege activities.

Hold and maintain

Dominant firms that have a hold and maintain strategy often try to suppress competition by controlling the market. Key products are patented; multiple competing brands are produced and marketed by the firm; prices are moderate; quality is apparent but not necessarily top-of-the-line; customer service is maintained. Reinvestment in the business is adequate to sustain low to moderate cost of production, meet production demand, remain technologically progressive, and grow at least as fast as the rate of new market growth to avoid any market share slippage. Given this strategy and level of intended reinvestment, financial resources are generally available for even the more costly OCM practices.

The hold and maintain strategy implies several HRM needs. The development of a stable, competent work force to ensure production efficiencies, marketing stability, and effective internal control is required. This suggests minimal turnover of valued employees and encouraging less effective employees to leave. It also suggests benefits for developing employee skills for future roles and informing them of OCM practices to encourage self-development. Finally, management continuity is desirable to maintain the leadership position, and competitive raiding must be defended against.

Each of the 13 OCM practices discussed has an intended benefit relating to one or more of the firm's HRM needs. The appropriate combination of OCM practices is likely to depend on other factors such as senior management preferences, the more salient needs of the firm with respect to OCM, and the skill and interests of the personnel staff who would design and operate the OCM systems. Practices are so indicated in Exhibit 3 by an A, B, C, rating system according to the benefits provided.

FAILING MARKET POSITION STRATEGIES

The final set of business strategies identified in Exhibit 2 are for firms of any size or market share in a failing position. Failure may be due to overall market conditions, industry failure, actions by competitors, or internal management. To the extent that a firm attempts to overcome a weak business position, one of the three low market share position strategies may apply (niche or specialist; superiority or prestige; growth). The primary difference between a firm in a failing position who is targeting their efforts to overcome the decline and a low market share position situation with respect to OCM practices is the likely lack of financial resources. Hence, only the least expensive OCM practices would be feasible for firms in a failing position with a niche/specialist, superiority/ prestige, or growth strategy.

Other than an attempt at stability through targeted efforts such as a niche/specialist or superiority/prestige strategy three strategies are viable for firms that are failing: hold and maintain, harvest, and diversify. No matter which strategy is pursued, few financial resources are likely to be available.

Example: General Electric closed 10 plants and reduced its workforce by 1,400 employees in 1984. The company was facing declining growth and had to make major changes to cope with over-capacity and under-utilized facilities. Consolidation was chosen as the means to maintain their competitive position. Programs for income maintenance, retirement, retraining, and placement were implemented to handle the movement of employees out of the plants slated for shut-down.

Hold and maintain

The hold and maintain strategy tries to stop the failure at its current level. Efforts are made to maintain sales, market share, profits, and competitive position for the short- to mid-term. Maintenance and developmental activities are reduced or stopped for personnel as well as capital resources. The corporate goal is to squeak by with as little loss as possible.

Human resources need to be managed in such situations to minimize turnover of critical personnel, encourage turnover of low performers, and maintain clear piloting of a rocky boat. The most productive way to minimize turnover in this situation is through providing developmental opportunities for key personnel. Counseling and guidance efforts are likely to be too long-term to yield immediate results and promotion opportunities are probably too limited to help reduce the departure of key people.

In order to reduce turnover via development activities, three OCM practices are possible: career planning, T&D activities, and developing mentor-protege relationships. The latter practice is likely to have the strongest and most immediate effect on key personnel. The offering of a limited number of training and development activities could satisfy the needs that some employees have for self-development as well as the firm's mid-range needs for skilled employees; however, the resources available may prohibit T&D activity.

The practices of promoting from within, establishing formal staffing policies, and having standardized criteria for promotion can lend stability to the internal management of the firm and encourage turnover of low performers. To the extent that resources are available, a firm could also conduct career and outplacement counseling to facilitate reduction in the number of employees. If this were done on a short-term basis until losses were stabilized, it could be an effective investment in maintaining a positive corporate image.

Harvest

A harvest strategy for weak businesses involves a minimum amount of reinvestment, short-term profit maximization, and extensive cash flow. This is generally operationalized through a reduction in the operating budget, cutting overhead costs, price increases or quality decreases, reduction in promotional expenses, curtailing customer services, and so on. The firm's HRM needs are minimal with the possible exceptions of maintaining a positive corporate image and providing employees with as secure a job as possible until the business is divested or liquidated. With these exceptions in mind, the financial resources generated in the harvesting of profits from the business could be spent on career and outplacement counseling services. This could yield the firm a stable position in the labor market and may serve to increase the amount of profitable harvesting that can be done by stabilizing its workforce.

Diversify

Diversification for a firm in a failing position is generally accomplished through analysis of what business the firm is in, and consideration of what related businesses it might enter, given its current managerial strength, production facilities, sales force, and channels of distribution. Once the new product areas are defined, management efforts and financial resources move from the failing business to the new business.

Since the firm plans to survive the failure, it needs to minimize turnover of key employees by promoting or transferring them to the new business. The firm's management must maintain as much control during the transition period as possible. Given the limited resources likely to be available, the firm can attempt to satisfy these needs through a job posting system and encouraging mentor-protege relationships. A job matching system or assessment center would not be feasible due to the high levels of ambiguity about the nature and duties of the positions in the new business. Since promotion from within, formal staffing policies, and standardized promotion criteria are each likely to reduce managerial flexibility in moving personnel into the new business, such practices are not recommended during the transition.

SUMMARY

Exhibit 3 summarizes which OCM practices are likely to satisfy the HRM needs most germane to various business strategies. OCM practices are ranked A, B, or C according to the number of needed benefits the practice would provide, and the likely availability of resources to develop or maintain the practice. Whether or not a firm following a particular strategy should implement all the OCM practices indicated is not specifically considered, although practices labelled "A" are highly recommended.

Many of the OCM practices have similar intended benefits, any one or pair of which could satisfy the firm's HRM needs if operationalized effectively. The OCM practice-strategy cells that are not filled with a letter indicate practices that are not as likely to satisfy critical strategic needs at a viable cost. This does not necessarily indicate that the OCM practice would be dysfunctional, rather that it may provide non-critical benefits, be of higher cost than is immediately practical, or partially compromise the benefits of other practices and desired outcomes.

For firms following one of the 10 strategies identified, Exhibit 3 indicates which OCM practices should be used, and which are likely to be infrequently used. Career planning, promotion from within, formal staffing policies, standardized promotion criteria, career counseling, outplacement counseling and mentor-protege relationships are recommended for more than half of the strategies listed. In contrast, the development of career paths, targeted development, assessment centers, and job matching systems are recommended for few strategies.

If OCM practices are to be effectively designed and implemented, they must take into account the firm's business strategy. OCM practices must be selected to satisfy specific HRM needs that stem from a particular strategy. When financial resources are limited, OCM practices that have low costs should be used—leaving the more expensive practices for better times. Even in the most severe financial situations, some OCM practices appear to be necessary to satisfy basic human needs. Financial considerations are only one of many issues to consider in planning OCD programs. In successful and profitable periods, a cadre of OCM practices are available; those that target to the firm's current and future needs should be identified and implemented.

REFERENCES

Hall, D. T., *Careers in Organizations,* (Santa Monica, CA: Goodyear, 1976).

Hall, D. T., and Associates, *Career Development in Organizations,* (San Francisco: Jossey-Bass, 1986).

London, M., and E. Mone. (eds.), *The Human Resource Professional and Employee Development,* (Westport, CT: Greenwood Press, 1987).

London, M., and S. A. Stumpf, *Managing Careers,* (Reading, MA: Addison-Wesley, 1982).

Schein, E. H., *Career Dynamics: Matching Individual and Organizational Needs,* (Reading, MA: Addison-Wesley, 1978).

Storey, W. D., *Career Dimensions I, II, III, IV,* (Croton-on-Hudson, NY: General Electric Company, 1976).

Thompson, A. A., Jr., and A. J. Strickland, III, *Strategy Formulation and Implementation: Tasks of the General Manager. Third Edition.* (Plano, TX: Business Publications).

AFTERWARD COMMENTS

Stephen A. Stumpf, New York University

I n the early 1980s, when Organizational Career Management (OCM) practices were supported widely by many firms, the thought of choosing the practices to fit an organization's line of business strategy was new and potentially viewed as an esoteric activity. It seemed that any practice that would develop and better use the growing number of human resources employed in organizations would benefit the people, and thereby the bottom line. The changing marketplace of the late 80s and 90s has shifted what was new and esoteric to something that is now believed by many who are experiencing these changes necessary for organizational stability and line of business survival.

In the article I outlined the intended benefits and costs of 13 OCM practices, identified the likely needs and financial resources available that are associated with 10 different business strategies, and then linked the OCM practices to these strategies. While I might alter some aspects of the information displayed in the article's three exhibits, the thrust of each exhibit remains the same—with increased emphasis on the changes in OCM practices necessary as a firm changes (or is forced to change) from one business strategy to another.

To simplify, the last five years has seen many firms move from a dominant position strategy to strategies associated with lower market share lines of business or failing lines of business. Many firms made such adjustments due to increase competition, declining market share, and a greater number of substitute products. Firms such as Citibank/Citicorp, The Sun Company, Metropolitan Life, American Express, and General Motors are firms that have experienced radical changes in the marketplace and altered their OCM practices accordingly.

While each line of business assesses its specific situation to identify the most useful OCM practices, some trends have emerged. Efforts to identify career paths and formal career planning systems have decreased, particularly for lines of business where the future is less known and more uncertain. Promotion from within and formalized staffing policies are on the rise, as are career counseling and outplacement counseling activities. Each of these activities places greater value on the existing human resources, even when downsizing is a necessary activity for organizational survival. The value of mentor-protege relationships continues to be promoted within organizations, yet firms have found ways to institutionalize this powerful career management practice.

In the past few years many of the "right fit" arguments made in the article have become HR drivers to accommodate dynamic business changes. Many firms in dominant positions implicitly assumed that they would continue in such positions for years to come. As their situation changed, so did their strategies. As their strategies changed, the HR department was called upon to facilitate the change and alter its OCM practices in the process. The result: explicit choices of OCM practices to fit their business strategies.

MANAGEMENT DEVELOPMENT

Given today's increasingly complex and turbulent business environment, companies need to ensure they have management talent that can thrive and lead through constant change. Leadership development becomes a critical part of their business strategy which must be integrated with other business activities and with the overall purpose of the organization.

In this section, the authors offer their insights and retrospectives on management and leadership development. Throughout the articles, several common "best practices" emerge, particularly in the area of experiential learning, that is, learning by confronting real issues in real environments.

Morgan McCall explores the practice of developing executives through work experiences. Drawing on a series of studies of successful high potential executives, he describes sixteen developmental experiences, the aspects that make them developmental, and the lessons learned. Most executive learning, according to McCall, takes place on the job through personal challenge. The development potential of a work experience is a function of the challenge it presents.

His Afterward comments offer lessons learned from attempts to apply principles set forth in the original article. He observes three obstacles to the effective development of executives through work experiences: the difficulty of actually connecting development activities to the business strategy, organizational pressure to accelerate leadership development, and leaving the learning from developmental experiences up to chance.

Starcevich and Sykes take a different tack to developing managers and executives. They discuss the advantages of internal advanced management programs and compare them broadly to the then-used university management development programs. Twelve years later they are still convinced of the utility of company-specific internal advanced management programs. They conclude that classroom-based management development alone, internal or external, is no longer adequate to develop leadership for today's complex business environment.

Trends in the business environment and in the internal workforce have fostered a movement toward transformational leadership. Sheppeck and Rhodes discuss the implications of this shift on what they view as significant changes in the nature of management development in U.S. corporations. The changes force a closer linkage between human resource practices, especially developmental activities, and business needs. They note that not enough emphasis is placed on why a person is given a particular assignment and what they should learn from it (what is its business purpose in light of the strategic direction of the company and their future leadership needs). They describe an emerging model, differing substantially from the traditional competency-based management training model, that focuses on effectively meeting the present and future leadership needs of an organization. Our best practices are reflected in the characteristics of the model, including a systematic approach to an individual's total career, integrated with emerging business needs, and a reliance on job experience as a means of developing leadership.

Many organizations tend to view management and executive development efforts as inherently individualized, giving little attention to how executive development can enhance organizational development and strategic implementation. Vicere and Graham discuss a more strategic paradigm than that of traditional executive development systems. This new approach, they argue, can be used to develop organizational culture, create commitment, foster strategic direction, and cultivate an environment for continuous improvement and innovation. The paradigm stresses executive development processes that are strongly connected to the strategic intent of the organization and its business units; a system that focuses on identifying and developing managerial talent to achieve its long-term strategic objectives. In his afterward Vicere discusses flexible education systems, which he sees as the next step in the new executive development paradigm.

Complex thinking is associated with higher levels of managerial performance and ultimately organizational effectiveness. Jean Bartunek and Meryl Reis Louis focus on strategies for developing managers' capacities for complex thinking. They describe what the HR professional can do to increase the cognitive complexity of managers in their organization through educational programs designed specifically for this purpose and through on-the-job experience. The authors contend that managers can place themselves in work situations that foster their own development allowing the elements of the work itself to be used to help develop complex thinking.

Five years after the publication of their articles the authors remain convinced of the importance of developing managers' capacities for complex thinking, especially given the increasing complexity and globalization of business. Unfortunately, as Bartunek and Louis point out, development efforts embedded in the workplace often are abandoned because of the substantial effort involved.

THE DESIGN OF WORK ENVIRONMENTS TO STRETCH MANAGERS' CAPACITIES FOR COMPLEX THINKING[1]

Jean M. Bartunek, Boston College and
Meryl Reis Louis, Boston University

Complex thinking is associated with a wide range of managerial skills from tolerance of ambiguity to effectiveness in group problem solving. Consequently, HR professionals have developed educational strategies aimed at expanding managers' capacities for complex thinking. In this paper, we summarize the characteristics of these educational strategies. In addition, we describe how naturally occurring events at work can be harnessed to achieve these same aims. We describe naturalistic strategies for fostering complex thinking in inexperienced newcomers, experienced newcomers, and experienced managers.

During the past several years, human resource professionals have come to appreciate the ill-structured, interdependent, messy, mutually causal, and otherwise complex nature of organizational life and managerial work. This appreciation has led to an interest in the processes by which people cope with such realities. In academia and in the corporate world, it is increasingly acknowledged that complex thinking is associated with higher levels of managerial performance and, ultimately, with organizational effectiveness. Weick for example, advises managers to "complicate yourself!" in order to tackle ill-structured, ambiguous organizational problems appropriately (1979, p. 261). Duhaime and Schwenk (1985) warn of the dangers of simplistic approaches to decision-making. Jacques (1986) notes that cognitively complex CEOs are able to be concerned not only about their own corporations, but also about

Reprinted from *Human Resource Planning*, Vol. 11, No. 1 (1988), 13-22.

[1] Professor Louis is grateful for the financial support of the Pacific Gas and Electric Co., Raychem Corporation and the Career Research Center at Columbia University.

shaping the societies in which their corporations function. Lepsinger, Mullen, Stumpf, and Wall (in press) suggest that managers who can act flexibly and reconceptualize problems should be more effective strategic thinkers. How can managers develop the capacity to think more complexly? That is, how can they learn to:

- view problems from several different perspectives;
- consider a variety of responses to these problems; and
- be cognitively and emotionally flexible in their implementation of innovations and of organizational strategy?

Managers who adopt and implement comparatively ill-defined innovations such as Quality of Work Life programs need the skills to (1) understand the varying attitudes different organizational members will have towards these innovations, (2) determine several possible responses when the inevitable snags in implementation occur, and (3) undertake steps that will enable the organization to learn new values and/or models of acting from the implementation experience (Cummings & Mohrman, 1987). Sometimes such learning involves a rethinking of appropriate organizational practices or of the innovation itself. All these skills reflect components of complex thinking.

Work conducted during the past few years provides sophisticated appreciation of processes that foster complex thinking. In this paper we describe components of such thinking and summarize several ways it can be developed throughout a manager's career.

In particular, we describe how cognitive complexity can be developed for newly hired managers and for more experienced managers, both in educational programs designed specifically for this purpose and "naturalistically," through coping with common work situations. Our goals are to identify what human resource professionals can do to increase the cognitive complexity of the managers in their organizations and to describe how managers can place themselves in work situations that foster their own development.

What is Cognitive Complexity?

The concept of cognitive complexity includes two primary components: differentiation and integration (Harvey, Hunt & Schroder, 1961). Differentiation refers to the ability to perceive several dimensions in a stimulus rather than only one, while integration refers to the ability to identify multiple relationships among the differentiated characteristics. Differentiation also often involves non-linear thinking, that is, the ability to move from one frame of reference to another to explore a situation. Integration often also involves seeing the patterns in the differential analyses, then making links where none may have existed before. In other words, cognitively complex managers can judge employees' performance on the basis of several differentiated dimensions (such as quality, speed, and collaborative ability). They can also integrate these dimensions to see patterned interrelationships among them. For example, a cognitively complex manager might recognize that a particular employee does higher quality work in collaboration with others than when working alone (Bartunek, Gordon, & Weathersby, 1983).

Cognitive complexity is reflected in a number of managerial actions, especially decision-making. Less complex managers make decisions using smaller amounts of information in linear ways to generate "good enough" decisions. More complex managers use larger amounts of information, they identify patterns in the information, and they generate several possible solutions. Obviously, the level of complexity managers demonstrate at any given time depends upon both the situation they face and their inherent abilities to differentiate and integrate information.

Cognitive complexity is associated with effective managerial behaviors other than decision-making. For example, it is positively associated with tolerance of ambiguity, the ability to assume a leadership role, and the capacity to empathize with people with very different cultural backgrounds. Cognitively complex people are also more able to work effectively in problem-solving groups and to resolve conflicts cooperatively. They are less likely to make errors when making organizational decisions. So, while cognitive complexity represents only one individual characteristic, its cultivation can enhance a broad range of desirable managerial capacities.

DEVELOPING COGNITIVE COMPLEXITY

How can managers' cognitive complexity best be developed? The usual assumption is that it is developed through educational programs. Our own work suggests that natural characteristics of the work setting can also be used to foster it. Next, we describe core principles related to developing cognitive complexity. Then we describe programs and natural strategies for fostering complexity. In particular, we focus on how to develop differentiation and integration.

Context for Development

Cognitive complexity isn't developed in familiar situations. It is developed in settings that are new and challenging. This is because in familiar, comfortable situations people have available routine, previously tested, and automatic "thought-saving" devices (Louis, 1980). In unfamiliar situations such devices are not yet available, so more cognitive effort is needed to understand such situations. Thus, a basic condition for the development of complexity, either in educational or "natural" work settings, is the experience of an unfamiliar, mind-stretching situation.

Differentiation and Integration

Developing complex thinking involves enhancing *differentiation*, the ability to perceive issues from multiple, yet specific and detailed perspectives. It also involves fostering *integration*, through which an overall understanding of the different perspectives and their interrelationships emerges.

How can differentiation be fostered? More specifically, how can managers learn to perceive from perspectives they do not ordinarily use, so the number of perspectives available to them is increased? There are at least two ways this can be accomplished. The first is learning to "get into the head" of people operating out of a different perspective. This involves setting aside one's habitual perspective and learning to think like people who usually take a different perspective. This can be facilitated by having people who typically take the different perspective help others learn it. For example, people in an accounting department might teach their perspective(s) to people in marketing, or people from one culture might introduce their perspective on problems to people from other cultures.

A second method for developing differentiation has come primarily from researchers interested in moral development (e.g. Kohlberg, 1969; Schlaefli, Rest, & Thoma, 1985). These researchers have found that differentiation can be enhanced by long-term programs that emphasize peer group discussions of controversial moral dilemmas. During these discussions, peers challenge each others' thinking and present differing points of view. These programs succeed in fostering moral reasoning in part because the opinions of the most cognitively complex group members tend to help other group members see new perspectives. This method can be used to develop more differentiated reasoning in several spheres, not only for moral development.

Integration can be accomplished through dialectical processes in which new syntheses are created from the interconnections among various perspectives. First people are exposed to different perspectives. Then they are encouraged to let knowledge of these perspectives lead to a new resolution, which incorporates elements of each. In corporate policy making, Mitroff and Emshoff's (1969) dialectical inquiry method for dealing with ill-structured organizational problems fosters integration. This method involves surfacing and challenging the conflicting assumptions that underlie particular action strategies and then integrating them for effective policy formulation.

EDUCATIONAL PROGRAMS DESIGNED TO FOSTER COMPLEX UNDERSTANDING

Training programs and workshops have been designed specifically to foster more complex understanding (e.g., Weathersby, 1980; Weathersby, Bartunek & Gordon, 1982). The components of these programs include

(1) the use of problem-centered designs, (2) a level of pedagogical complexity that both supports and challenges the developmental capacities of participants, and (3) the presentation of multiple perspectives with provisions to integrate them, especially with experience.

Problem-Centered Designs

The most viable strategy in workshops or training sessions is to focus on problems of concern to the participants (rather than on concepts of interest primarily to presenters). Problem-oriented training can take into account participants' current knowledge, experience, and concerns, and can use concepts to illuminate ways of viewing various problems. The problems can then be investigated through the lenses provided by several perspectives. For example, problems of declining productivity can be understood more complexly by being addressed as problems of communication, motivation, leadership style, and organizational design.

Appropriate Level of Complexity

It is important to match the content and structure of the training to the participants' developmental level by making the training slightly more complex and demanding than participants' usual level of response. Thus, the appropriate type of training environment depends on the participants' present levels of complexity. People who exhibit lower levels of complexity usually require a more structured approach, the presentation of fewer perspectives, and more authority-centered instruction than do participants who exhibit greater complexity.

Presentation of Multiple Perspectives and Opportunities to Integrate Them

There are several ways to present multiple perspectives that provide opportunities for integration. As suggested above, particular problems can be identified, and these can then serve as the focus of a discussion that incorporates diverse views. Participants from different backgrounds can be asked to describe situations or problems as they would be understood or addressed from their own perspective. Personnel from different functional areas might work together to illustrate ways in which their perspectives might complement each other. Organizational simulations such as the Looking Glass (e.g., Kaplan, Lombardo, & Mazique, 1985) Metrobank, Investcorp, or the Northwood Arts Center (Stumpf, in press) can enable participants to apply knowledge from various functional areas to a single complex situation. Finally, a cyclic approach can be used in which two or more ways of addressing the same issue are presented—first independently, then in conjunction with each other, and finally in a planning or action-oriented context.

NATURALISTIC STRATEGIES FOR DEVELOPING COMPLEXITY AT WORK

Work Environment Characteristics That Might Foster Complexity for Newcomers

While educational strategies can be used to foster complex thinking, they are certainly not the only avenues available. Our work and that of others (e.g., McCall 1988) suggest that aspects of the natural work place environment may also foster such development.

In the workplace, as in training programs, a complex environment that demands cognitive effort is likely to foster complexity. One example of a complex environment is the novel or unfamiliar situation. Let us look at one occasion that is likely to involve substantial novelty—the experience of being a newcomer when beginning a new job. At the beginning, organizational newcomers find themselves unable to use their previously developed ways of interpreting their experiences. They are forced to develop an awareness of new elements of their work situation (differentiation) and an appreciation of how to interpret these elements and their relationships (integration).

Organizational newcomers need to master elements associated with two domains of an unfamiliar setting: the organizational domain and the job domain. Thus, organizational entry involves two cycles of differentiation and integration; first, a general, global cycle associated with mastery of the organizational domain and then a situation-specific (job) cycle. The extent to which each domain is experienced as a salient, unfamiliar situation depends on the newcomer's level of experience. For *inexperienced newcomers,* those without substantial full-time work experience, the salient, unfamiliar situation is likely to be the overall organizational context. They first notice the new, individual elements of the work place and then develop a rudimentary appreciation of the overall context, a global integration. *Experienced newcomers* on the other hand, those who already have substantial work experience when entering a new job, are already likely to have an overall picture of the work world; their primary concern is understanding the components of the job. As they develop an understanding of the individual job components, they can also generate a situation-specific integration of these components. (Of course, the extent to which the new setting is similar to their previous setting will also affect whether the job or overall organizational context is experienced as the salient situation.)

As we can see, then, differentiation and integration tasks are a normal part of entering a new work setting, for both experienced newcomers and inexperienced newcomers. However, the particulars of these tasks differ for the two groups.

How can the work environment "naturalistically" affect the development of cognitive complexity? Our research has focused on two types of characteristics: characteristics of the overall transition situation (such as the newcomer's interaction with peers) and characteristics of the job. Transition characteristics should be most important for developing cognitive complexity in inexperienced newcomers. Job characteristics should be most important for developing cognitive complexity in experienced newcomers.

Inexperienced newcomers can be given chances to communicate more with senior organizational members and to learn from them alternative ways of making sense of the organizational situation. This will help them build frameworks for understanding general characteristics of the world of full-time, permanent employment. Such interactions provide inexperienced newcomers with a differentiated view of global dimensions and examples of how others integrate these.

Experienced newcomers have a more developed global perspective. For them, job characteristics such as task variety (carrying out several different parts of work) and task identity (doing a whole task or, at least minimally, seeing how the work fits into the whole) foster situation-specific differentiation and integration. They offer the opportunity to expand one's perspective on aspects of a task and/or to integrate these aspects into a whole.

In a recent study (Bartunek & Louis, 1986) we collected data from several hundred graduates of full time MBA programs. Of these, 59% had no full-time, career-related work experience prior to their MBA program (inexperienced newcomers) and 41% had some full-time, career-related work experience (experienced newcomers). We asked these MBA graduates to rate the availability and helpfulness of several transition characteristics (e.g., a buddy relationship with a senior co-worker, onsite formal orientation sessions, offsite training programs) and several job characteristics (e.g., task identity and task variety). We also measured the complexity of their decision-making. We determined the impacts of job characteristics and transition characteristics on the decision-making complexity of both the experienced and inexperienced newcomers.

As we had expected, transition characteristics had more impact on the complexity of inexperienced newcomers' decision-making, while job characteristics had more impact on the complexity of experienced newcomers' decision-making. The two transition characteristics that had the greatest positive impact on inexperienced newcomers' complexity were daily work-related interactions with more experienced peers and the presence of a secretary or other support staff. Some transition characteristics (the presence of other new recruits and a buddy relationship with a more senior co-worker) decreased inexperienced newcomers' use of complex decision making. On the other hand, job characteristics had the greatest positive impact on the experienced co-workers. Task variety, in particular, both increased the likelihood of using a complex decision style and decreased the likelihood of using a simple decision style.

Thus, formal training programs are not the only means of increasing new employees' cognitive complexity; natural elements of the work place, if designed appropriately, may also have positive effects. But, as our results indicate, experiences at work may have negative effects on the use of complex decision styles as well.

Developing the Cognitive Complexity of Experienced Professionals and Managers

Natural characteristics of the workplace can affect the cognitive development of experienced managers, of "old-timers" as well as of newcomers. Because people's concerns change over time, the characteristics of work environments that foster the development of cognitive complexity among experienced managers differ from the characteristics that foster the development of cognitive complexity in newcomers.

Katz's work (1980) suggests a way of understanding the difference between experienced and inexperienced managers. Katz suggests that over the course of several years, characteristics of an employee's job come to have less and less effect on the employee's attitudes; other aspects of one's role at work, such as interpersonal relationships, pay, and working conditions come to be more important. The reason job characteristics lose their impact is that, with extended job longevity, people's perceptions of their present conditions and their future possibilities become increasingly impoverished (or, in our terms, cognitively simple). Over time even the most demanding job characteristics come to be experienced as customary and less interesting and exciting if they do not change in any substantial way.

Besides encouraging participation in training programs aimed at managerial skill development, what can be done in these circumstances to foster cognitive complexity? While as yet no research has been conducted directly investigating this question, we can propose two types of activities that should have positive effects. These proposals are based on the assumption that an attempt to foster the cognitive complexity of experienced managers should take into account both the tendency of jobs to become "old" if there are no changes in them and the increased concerns of experienced managers regarding interpersonal relationships. The proposals focus on participation in employee involvement programs such as quality circles, and on membership in project teams.

Participation in Employee Involvement Programs Such as Quality Circles

Quality circles are groups of employees who meet regularly in order to improve their work setting in some way. They are usually members of the same department, or people who perform similar jobs. A supervisor of the work group is often the facilitator. The members receive training in problem-solving, statistical quality control, and group process. The basic activity of the quality circle is to select and recommend solutions for problems of the work place, including equipment malfunction, quality control, and communication difficulties.

When properly structured, quality circles offer experienced managers and other employees the potential for developing their cognitive complexity. Just as particular job characteristics are responsive to experienced newcomers' concerns about understanding their jobs, participation in quality circles may respond to experienced employees' concerns about improved interpersonal relationships. Within this natural context, they offer the potential for increased differentiation and integration. First, simply because the members form into groups, quality circles offer the possibility for experienced managers to see other perspectives in addition to the one with which they typically operate. In addition, since the members formulate problem statements and potential solutions, there are opportunities to integrate the different perspectives presented. However, while quality circles offer this potential, they do not necessarily increase members' cognitive complexity. Just as the effects transitions have on inexperienced newcomers depend on particular characteristics of the transitions, so too do the effects of quality circles depend on particular characteristics of the quality circle groups. In particular, participants must really have an opportunity to voice a variety of perspectives, and the group must work together to formulate integrated responses to problems. Otherwise, the needs experienced managers have for improved relationships might be met, but their cognitive complexity will not increase.

Project Teams

It is possible to design work for experienced managers in such a way that meets their needs for improved interpersonal relationships *and* increases their cognitive complexity. One way is by assigning them to long-term project teams that convene around a whole task for which the team is responsible. Working as a member of such a multi-person team presents people with several experiences that may stimulate cognitive complexity. First, the new task itself represents a new perspective. Second, the task is likely to be experienced as having a fairly clear beginning, middle, and end; thus the potential for integration of different components is present. Third, such a task requires that team members who come from different departments and functional areas learn each others' perspectives and develop a common view of means and ends (Louis & Hall, 1987). This last characteristic is a direct parallel to training programs in which people are led to take another's perspective as practice in differentiation and integration.

As was the case with quality circles, project teams offer a naturalistic context in which cognitive complexity may or may not be developed. The development of cognitive complexity will depend in part on the extent to which different departmental and functional perspectives really are heard and integrated in project team work.

SUMMARY, IMPLICATIONS AND SOME CAUTIONS

We have suggested several ways to increase differentiation and integration, and thus to foster the cognitive complexity of managers, professionals and others engaged in work activities in organizational settings. We have described how formal training programs and "natural" elements of the work itself can be used to help develop complex thinking. The elements we suggested for facilitating increased differentiation and integration are shown in Exhibit 1.

Exhibit 1
Means of Fostering Differentiation and Integration

	Differentiation	Integration
Training Programs	-presentation of multiple perspectives -participants from different backgrounds describe problems from their perspective -trainers from different departments work together	-a cyclic approach in which different concepts are presented independently, then in conjunction with each other, then used jointly in a managerial setting
Naturalistic Strategies		
Inexperienced Newcomers	-transition characteristics that make newcomers aware of many individual elements of the work place	-transition characteristics that help newcomers develop appreciation of the overall context of work
Experienced Newcomers	-job characteristics that allow newcomers to carry out different parts of a task	-job characteristics that allow newcomers to see how individual tasks fit into the overall work of the organization
Experienced Managers	-group involvements in which experienced managers learn other individual or departmental perspectives on organizational problems or work	-group involvements in which experienced managers work with representatives from other departments to solve common problems or conduct joint projects

Overall, the list of characteristics in Exhibit 1 indicates that there are several ways cognitive complexity can be fostered throughout a person's worklife. There are undoubtedly other means than those we have listed here. The major point is that different elements of the work place should be structured in ways that encourage employees to learn new perspectives and learn ways of creatively integrating these.

Implications

It is unlikely that companies will offer large numbers of workshops or training programs specifically aimed at fostering more complex thinking and decision-making. However, companies do offer various types of workshops and training programs to teach specific managerial skills. Our work suggests that these training programs can also foster complex understanding, as long as the pedagogical elements we have described are built in.

In addition, all organizational newcomers experience transition characteristics and have jobs that have some particular types of job characteristics. Managers have frequently thought about these transition characteristics and job characteristics in terms of how they socialize new employees into the company. They have not frequently thought about the fact that these characteristics not only socialize their professional and managerial employees, but they also affect the likelihood that employees will learn to approach problems more complexly. Our work suggests that the work environment and the job can be designed to socialize newcomers and to develop their capacity for complex understanding.

Finally, the work environment can also foster or retard complexity in experienced managers. The typical occasions for learning—training workshops and orientation seminars—can be used to develop complex understanding; but in addition, normal, day-to-day work experiences can foster such understanding. Thus, we encourage human resource managers to devise ways in which complex understanding can be developed throughout the course of employees' work lives.

Some Cautions

We have suggested several ways in which cognitive complexity may be increased, but we do not mean to indicate that managers should respond complexly to every problem they encounter; nor do we think that substantially increasing complexity is easy.

As McCall and Kaplan (1985) have shown, it is sometimes important for managers to take quick, decisive action on problems. Such action will customarily be of relatively low complexity and be based upon relatively small amounts of information. However, McCall and Kaplan also point out that quick action sometimes makes finding long-term solutions to problems more difficult. *Effective* quick action recognizes the complexity of the problem involved, and includes steps that allow more detailed, complex solutions to be later developed, if they become necessary. So, even while complex action is not always required, the capacity for complex action is crucial.

While there are several aspects of work that should be associated with increased cognitive complexity, creating any fundamental change in this capacity is not easy. Early theories of human development tended to view complexity as a capacity that, once developed, would always be present. More recent research indicates clearly that even if people are cognitively complex at one point, events in their lives (such as work characteristics that never change) can make them more cognitively simple over time. Moreover, the simple temporary provision of some components fostering complexity will not have major, long term effects.

The development of complexity requires an effort spanning several years and encompassing several aspects of life. It is not enough for a new manager simply to have a job with high task variety for a short time, or for project teams to work together only on one minor task. For cognitive complexity to be fostered in any sustained way, enduring effort and exposure to a stretching environment are required. This is clearly a difficult task. Nevertheless, the benefits to both managers and their organizations in terms of gains in managerial talents seem worth the effort.

REFERENCES

Bartunek, J.M., J.R. Gordon, & R.P. Weathersby, "Developing 'Complicated' Understanding in Administrators." *Academy of Management Review*, 8, 1983, pp. 273-284.

Bartunek, J.M. & M.R. Louis, "Information Processing Activities Associated with Organizational Newcomers' Complex Thinking." *Best Papers Proceedings of the Academy of Management*, 1986, pp. 56-69.

Cummings, T.G., & S.A. Mohrman, "Self-designing Organizations: Towards Implementing Quality-of-Work-Life Innovations." In R. Woodman & W. Pasmore (Eds.), *Research in Organizational Change and Development* (pp 275-310). (Greenwich, CT: JAI Press 1987).

Duhaime, I.M., & C.R. Schwenk, "Conjectures on Cognitive Simplification in Acquisition and Divestment Decision Making." *Academy of Management Review*, 10,1985, pp.287-295.

Harvey, O.J., D.E. Hunt, & H.M. Schroder, *Conceptual Systems and Personality Organization*. (New York: Wiley 1961).

Jaques, E., "The Development of Intellectual Capability: a Discussion of Stratified Systems Theory." *Journal of Applied Behavioral Science*, 22,1986, pp. 361-383.

Kaplan, R.E., N.M. Lombardo, & M.S. Mazique, "A mirror for managers: using simulation to develop management teams." *Journal of Applied Behavioral Science*, 21, 1985, pp.241-254.

Katz, R. (1980), "Time and Work: Toward an Integrative Perspective." In B.M. Staw & L.L. Cummings (eds.). *Research in Organizational Behavior*, 2 (pp. 31-127). (Greenwich, CT: JAI Press 1980).

Kohlberg, L. (1969), "Stage and Sequence: the cognitive Development Approach to Socialization." In D. Goslin (Ed.), *Handbook of Socialization Theory and Research* (pp. 347-389). (Chicago: Rand McNally 1969).

Lepsinger, R., Mullen, T.P., Stumpf, S.A., & Wall, S.J., "Large Scale Management Simulations: a Training Technology for Assessing and Developing Strategic Management Skills." In *Advances in Management Development*. (New York: Praeger, in press).

Louis, M.R., "Surprise and Sense-making: What Newcomers Experience in Entering Unfamiliar Organizational Settings." *Administrative Science Quarterly*, 25, 1980, pp.226-251.

Louis, M.R. & D.T. Hall, *On Taking Project Work Seriously.* Manuscript under review. 1987.

McCall, M., "Developing Executives Through Work Experiences." *Human Resource Planning*, Volume II, No. 1 (1988).

McCall, M. & R. Kaplan. *Whatever it Takes: Decision-makers at Work.* (Englewood Cliffs: Prentice-Hall 1985).

Mitroff, I.I., & Emshoff, J.R., "On Strategic Assumption-making: A Dialectical Approach to Policy and Planning." *Academy of Management Review*, 4, 1979, pp.1-12.

Schlaefli, A. J.R. Rest, & S.J. Thoma, "Does Moral Education Improve Moral Judgment? A Meta-analysis of Intervention Studies Using the Defining Issues Test." *Review of Educational Research*, 55, 1985, pp. 319-352.

Stumpf, S.A., "Business Simulations for Skill Diagnosis and Development." In M. London & E. Mone (Eds.), *The HR Professional and Employee Career Development*. (Westport, CT: Greenwood Press, in press).

Weathersby, R.P., "Education for Adult Development: The Components of Qualitative Change." *New Directions for Higher Education*, 29,1980, pp. 9-22.

Weathersby, R.P., J.M., Bartunek, & J.R. Gordon. "Teaching for 'Complicated' Understanding." *Exchange: The Organizational Behavior Teaching Journal*, 7, 1982, pp. 7-15.

Weick, K., *The Social Psychology of Organizing.* (Reading, MA: Addison-Wesley 1979).

AFTERWARD COMMENTS

Jean M. Bartunek
Meryl Reis Louis

E vents that occurred after our paper was published are relevant to the arguments we made and suggest both means of and potential problems in fostering managers' capacities for complex thinking. *Workforce 2000* (Boyett & Conn, 1991), for example, and the need it makes evident for both appreciating and fostering cultural diversity within a workplace, indicate how important it is for managers and other organizational members to be able to operate out of multiple cultural perspectives. The increasing globalization of business makes it clear that managers need to appreciate multiple ways of operating beyond their workplace as well as within it. At the same time, increased racial tensions in the U.S., the complete breakdown of some Eastern European countries, unification problems in the European community, and several other less dramatic events, demonstrate that it is easier to appreciate multiple perspectives than to achieve this.

In the past few years a number of initiatives have been undertaken that are aimed at fostering managers' more complex thinking. These include, among others, Robert Quinn's text and series of workbooks that foster executives' capacity to act "beyond rational management" (cf. Quinn, 1990) and the Center for Creative Leadership's attempts to develop mangers' character so they can appreciate the more complex realities they encounter as they advance in their careers (Kaplan, 1990). Such efforts should be supported and expanded.

An additional dimension of the complexity in managerial thinking has emerged in the past decade. The role of intuitive knowledge as a supplement to rational/analytic thought has become widely acknowledged. And now the role of a more fundamental source of meaning, spiritual insight, is beginning to appear in the talk and writings of management practioners and scholars alike.

But these trends toward complexity in managerial thinking are counterbalanced by other events. For example, in our paper we describe quality circles as examples of means through which organizational members might learn to operate more complexly. Today there are relatively few companies employing quality circles in the U.S.. The reasons for their decline is complex, but include what happens when any fad is embraced and implemented without thorough grounding. In some settings, when corporations understood the commitment quality circles would take they were abandoned. Attempts to foster Total Quality Management, a similar approach, have often met the same fate. What will happen to attempts to foster cultural diversity? When corporate leaders see how difficult this truly is will they be willing to continue the effort?

In sum, five years after our paper was published we remain convinced of the importance of developing managers' capacities for complex thinking. We are encouraged that some creative means for pursuing aspects of this cause have emerged. But we are concerned that as people realize the effort it requires they may abandon the effort.

REFERENCES

Boyett, J., & Conn, H.P. (1991), *Workforce 2000*. New York: Dutton.

Kaplan, R. E., "Character change in executives as 'Re-form' in the pursuit of self-worth." *Journal of Applied Behavioral Science*, 26, 1990, pp. 461-482.

Quinn, R. E., *Beyond Rational Management: Mastering the Paradoxes and Competing Demands of High Performance*. (San Francisco: Jossey-Bass 1990).

DEVELOPING EXECUTIVES THROUGH WORK EXPERIENCES[1]

Morgan W. McCall, Jr., Center for Creative Leadership

E xecutive development, often considered solely in terms of educational programs, actually occurs primarily through on-the-job experiences. Surprisingly little research exists, however, on the kinds of experiences that make a difference, or on the difference they make. This paper summarizes a series of studies of successful, high potential executives that addressed these issues. It describes 16 developmental experiences, the elements that made them developmental, and the lessons executives said they learned from them. Making better use of experience is a significant challenge for organizations that are serious about the development of executive talent.

"I learned to take risks on people and to keep my cool as a leader. I learned the importance of a leader's ceremonial role to subordinates .... how to manage a large team harmoniously, and the importance of a company 'culture'." (Lindsey, Homes, & McCall, 1987)

"I had to learn to work with two customer systems and sales forces almost overnight. I learned how to balance the needs of the company with risk to the project and to myself, how to manage upward effectively, and how to build and maintain a motivated team." (Lindsey et al., 1987)

These two executives were not describing what they had learned from a job assignment, nor from a management seminar or from reading the

Reprinted from *Human Resource Planning*, Vol. 11, No. 1 (1988), 1-11.

[1] This paper is based on a series of studies, a comprehensive report of which appears in Lindsey, Homes, and McCall (1987). The author wishes to acknowledge the many people who played a significant role in these research projects, especially Mike Lombardo, Esther Lindsey, Randall White, Ann Mornson, Joan Kofodimos, and Virginia Homes. Bill Drath, Esther Lindsey, and Steven Stumpf have my gratitude for their many useful comments on this manuscript.

latest management text. They were describing lessons learned from starting an operation from scratch. Even though commitment to developing managerial talent is often measured by the size of a training budget, the role the classroom plays in the development of executive skills is unclear. A recent article by Short (1987) reported that the "corporate classroom" is budgeted at over $40 billion for its more than 8 million "students." Bennis and Nanus (1985) put the figure between $30 and $40 billion. Kotter (in press), in a recent study of 15 corporations well known for the quality of their executive cadre, concluded that "as important as formal training can be, it never seems to be the central ingredient in development at these firms. It may be rather obvious that if people spend 98-99% of their work time on the job, and only 1-2% (at most) in formal training, that most learning must occur on the job."

The two executives quoted above and their corporations took substantial developmental risks in these assignments. Unlike the relatively tangible cost of educational programs, the expense of on-the-job development is difficult to calculate. That it can be astronomical is reflected by the following comment from a member of the executive committee of a major corporation:

> "I assigned him to that job because I thought he would learn from it. He clearly wasn't the most qualified candidate. I figured if he couldn't cut it, it would cost us two million. In a two billion dollar business, we could afford it."

While it may be obvious that executives learn on the job, relatively little is known about such learning. A recent review "revealed no systematic body of research focused on what experiences or events may be important in managers' careers" (McCauley, 1986, p. 2). However, this review did identify several studies showing that early job challenge, early broad responsibility, early leadership opportunities, and task force and staff assignments can have developmental significance.

In Kotter's study (in press), the better firms made use of a broad array of developmental experiences, "including adding responsibilities to jobs, creating special jobs, using inside and outside training, transferring people between functions and divisions, mentoring and coaching employees, giving those people feedback on progress, and giving them instruction in how to manage their own development."

What evidence there is indicates that work experiences are critical for developing managerial talent. But some stubborn questions remain, including three that I can address here. To make effective use of work experiences, we must first understand, "What makes an experience developmental?" Research to date suggests that job challenge is crucial to development, but it tells us little about the kinds of experiences that develop

SHARED WISDOM

executives. Not all experiences are equally challenging: What makes the difference and what differences does it make?

Second, "What can experience teach?" It's one thing to talk about the importance of exposure, breadth, and visibility, but what specifically might someone learn from such developmental experiences?

Finally, even if we knew what makes an experience developmental and what a person might learn from it, "How can we design systems to take advantage of our knowledge?" Can we do a better job of strategically managing the careers of executives than simply providing periodic job rotations?

Job Challenge

Why is it that so many of the most successful corporations emphasize job challenge for developing managers (see, for example, Hall, 1976)? Kotter (in press) concludes that "challenging entry-level jobs help attract good people in the first place, and challenging promotion opportunities help firms hold onto those people . . . The challenges, in turn, both stretch people, and allow them, often early in their careers, to exercise some leadership. And that, of course, is at the heart of development."

If good people want challenge, and if challenge is at the heart of development, then what is challenge? The answer is not as obvious as it seems. A longitudinal study at AT&T (cited in McCauley, 1986, p. 4), used four characteristics to examine the challenge of managerial jobs. A single index was created by combining measures of "job stimulation and challenge, supervisory responsibilities, degree of structure of assignments, and degree to which the boss was an achievement model." They found a significant relationship between early job challenge (as reflected by these characteristics) and subsequent managerial success. By implication, then, challenging jobs are those that require people to supervise others, are relatively less structured, and involve working for a good boss. This leaves me with the unsettling feeling that there must be more to challenge.

Our studies (Lindsey, et al, 1987; McCall & Lombardo, 1983) looked a little deeper. We examined 616 descriptions of experiences that made a lasting developmental difference to 191 successful executives from six major corporations. We were able to identify 16 types of experiences or "key events," including (a) assignments, (b) other people, (c) hardships endured, and (d) other events (*see Exhibit 1*).

These key events can help us to understand what underlies the challenges that make work experiences developmental. Consider five kinds of assignments identified in Exhibit 1. These are *not* distinguished by title, Hay points, function, business unit, status, salary, hierarchical level, or product line. Rather, they reflect dramatically different managerial challenges. In three of them—starting from scratch, turnarounds, and large scope jobs—the manager is clearly in charge and has line responsibility. The other two, project/task force assignments and line-staff switches, put a premium on persuasion, that is leading without formal authority or position power.

EXHIBIT 1
16 Developmental Experiences

Assignments

•**Starting from Scratch**—building something from nothing
•**Fix It/Turn It Around**—fixing/stabilizing a failing operation
•**Project/Task Force**—discrete projects and temporary assignments done alone or as part of a team
•**Scope**—increases in numbers of people, dollars, and functions to manage
•**Line To Staff Switch**—moving from line operations to corporate staff roles

Hardships

•**Business Failures and Mistakes**—ideas that failed, deals that fell apart
•**Demotions/Missed Promotions/Lousy Jobs**— not getting a coveted job, or being exiled
•**Subordinate Performance Problem**—confronting a subordinate with serious performance problems
•**Breaking A Rut**—taking on a new career in response to discontent with the current job
•**Personal Traumas**—crises and traumas such as divorce, illness, and death

Other People

•**Role Models**—superiors with exceptional (good or bad) attributes
•**Values Playing Out**—"snap shots" of chain-of-command behavior that demonstrated individual or corporate values

Other Events

•**Coursework**—formal courses
•**Early Work Experiences**—early non-managerial jobs
•**First Supervision**—first time managing people
•**Purely Personal**—experiences outside of work

See Lindsey et al., in press for complete definitions.

When "other people" were identified as the pivotal force in developmental experiences, their role was surprisingly narrow. Virtually all of the significant other people were bosses or hierarchical superiors (not subordinates, peers, friends, spouses, or gurus, as some might expect), with the primary variability coming in how long the manager was exposed to the particular boss (from a few minutes to several years), and whether the boss was exceptionally good (about 2/3) or exceptionally bad (about 1/3). Having a good boss seemed to matter most in a manager's first supervisory job and in big scope jobs. In other situations, for example in start ups, it was often the absence of supervision, not the qualities of the boss, that allowed development to occur.

In addition to developmental work experiences based on assignments and other people, executives discussed five kinds of experience we categorized as hardships (see Exhibit 1): Being set back by mistakes or distasteful jobs, being forced into all-or-nothing career decisions, being confronted with difficult personnel problems, or dealing with traumatic personal events. These were experiences that forced their victims to dig deep and confront a level of self not usually dealt with in other kinds of situations.

The Elements of Job Challenge

The "elements" that make up these developmental events write the encyclopedia of job challenge. Content analysis of the hundreds of experiences described by executives surfaced eight fundamental challenges: bosses, incompetent or resistant subordinates, dealing with new kinds of people, high status, business adversity, scope and scale, missing trumps, and degree of change.[2]

Bosses were a particular challenge when managers had to adapt to their bosses' ogre-like qualities or stylistic differences. Bosses were also developmental if they modeled an exceptional skill or attribute, and in certain jobs where the manager needed and got the boss's advice and support. It was by learning to adapt to a variety of bosses that executives developed the ability to deal effectively with a diverse array of people in authority.

While both good and bad bosses could create a developmental work context, managing competent subordinates was seldom mentioned as a developmental experience. The challenge came in overcoming *incompetence and resistance from subordinates,* or in having to build an effective team from scratch. There were also developmental challenges in learning to manage former peers or bosses, or older or more experienced employees. These kinds of situations led to the realization that no "one way" of leading would work all the time. These experiences forced the development of alternative approaches to fit various situations. As one executive learned, "You can't fire everybody."

One's boss and subordinates are obviously important to executive development, but learning potential was increased every time managers worked with *types of people they had not dealt with before.* Higher level executives, clients, suppliers, unions, vendors, governments, people from other cultures, and joint venture partners were among the new relationships executives frequently confronted and learned from.

Simply dealing with these people could be challenging, but the developmental ante was further raised when managers had to do the dealing without any formal authority over them, and when there was no requirement to cooperate. As was true with bosses and subordinates, encounters with these different kinds of relationships led managers to develop new skills to deal with various situations. Negotiating with a union and working with a joint venture partner are not the same thing.

Yet another developmental aspect of experience was *playing for high stakes,* for example: being out on a limb with a project highly visible to top management, working against a tight deadline, taking a huge financial

---

[2] Research is in progress to systematically measure these characteristics of experience. Preliminary support for the content analytic results can be found in McCall & McCauley, 1986.

risk, and maybe having to go against one's bosses' preferences or advice. Managers had to learn to cope with the pressures, handle the risks, and take effective actions in the face of enormous consequences.

Managers are responsible for the performance of the business, consequently job challenge increases along with *business adversity*. The developmental demands described by executives increased as markets went sour, suppliers or customers went out of business, competitors seized the moment, unions went on strike, the economy changed unpredictably, natural resources ran short, technology changed, or equipment failed. Responding to these kinds of situations taught critical lessons: how to take action quickly, how to cope with ambiguous problems, how to make choices without sufficient information, and how to play for big stakes.

As one takes on responsibility for more people, dollars, functions, products, markets, or sites, *scope and scale* emerge as a major challenge. Particularly for managers who have developed personal leadership skills, changes in scope present countless demands to learn to "lead by remote control," to find ways to run things when it's impossible to keep one's arms around them.

In many of their significant learning experiences, managers came into the situation with *at least one missing trump*. They routinely faced unfamiliar functions, businesses, products, or technologies, sometimes they were too young, had the "wrong" background, or had to master computerese or financialese or legalese. Some found themselves in foreign countries, unable to speak the language or communicate with the people they managed. In all these cases, the challenge was not to let the missing trumps do them in; the development was in learning how to work around a significant disadvantage.

Not surprisingly, challenge also seemed proportional to the *degree of change* a new situation presented to the individual. People were promoted two or more levels at once, moved into new businesses, or plucked from years on the line into some technical staff assignment with no subordinates and no clear bottom line. Hot shots found themselves exiled to less significant jobs, free-wheelers got bridled by a hands-on boss, fix-it managers were sent to start something up. In these situations, managers had to find ways to deal with huge and usually unexpected change. From the feeling of being overwhelmed, they developed the ability to adapt.

Making Use of Job Challenge

The message of this study is simple. There were identifiable and categorizable things that executives said challenged them. Meeting these challenges left little choice but to learn and develop new abilities. In this respect, development came from inside, from individual desire to succeed. This leads us to our first rule: development is not something you can do to, or for, someone. Development is something people do for themselves. On the other hand, a lot can be done to provide talented people with the kinds of challenges that will give them opportunities to develop new skills. This leads to our second rule: The developmental potential of a work experience is driven by the challenges it presents; exposure to a different function, product, division, or the like is not enough. While the exposure can be useful, even enriching, what matters is what one is doing while being exposed.

What Work Experiences Can Teach

"There is no simple formula, no cookbook that leads inexorably to successful leadership....Learning to be a leader is somewhat like learning to be a parent or lover; your childhood and adolescence provide you with basic values and role models. Books can help you understand what's going on, but for those who are ready, most of the learning takes place during the experience itself." (Bennis & Nanus, 1985, p. 223)

To say an experience is developmental begs the question, "developmental of what?" As we studied what executives learned from their most developmental experiences, we found many examples of "exposure" learning—gains in cognitive knowledge of technical or business issues. But such lessons are just the beginning, representing only two of what turned out in our content analysis to be thirty-four categories. Just as experience is highly differentiated, its lessons pertain to a broad spectrum of skills, abilities, attitudes, philosophies, perspectives, knowledge, and values. This overwhelming array of bits and pieces, the puzzle-pieces of managing, can be arrayed into the five clusters shown in Exhibit 2: (1) Setting and Implementing Agendas; (2) Handling Relationships; (3) Basic Values; (4) Executive Temperament; and (5) Personal Awareness.

The lessons in the first cluster relate to obtaining the knowledge and skills needed to set and pursue agendas. John Kotter (1982) observed that effective general managers were able to set agendas for themselves and their businesses that consisted of "loosely connected goals and plans." Their agendas included issues covering a variety of time frames, a broad range of business issues, and both "vague and specific goals." These agendas were not usually written and were only loosely related to formal plans (Kotter, 1982). Lessons that enable managers to form agendas are those that teach business and technical knowledge, organizational design skills, how to think broadly and accept responsibility for direction, and finding alternative ways to accomplish one's ends.

The second cluster of lessons shown in Exhibit 2 are related to handling relationships. The kinds of relationships an executive must deal with are quite diverse. While all the lessons in this cluster require the ability to understand the other person's point of view, there is no such thing as "a man for all interpersonal seasons." The ability to work effectively with one group does not guarantee that a manager is equally adept with other constituencies.

Basic values, the third cluster of lessons, refers to the development of moral and philosophical perspectives on how people should be treated and the standards of conduct appropriate in a leadership role. Here executives hone and shape their fundamental values based upon their work-related experiences.

Executive temperament, or "what executives are made of" describes the fourth constellation of lessons. Coping with ambiguity, persevering through adversity, rolling with the punches, and making tough decisions are part of the daily menu of executive life. These abilities may spring from the common root of self-confidence.

Finally, five lessons form a personal awareness theme. At various points in their careers, many of the executives we studied came to grips with what they really liked to do, what they were going to do with their careers, and the sacrifices they were willing to make in their personal lives to achieve their ambitions. Many aspects of development require self-awareness: By recognizing and accepting their blind spots and weaknesses, these managers learned to direct their own development and realistically assess their aspirations.

There is not space here to fully define each of the thirty-four lessons shown in Exhibit 2, or to explore the subtleties within and among them (for that, the reader is referred to Lindsey et al., 1987). There are a number of conclusions, however, that have implications for using experience as a way of strategically developing executive talent. Among them are the following:

1) Different kinds of experience can provide opportunities to learn quite different things (these are summarized in Exhibit 2). There is a technical or business lesson to be learned from almost any assignment, but such lessons are seldom the primary lessons learned from a truly developmental experience. It is crucial, therefore, to think seriously about what a person might learn from a particular experience and not to stop at the "exposure" level.

2) A job that is incredibly developmental for one person can be largely redundant in the growth of another. However obvious that is, it is still tempting to think of development in absolutes—that through this experience a person learns "x", regardless of the person who goes through it. Our data show two things bearing on this issue. First, executives with repeat experiences (e.g., two turnarounds) learned fewer, and usually similar, lessons the second time. Second, executives who became "specialists" by virtue of successful repetition (e.g., "start up" managers) sometimes

derailed later in their careers because they failed to develop the broader array of skills required to handle other kinds of situations.

Exhibit 2
Executive Leadership Qualities And The Experiences
Associated With Them

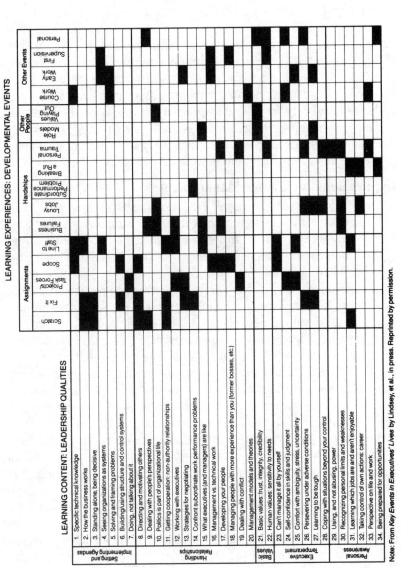

Note: From *Key Events in Executives' Lives* by Lindsey, et al., in press. Reprinted by permission.

3) There can be no guarantee that an individual will learn the lessons that an experience offers. Even companies that make extensive use of developmental assignments often fail to consider what they might do to help individuals learn. It's as if the sink-or-swim approach we associate with selection has been applied to development, too: throw them in and leave the learning outcome up for grabs. Even if development is ultimately up to the individual, we think a great deal could be done to help people make more of the job experiences they have. At the simplest level it might mean giving managers time between assignments to reflect on what they've just been through (as opposed to showing up on Monday to take over New Guinea operations). It could also mean providing a structured experience after a significant assignment to help a person make systematic sense of it. A great deal of thought and effort goes into designing classroom experiences, and it will probably require at least as much effort to take advantage of key work experiences. Sometimes executives do not stay in important assignments long enough to learn much from them at all (Gabarro, 1987)!

Implications for Career Management

It is clear that effective use of work experience for development will be difficult unless the culture of the corporation supports the practice. A supportive culture is more than a statement of mission and values endorsing development. It is an environment in which *at least* the following four concrete things happen.

1) Executives risk a portion of the bottom line to put talented people in jobs for which they may not be fully qualified. Such decisions are common, and the developmental choice is made on purpose. Placement decisions are a behavioral reflection of management's recognition that a person fully qualified for a job is the least likely to develop in it.

2) Managers are allowed—encouraged—to take risks and make mistakes. Mistakes aren't fatal as long as they aren't repeated, they result from real effort to do something new and beneficial, and they teach the manager something useful. Because managers need to take responsibility for their mistakes, the organization may need to use temporary punishments ("penalty boxes"). There are many examples of people taking reasonable risks, both in business decisions and in career moves. Interestingly, this propensity toward taking reasonable risks and tolerating failure is a characteristic of the "excellent" firms described by Peters and Waterman (1982).

3) Movement across organizational boundaries occurs regularly and easily. There are formal or informal mechanisms for identifying talented managers in other parts of the organization and for keeping them challenged even when that means crossing barriers. Because they identify with the larger corporate entity, managers do not have to protect their turf, and they do not tolerate games of "pass the turkey."

4) Developing executive talent is accepted as a line responsibility—commitment is demonstrated by the amount of time executives devote to it. Sometimes very serious incentives (such as a percentage of the bonus) are attached to achieving developmental goals.

One could list other characteristics of a culture that supports development, but the main point is that the behavior of executives is a clear demonstration of their commitment. People do not have to search to find examples of significant developmental moves. Action signifies their commitment—rewards and reprimands are consistent with developmental moves. In organizations where contrary patterns exist—where the folklore, for example, is replete with examples of fatal mistakes—the more practical human resource approach might be to emphasize selection and leave development to the occasional unsung hero. In these organizations, nothing short of a significant cultural shift, usually requiring several years of intense senior management effort, will work well.

If the organizational culture is at least partially supportive of development, the next step is doing something. While there is no "right" answer, effective development begins with the basic business strategy of the company. Take, as an example, whether or not to have a high-potential talent pool. In a conglomerate that has opted to be a holding company driven by financial criteria, the idea of developing executive talent for the corporate staff is moot. Any decisions on talent pools would best be left to the business units. However, a company that wants or has a strong corporate identity, but has numerous business units, needs some way to identify corporate resources across its many parts.

The salience of business strategy for executive development is even more pronounced in the case of cross-boundary movement. Our findings strongly suggest that variety in assignments over time is very important to development. Such variety is often attainable only through moves that cross functional, product, or business boundaries—leaps that sometimes defy past practice, and that almost always entail great risk to those who leap. Such moves should not be made lightly or because "it seems like a good idea." Rather we suggest that the business strategy dictates the need for such moves and the degree of acceptable risk associated with them. One company we work with has a strategic plan that calls for a new product line that will require the particular expertise held by two traditionally separate parts of the business. Success will depend upon finding managers for the new enterprise who are hybrids of these two parts, and this seems to justify the risk of developmental boundary spanning. Another company anticipates strategic realignment that will place a premium on skills most readily developed in a small part of the business historically considered a dead-end. Once again, the strategy dictates breaking boundaries for the sake of developing people for the future.

Business strategy affects development in more subtle ways as well. Research suggests that "growing" a general manager takes 10 to 20 years (Kotter, 1982), and there are no shortcuts. Confidence in business plans that go beyond five-year projections is low, at best, and obviously one cannot expect better accuracy with human resource strategy than with the business plan itself. Given the uncertainty of the future, it makes sense to insure that a variety of managerial styles and abilities are in the corporate pool. Business strategies can work against this if they result in the reduction of opportunities for people to:

- have responsibility for multiple functions and a bottom line at a relatively early age (e.g., to run small business units);
- roll-out or start up operations (e.g., Bechtel reportedly takes on small, uneconomic projects just to give high potential managers a whole job early);
- take responsibility for solving significant organizational problems and requiring people to reach their particular technical or functional specialties.

In our vernacular, we are suggesting that a developmentally oriented company will find ways to keep start-ups, turn-arounds, big-scope assignments, and meaningful projects and staff jobs available for its high potential people, even if short term business objectives suggest that it is inefficient to do so. And that is the crux of the argument—*having* managerial talent to run the business is just as significant as making optimal business and financial choices. Whether a corporation chooses to develop its own talent, or to refine its selection procedures to choose talent as needed, is itself a crucial strategic business decision.

The procedures used to develop executive talent through on-the-job experience must make sense in the context of a particular organization's culture and business strategy, so offering general advice is tricky. Nevertheless, we can identify several elements that are likely to be present in a career management system. The conclusions we have drawn from our research and from working with corporations on executive development issues suggest that a solid system will have many of the components described below.

A. A means for identifying and tracking high potential people across the corporation and all levels of the hierarchy. Whatever system is used, it will be characterized by frequent updating and fluid membership;

B. A mechanism for assessing and facilitating self-assessment of accomplishments, career experiences, and demonstrated learning over time;

C. A means of identifying developmental jobs throughout the company, a means for keeping track of them and what they might teach, and procedures for unblocking key assignments without losing solid performers in the process;

D. A way to ensure that placement decisions are made in light of developmental as well as business interests, and that line managers take reasonable risks for developmental purposes;

E. A way of keeping the managers who make placement decisions informed of available candidates from other parts of the business, and provisions for keeping track of the high potentials as they move to new assignments, particularly when they go overseas;

F. A tangible reward system for executives who identify and develop their people and who allow good people to move across boundaries in the interest the corporation;

G. A program geared to helping talented managers get the most out of the work experiences they have, possibly including such things as coaching or training interventions at crucial times, or readily available training and educational opportunities that support and help to synthesize what is learned on the job;

H. A human resources staff intimately knowledgeable about the business of the corporation, the demands of executive jobs, the pool of managerial and executive talent needed, and ways to work effectively as resources to line management.

Elegant formal systems do not guarantee effective executive development practice. Rigid career paths, forced mentoring and coaching programs, lockstep rotation plans, catalogs of training programs, and elaborate succession planning tables may actually be counter-productive. Our studies suggest that the development of executive talent is highly individualized. While no one would suggest that the processes should be random or devil-may-care, rigidity is not the answer either. Much as the success executive is pragmatic, flexible, and action-oriented, we believe a system to develop such people should have those same characteristics.

REFERENCES

Bennis, W., and B. Nanus, *Leaders: The Strategies for Taking Charge.* (New York: Harper and Row, 1985.)

Gabarro, J. J., *The Dynamics of Taking Charge.* (Boston, MA: Harvard University Press, 1987.)

Hall, D. T., *Careers in Organizations.* (Pacific Palisades, CA: Goodyear Publishing Company, 1976.)

Kotter, J. P., *The Leadership Factor.* (New York: The Free Press, 1989.)

Kotter, J. P., *The General Managers.* (New York: The Free Press, 1982.)

Lindsey, E. H., V. Homes, and M. W. McCall, Jr., *Key Events in Executives' Lives.* (Greensboro, NC: Center for Creative Leadership, 1987.)

McCall, M. W., Jr., M. M. Lombardo, and A. M. Morrison, *The Lessons of Experience.* (Lexington, Mass: Lexington Books, 1988.)

McCall, M. W., Jr., and M. M. Lombardo, *Off the Track: Why and How*

Successful Executives Get Derailed. Technical Report No. 21. (Greensboro, NC: Center for Creative Leadership, 1983.)

McCall, M. W., and C. D. McCauley, "Analyzing the Developmental Potential of Jobs." Presentation at the Annual Meetings of the American Psychological Association. Washington, DC, August, 1986.

McCauley, C. D., *Developmental Experiences in Managerial Work: A Literature Review.* Technical Report No. 26. (Greensboro, NC: Center for Creative Leadership, 1986.)

Peters, T. J., and R. H. Waterman, Jr., *In Search of Excellence.* (New York: Harper and Row, 1982.)

Short, A., "Are We Getting Our Money's Worth?" *New Management,* 4, Winter, 1987, pp. 23-26.

AFTERWARD COMMENTS

Morgan W. McCall, Jr., University of Southern California

O ur research on the developmental experiences of successful executives generated a lot of activity. Not only has there been new research on the general theme of learning from experience, but corporations have solicited my participation in their efforts to improve leadership development. Direct experience, it turns out, is a powerful teacher even for researchers. So powerful and with so many lessons, in fact, that limiting the scope of this retrospective was difficult.

I offer three general lessons from my work on developing executives through work experiences: 1) Commons sense is often harder to apply than one would expect; 2) the pressure to find shortcuts to executive development is so pervasive that selection may become the only viable option; and 3) incredible amounts of experience are wasted because little is done to enhance the learning that is possible from a development assignment.

Common Sense Masks Uncommon Sense

Our research confirmed what executives instinctively knew: leadership skills are learned from experience. What we had to offer was a reasonably thorough understanding of which kinds of experience were particularly important to developing executive skills and what lessons those experiences potentially taught. But the truth seemed less compelling precisely because it was so obvious. "We already move people around to develop them, thank you. We already rotate people through staff assignments or put them on major projects—there's nothing new here." Instead of using this understanding to hone their skills in development, organizations all too often ended up merely justifying their current practices or, worse, doing nothing further. But it's a long way from rotating people or doing succession planning or sending executives overseas to using experience thoughtfully for development purposes. Common practice can benefit enormously from consideration of *why* a person is given a particular assignment, what one hopes a person will learn from it, and what consequences are attached to learning or failing to learn.

Connecting development activities to the business strategy also turns out to be easy in theory but extremely difficult to practice. Choosing assignments on the basis of future leadership needs—acting on the sure knowledge that the experiences that created today's leaders are not the same experiences creating the leaders of the future—may be common sense, but it is an uncommon behavior.

Searching for Shortcuts

The fact that an organization takes an interest in developing leadership often means it has discovered an urgent need for leaders. Thus the stimulus to improve is also a stimulus to move quickly. The pressure to accelerate development can be enormous, generating confusion between the potential gains in efficiency from using assignments effectively and the misleading notion that all skills can be learned "faster" as a result of the efficiency. Truth is, by avoiding sloppy use of assignments for development substantial efficiency can result. But it takes a long time to learn some of the critical leadership skills; one cannot compress the learning cycle. If it takes two years to learn a certain skill, efficiency in getting a person in the right assignment to learn it does not reduce the time it takes to learn it—only the time it takes to get the opportunity. This is not to say that coaching and other activities might not speed up the learning process, but some things simply take time.

So, when I point out that even with all this knowledge it still takes a long time to develop leaders (any efficiency gained through effective disposition of assignments is needed to provide the time to learn a broader array of skills), the pressure for shortcuts inevitably forces the selection issue. What is really wanted, it turns out, is to find the needed leaders now, not develop them. Assignments, after all, can be viewed as tests just as easily as they can be seen as developmental experiences. "If you have the right stuff, we'll see it." And if you already have it, there's no need to spend time developing it.

If an organization has vast resources of undiscovered leadership talent, then improving selection and assessment practices is extremely wise. If, however, future leadership must be developed rather than discovered, then the promised shortcut of selection can turn into a regrettable detour. It is the search for the "miniature" leader that leads early identification astray—I firmly believe that executive leadership skills are in large part learned and that we should be seeking people who are most able to learn from the experiences we will give them. If skills are in fact developed from experience over time, then those skills are not necessarily present early. A selection strategy, then, is looking for something that isn't there.

Leaving Learning to Chance

Even when we get it right—we identify a talented person and get him or her into the best assignment for developing a particular skill—there is tendency to drop the ball on the goal line. A business does not exist to develop people. When a talented person is given an assignment, even a developmental assignment, effective job performance is the priority. We tend to forget (or overlook) that doing the job effectively and learning developmental lessons are likely to be two different issues. We accept that when *performance* is the issue, people need clear goals and accountability. Development requires no less, yet it is rare to find organizations that set explicit learning goals for job assignments and then hold people accountable for attaining them. Often discussions of development focus on coaching, providing resources, and giving feedback, forgetting some of the fundamentals of human behavior. People need to know what is expected of them, and those expectations must be measured and rewarded. If you want growth, you have to define it, measure it, and hold people accountable for it.

In summary, the same kind of experiences are important and teach the same things whether we are talking about corporate executives or physicians who become managers, whether the company makes washing machines or flavored water. The knowledge that really matters is not at the deceptively simple level—rotate people across jobs, keep them challenged, expose them to key business areas. While all of these strategies have some merit, in and of themselves they miss the point. Using assignments effectively for development is a way of thinking, not a series of practices. It seems like common sense: know what it is you are trying to develop, identify experiences that possibly teach it, find a way to get the right person in it at the right time, hold him/her accountable for growth as well as performance, and do it again for next assignment. Is that rotation? Keeping people challenged? Exposure? Surely it is all of those, but with a purpose. And the purpose is dictated by the business and its future direction. The kinds of experiences executives need to prepare them for the future are the ones they are having (or should be having) now.

MANAGEMENT DEVELOPMENT: REVISED THINKING IN LIGHT OF NEW EVENTS OF STRATEGIC IMPORTANCE

Michael A. Sheppeck and Clifton A. Rhodes, Honeywell Inc.

As Bennis (1993) noted, at the end of the 1970s and the beginning of the 1980s was a hard time for the United States. We suffered from "gaps" in leadership, productivity, and commitment to our institutions. While not everyone placed the sole responsibility for our economic decline on management, many did. In effect, a renewed emphasis was placed on management and particularly the notice of leadership. People such as Lee Iacocca and others caught our attention. There was a great yearning for the leaders of old.

This article deals with what the authors view as significant changes in the nature of management development in U.S. corporations. Of particular interest is an emerging model for growing future leaders or executives, which we call leadership development. We begin by outlining the challenges for human resource planning them have fueled this development model. We then compare the leadership model with the traditional management training model, using examples from a major U.S.-based company, Honeywell, Inc. We also use Honeywell to document the process of evolution toward leadership development. We conclude the article with some personal observations on lessons from the Honeywell experience and future trends in the management development arena.

The forces reshaping the American scene have been well documented (Bennis, 1983; Naisbitt, 1984; Yankelovich, 1981). Several of these forces have impacted the utilization of human resources in American companies and the operating style of managers. They have forced a closer linkage of human resource practices, especially development activities, with business needs. Some of the most important changes are these:

Reprinted from *Human Resource Planning*, Vol. 11, No. 2 (1988), 159-172.

- Changing nature of U.S. demographics: more women, minorities (US Department of Labor, 1984) and a greater heterogeneity of personal values (Massey, 1979).
- Employee expectations out of line with the U.S. economic position in the world (The Productivity Letter, 1986a).
- Slowed productivity growth and eroding market share (Bennis, 1983; The Productivity Letter, 1986b).
- Changing advancement opportunities for all employees and managers in particular (Business Week, 1983).
- An emphasis on information, automation, and robotics (Industry Week, November 10, 1986).
- Need for greater technical vitality in R&D and engineering ranks.
- Commitment and leadership "gaps" (Bennis, 1983).

These trends, and the last one in particular, have turned the spotlight on corporate management practices and led to a renewed search for "leaders." The publication of books such as *The One Minute Manager* (Blanchard and Spencer, 1981), *In Search of Excellence* (Peters and Waterman, 1982) and *Lenders* (Bennis and Nanus, 1985) further underscore the intensity of the search.

The most recent thinking regarding leadership centers on the transformational or visionary leader (Bennis 1983; Tichy and DeVanna, 1986; Bennis and Nanus, 1985). This view differs from older trait and power theories by emphasizing:

- The creation by the leader of a clear vision for action,
- Active involvement of the leader as a change agent in the organization,
- Clear communications by the leader regarding vision and action to all others in the organization,
- The building of trust and the belief in people,
- An emphasis on values (both personal and organizational),
- A strong sense of self-understanding and self-esteem.

MANAGEMENT DEVELOPMENT APPROACHES

The transformational approach to leadership has prompted a serious change in thinking regarding management development. The emerging model, referred to simply as "Leadership Development" in this article, differs in significant ways from the older "Management Training" model.

Management Training Model

The Management Training model has been the dominant approach to management development for the last several decades. The objective of this approach is to provide for the acquisition of managerial competence in a smooth, uninterrupted fashion. Typically, this approach focuses on adult learning, particularly learning in a classroom setting (Knowles, 1984). Other characteristics include utilization of competency guidelines for skill acquisition (Boyatzis, 1982; Hughes, 1978) and a more "prescriptive" approach (Pouliot, 1984) for determining educational activities.

An excellent example of this approach is the educational component of Honeywell's management development model. This model focuses on the various levels of management, stages in the development of an individual at each level (i.e., stages in the learning process), and a set of fundamental management competencies (see Exhibits 1 and 2).

The model holds that individual managers go through a four stage learning cycle. The first stage deals with *entry* to the organization or a new job, where the individual's primary focus is on orientation and getting to know the organization. As an individual progresses he/she begins to move through the *skill building* stage. This stage is concerned with acquisition of the basic knowledge and skills required for performance in the managerial job. Over time the individual moves into the *performance* stage. This is typically the most productive stage in an individual's tenure on a given job. In this stage, the individual has achieved his/her optimum level of performance. Finally, some individuals move into the *mastery* stage. In this stage, the individual, while continuing to perform at a high level, also begins to act as a consultant or mentor to those around him/her. The individual shows expertise well beyond the specific skill needs of the job.

Individual managers move through the four stages at their own pace. The Honeywell experience shows that most managers are promoted to new jobs or higher level jobs while they are in the performance stage of their cycle. At that point, the cycle begins anew at the entry or orientation stage.

By utilizing the model it is possible to determine a set of internal and external educational programs suited to managers at various times in their development (see Exhibit 3). As the exhibit shows, formal education typically deals with the skill building and performance stages. The entry and mastery stages have such unique characteristics that on-the-job experience, with a small amount of very specific training, seems to be the best mode of development. As the Exhibit 3 further shows, at Honeywell an introductory program (e.g., Introduction to Supervision and Middle-Manager Development) is provided for individuals during their skill-building stage. Subsequently, roughly two or three years later, individuals are encouraged to attend an advance program for their specific managerial level and their stage in the learning cycle. When used consistently and rigorously, this approach to management development has been very effective in developing basic managerial skills at all levels in the management hierarchy.

EXHIBIT 1
Honeywell Management Development Model

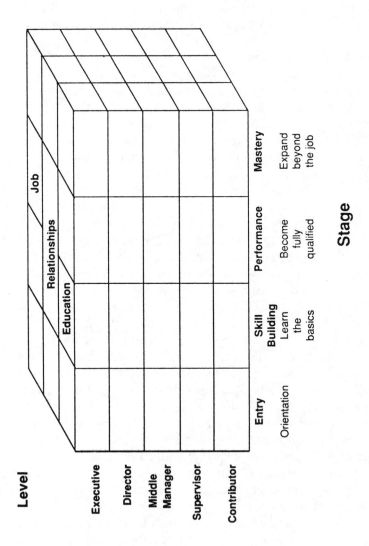

EXHIBIT 2
Management Competencies

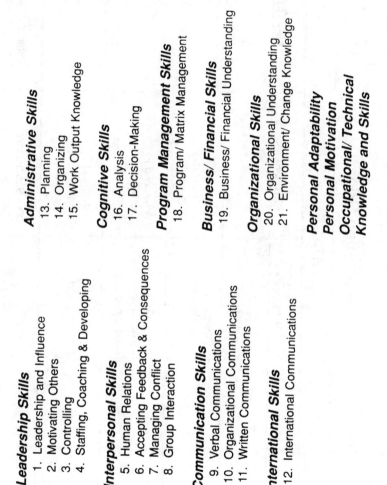

Leadership Skills
1. Leadership and Influence
2. Motivating Others
3. Controlling
4. Staffing, Coaching & Developing

Interpersonal Skills
5. Human Relations
6. Accepting Feedback & Consequences
7. Managing Conflict
8. Group Interaction

Communication Skills
9. Verbal Communications
10. Organizational Communications
11. Written Communications

International Skills
12. International Communications

Administrative Skills
13. Planning
14. Organizing
15. Work Output Knowledge

Cognitive Skills
16. Analysis
17. Decision-Making

Program Management Skills
18. Program/ Matrix Management

Business/ Financial Skills
19. Business/ Financial Understanding

Organizational Skills
20. Organizational Understanding
21. Environment/ Change Knowledge

Personal Adaptability
Personal Motivation
Occupational/ Technical Knowledge and Skills

EXHIBIT 3
Education Grid Stage

Education Grid

LEVEL	STAGE			
	ENTRY	SKILL BUILDING	PERFORMANCE	MASTERY
EXEC		Aspen Institute		
DIR		Director Development	Advanced Program For Directors (Exeter)	
MID LEVEL		Middle Manager Development	Advanced Program For Middle Managers	
SUP		Introduction to Supervision	Advanced Program For Supervisors	
IND. CONTRIB.	Honeywell Orientation	ACE After-Hours Education	Pre-Supervisory Courses	Company Sponsored Degree Programs

The learning model shown in Exhibit 1 has many uses. For example, as suggested above, the learning stages concept is typically used in succession planning. At Honeywell, the typical manager progresses through the first three stages in a three to five year period. At that point, managers are ready for movement to new lateral jobs or promotion to higher level jobs. Individuals who have not progressed from skill building to the performance stage usually are not seen as "promotable" within the organization.

The competencies identified in Exhibit 2 are used to continually check the applicability of training programs offered for all levels of managers. In other words, educational objectives for each program are clearly linked to the various critical competencies identified in the exhibit. Thus, the competencies foster an informal needs analysis on an ongoing basis. Finally, the competencies and learning stages are also used in management staffing. The competencies serve as benchmarks for the identification of individuals with managerial talent. The concept of learning stages helps in the assessment of individuals outside the organization who are being considered for selection. An effort is made to identify individuals who are clearly in the performance stage on their current jobs and, therefore, can make the greatest contribution to the company at the time they are hired.

Leadership Development Model

As noted earlier, trends in the external environment and the internal workforce have fostered a movement toward transformational leadership. Bennis and Nanus (1985, p. 21) define transformational leadership in terms of the wise use of vision and judgement. The distinction between transformational leadership and management revolves around effectiveness (i.e., doing the right thing) versus efficiency (i.e., mastering the various routines of management life).

All types of businesses require an emphasis on leadership development. At the same time, however, the specific qualities of leadership that are emphasized may vary. For example, in the high-tech sector, leadership is required to create a vision for growing a competitive organization in an increasingly difficult marketplace. On the other hand, in the manufacturing sector, the likely emphasis is on leadership to transform organizations into very efficient and cost-conscious operations.

In the development arena, the movement toward the leadership model has been furthered by the realization that management growth is most impacted by job experiences and interpersonal relationships (with boss, peers, subordinates, and professional community). The 1985 Honeywell Job and Relationship Study, a research project involving over 4,000 Honeywell managers, suggested that job experiences and relationships account for approximately 80% of a manager's post-educational learning. A similar study conducted by the Center for Creative Leadership (CCL) (1985) shows nearly identical findings. CCL found that experiences accounted for approximately 50% of all post-educational learning, with relationships accounting for 30% and educational experiences accounting for 20%.

Interestingly, Honeywell found that managers would like to see slightly more emphasis placed on educational experiences. The recommendation is that managers should be attending educational programs at very specific times in their careers. For example, when an individual moves from individual contributor to supervisor, he/she should attend a program on the essential survival skills of appraisal, coaching and recognition. Likewise, when an individual moves from supervisor to middle-manager, he/she should attend training on interdepartmental cooperation and the use of power and influence. These findings have led Honeywell to refocus its leadership development efforts to emphasizing the use of multiple growth avenues. The objective of the new leadership development model is to create a management system that ensures that the present and future leadership needs of the organization are effectively met. This management system utilizes both educational and on-the-job experiences as prime modes of development. Additional characteristics of the leadership development approach are as follows:

- The belief that a systematic approach to an individual's total career (a focus on career in addition to competency) is essential for effective leadership development.
- The utilization of human resource planning (determining future leadership requirements) as an aid in career development planning.
- Strong involvement by executives, i.e., the "diagnostic" approach as outlined by Pouliot (1984).
- Reliance on job experiences, relationships, and classroom education as the prime drivers of development and growth.
- A focus on visioning, ethics, and the management of change as key development outcomes.
- A long-term objective to develop a pool of leadership talent rather than rely on individual succession planning as the modus operandi for development.

In Honeywell the evolution toward leadership development has involved two other important ingredients. The first is the Human Resource Development Board, which was formed in 1984 to further emphasize and legitimate development from a senior management perspective. The Board has been instrumental in refocusing attention on the importance of a long-term perspective and commitment to leadership development. The second ingredient is the creation of a "people development" award for managers. The Lund Award—named after a prominent retired Honeywell executive known for his skill and commitment to developing people—has become a prestigious company-wide award for recognizing the importance of people development.

Honeywell is currently exploring the addition of other elements to its leadership development approach. One example comes from General Electric, which has developed a series of special topic leadership workshops. These workshops bring together a sponsoring GE executive, high level managers dealing with the topic in question, and a noted expert or educator. The objective is to provide state-of-the-art information and the opportunity for joint problem-solving under the sponsorship of a key executive. GE's actions, like those of Honeywell, point to a leadership development approach based more on visioning and meeting emerging business needs than on strict management competence. We believe this is the trend for the future.

PROCESS OF EVOLUTION

Any organization attempting to develop its management cadre will typically experiment with various approaches. Factors such as senior management commitment, resource constraints, business conditions, and participant interest often dictate what an organization eventually does in the development arena. The evolution of leadership development at Honeywell serves to illustrate some of these forces for change.

The Move from Early Approach to Management Training

The early approach to development in Honeywell was characterized by decentralization, few systems at either the corporate or operating division level, a classroom training focus, and an emphasis on "within function" careers.

While limited, this early approach did provide a baseline for several important lessons. For one, a more systematic training approach, using a time-based and learning-based model, was needed to capture and channel managers' attention regarding their own development. The learning cycle model together with the identification of specific training courses offered at various stages helps managers to understand what they should be doing at each stage of their career. In addition, this structured approach allows senior management to gauge training effectiveness by determining how many individuals are attending programs of various types.

Another important lesson was that competency-based approaches are a required foundation for future management development. In other words, managers need to have a clear and solid grasp of management fundamentals before they can deal with the more abstract concept of leadership. Nevertheless, we have found the management training approach, when taken by itself, falls short of the gains realized through the more powerful concept of leadership development.

A study by a leading management consulting firm identified deficiencies in Honeywell's approach to management development as the company entered the uncertain and challenging time of the 1980s. The study spurred the interest of senior management and resulted in a number of actions that moved management development from competency training toward leadership development. These actions included baseline research on internal methods for developing managers, construction of a Management Development Center dedicated to fostering management growth, the formation of the Human Resource Development Board, and establishment of the Lund People Development Award.

While these actions were taking place, human resource planning both at the corporate and operating division levels was coming of age. HRP focused senior management's attention on key human resource issues confronting the company, including the issue of leadership development. The immediate result was a mandatory training policy for new supervisors (sponsored by the Human Resource Development Board) and the implementation of the Job and Relationship Study. These initiatives were followed by significant challenges in the company's succession planning/high talent system. The revision of this system has become the current priority and key plank in Honeywell's leadership development platform.

Executive Career Planning and Development Process

Honeywell's executive career planning and development process focuses on a small number of candidates (approximately 150) for senior management positions. The system emphasizes career development through stretch assignments and other developmental events. As shown in Exhibit 4, the system identifies three distinct groupings of managers. Group A consists of current General Managers running divisional operations and senior functional staff at the corporate level. It is expected that these individuals could become executives within one to five years. Group B is made up of current Directors who are enroute to becoming Vice Presidents and who could become General Managers within one to five years. Finally, Group C is made up of Middle Managers who are viewed as prospective Directors and who could become General Managers within the next six to ten years.

A stringent set of job performance criteria, leadership attributes, and past experiences are used to select individuals for the executive career planning process. Exhibit 5 shows the performance benchmarks used as criteria for entering the career planning and development process. The benchmarks represent business-oriented accomplishments that individuals must show on their present and past jobs. The items go in progression from Group C, to B, and finally to Group A.

SHARED WISDOM

In addition, a "Career Planning Guide" (Exhibit 6) is used both to gauge an individual's experience to date and to suggest future stretch activities for development purposes. It is not anticipated that every individual will have the experiences outlined in the Guide. However, the items do serve as convenient benchmarks for determining relevant experiences for an executive career.

The Guide specifies the various functions an individual should have experienced over time; how many businesses within the company he/she should have worked in; the various types of business life cycles he/she should have experienced; and finally, several different contexts that have meaning within the company.

All A, B, and C group members are eventually informed of their status in the process. However, given the decentralized nature of the company, actual communication is left to the discretion of individual divisions. This results in the communication process taking longer to unfold in some parts of the company than others. It is expected that membership in the A, B, and C groups will remain relatively stable over time. Nevertheless, changes (i.e., individuals going on and off the list due largely to promotions or failure to evidence consistently outstanding performance and personal growth) can occur because group membership is reviewed annually.

Senior executives play a major role in the career planning process by sponsoring a small number of Group A, B, and C individuals within their respective businesses. Sponsorship focuses principally on the system of identification for Group A, B, and C members. The senior executives are committed to this system and must facilitate and control the identification process in their respective businesses. In addition, they have a coaching role for A and B level participants. The immediate managers of these individuals have the primary coaching/development responsibility. However, senior executives lend their attention and support to the process. Group C members are managed in the system exclusively by their divisional general managers. In effect, senior executives "sponsor" the overall program and have final corporate responsibility for the identification and evaluation of all A, B, and C group members. Finally, each operating unit of the company is encouraged to establish a similar process for critical job families or functions.

Establishment of the executive career planning and development process has also led to greater emphasis on educational experiences that provide key managers with a broader business perspective. Programs such as those offered by Aspen and the Brookings Institute and mini executive courses at Harvard, Stanford, and MIT are being systematically used in the long-term development of future executives. In this way, Honeywell's executive career planning and development process incorporates the job and educational experiences that are central to the leadership development approach.

EXHIBIT 4
Structure

Structure

The process & requirements have been structured for 3 categories or levels of candidates.

Group	Current Level	Readiness
A	GM & Senior Functional Staff	Exec 1-5 yrs.
B	VP ← Dir	GM 1-5 yrs.
C	Dir ← MM	GM staff 1-5 yrs. GM 6-10 yrs.

EXHIBIT 5
Performance Benchmarks

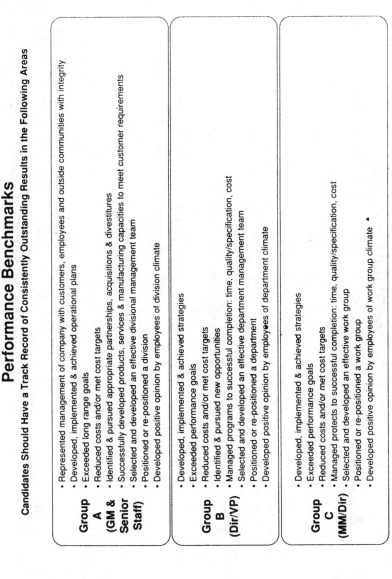

Performance Benchmarks

Candidates Should Have a Track Record of Consistently Outstanding Results in the Following Areas

Group A (GM & Senior Staff)
- Represented management of company with customers, employees and outside communities with integrity
- Developed, implemented & achieved operational plans
- Exceeded long range goals
- Reduced costs and/or met cost targets
- Identified & pursued appropriate partnerships, acquisitions & divestitures
- Successfully developed products, services & manufacturing capacities to meet customer requirements
- Selected and developed an effective divisional management team
- Positioned or re-positioned a division
- Developed positive opinion by employees of division climate

Group B (Dir/VP)
- Developed, implemented & achieved strategies
- Exceeded performance goals
- Reduced costs and/or met cost targets
- Identified & pursued new opportunities
- Managed programs to successful completion: time, quality/specification, cost
- Selected and developed an effective department management team
- Positioned or re-positioned a department
- Developed positive opinion by employees of department climate

Group C (MM/Dir)
- Developed, implemented & achieved strategies
- Exceeded performance goals
- Reduced costs and/or met cost targets
- Managed projects to successful completion: time, quality/specification, cost
- Selected and developed an effective work group
- Positioned or re-positioned a work group
- Developed positive opinion by employees of work group climate

EXHIBIT 6
Career Planning Guide

Career Planning Guide

Assignments Should Be Selected To Provide A Full Range Of Experiences

Group	Functions	Businesses	Business Life Cycles	Business Context	Readiness
A VP/GM & Senior Staff	1 each from... • Operations **and** -Engineering -Manufacturing -Program Mgnt. • Field **and** -Marketing -Field Sales -Field Ops. • Staff, esp. -Finance -Int'l. Project	2+ Int'l	3 of ... •Start-up •Fast growing •Mature •Retrenching/ Phase out •Troubled	2 of ... •Complex •Large Size •High Technology •Service	Exec 1-5 yrs.
B VP ← Dir	1 each from... • Operations **and** -Engineering -Manufacturing -Program Mgnt. • Field **and** -Marketing -Field Sales -Field Ops. • Staff, esp. -Finance -Int'l. Project	2	2 of ... •Start-up •Fast growing •Mature •Retrenching/ Phase out •Troubled	2 of ... •Complex •Large Size •High Technology •Service	GM 1-5 yrs.
C Dir ← MM	1 each from... • Operations **and** -Engineering -Manufacturing -Program Mgnt. • Field -Marketing -Field Sales -Field Ops. • Staff, esp. *Desirable* -Finance -Int'l. Project	1 or 2	1 of ... •Start-up •Fast growing •Mature •Retrenching/ Phase out •Troubled	1 of ... •Complex •Large Size •High Technology •Service	GM staff 1-5 yrs. GM 6-10 yrs.

Using all this information to chart a career plan for an individual is more art than science. The individual's past experiences, stage in the career-cycle model, past education, and current job level and duties dictate what development activities should take place. As noted above, the prime focus is on utilizing job experience as the main development avenue. Therefore, individuals are encouraged to accept positions that help them broaden their perspective of the various Honeywell businesses, and the various functions in each business. In addition, they are encouraged to attend various educational activities to broaden their business background, develop specific managerial skills and tools, or develop a broader, more liberal view of world events.

Responsibility for the process of summarizing and analyzing an individual's experiences in order to prescribe developmental events is assumed by key human resource and senior line executives in conjunction with the target manager. This process ensures that individuals obtain the types of development they require in a manner acceptable to them.

IMMEDIATE LESSONS AND FUTURE TRENDS

A number of lessons have been learned from Honeywell's recent management development efforts:

- A certain amount of trial-and-error is to be expected and fostered in shaping an effective management development system.
- A paradigm shift is necessary. Senior management and development professionals must embrace a new philosophy of development that shatters many tenets of the traditional competency training model.
- Senior management understanding and commitment to the development process is vital.
- Human Resource Development practitioners must understand and effectively utilize the latest developments in their craft. Senior managers are capable of seeing through thinly veiled confidence and will not support efforts they feel are not thoroughly grounded in theory and practice.
- The objectives of the development process must be clearly articulated and directly tied to current and future business needs.
- Communication to all management levels of the mission, issues, and strategies of development cannot be overdone.

Thus far this new approach to development has been well accepted throughout the company. Implementation has gone very well, particularly with respect to commitment by divisional and corporate executive management. The real test, however, is whether over time future leaders are effectively reassigned across divisional and business boundaries. The critical success factor in this change process, as in most others, is executive commitment and willingness to consciously "work" the new system.

While specific management development efforts vary considerably in American companies, the new emphasis on leadership development is clear. Listed below are a number of related trends we believe will pervade management development in the 1990s:

- Management development will continue to be driven by an organization's culture and management style. Savvy Human Resource Development practitioners must be prepared to blend recent advances in individual development with an organization's current stage of development.

- Broadening the manager's perspective on issues beyond planning, doing and controlling will grow in importance. Well-rounded leaders who understand both the ethics and the economics of today's world will have the greatest chance of guiding their organizations toward success in the future.

- Effective visioning and management of change will be key success factors for our future leaders. Development will focus on enhancing these leadership capabilities through on-the-job experiences, relationships with others, and classroom training.

- Senior management involvement in providing focus and direction to development activities will continue to grow.

- Emphasis on the whole person and the whole career, rather than simple skill training, will be the hallmark of future development efforts.

Organizations moving in the direction of these trends will benefit from having more effective leaders and a greater chance of success in the global marketplace of the 1990s.

REFERENCES

Bennis, W., "Four Traits of Leadership." *The May Report,* December, 1983.

Bennis, W., and Nanus, B., *Lenders: The Strategies for Taking Charge.* (New York: Harper & Row, Publishers, 1985).

Blanchard, K. and Johnson, S., *The One Minute Manager.* (New York: Berkeley Books, 1983).

Boyatzis, R., *The Complete Manager.* (New York: Wiley, 1982).

Business Week, "A New Era For Management." April 25, 1983. pp. 50-80.

Center for Creative Leadership, *Developing the Executive Resource: Making the Most of Job Experiences.* (A course offered November 13-15, 1985, Greensboro, NC).

Hughes Aircraft Company, *Research and Development Productivity: An*

Investigation of Ways to Evaluate and Improve Productivity in Technology-Based Organizations, 2nd ed. (Culver City, CA: Hughes Aircraft Company, 1978).

Industry Week, "Map-Top, Tying It All Together." November 10, 1986, pp. 46-102.

Knowles, M., "Adult Learning: Theory and Practice." In L. Nadler (Ed.)., *The Handbook of Human Resource Development.* (New York: John Wiley & Sons, 1984).

Massey, M., *The People Puzzle—Understanding Yourself and Others.* (Reston Publishing Co., 1979).

Nasibitt, J., *Megatrends.* (New York: Warner Books, Inc., 1984).

Peters, T. and Waterman, Jr., R., *In Search of Excellence: Lessons From America's Best Run Companies.* (New York: Harper & Row, 1982).

Pouliot, L., "Executive Management and Supervisory Programs." In Nadler (Ed.)., *The Handbook of Human Resource Development.* (New York: John Wiley & Sons, 1984).

The Productivity Letter, "Questions and Answers." American Productivity Center, December 1986a, 6(6), p. 4.

The Productivity Letter, "Journalist Halberstam Addresses America's Industrial Challenge." American Productivity Center, December 1986b, 6(6), p. 4.

The Productivity Letter, "Newsweek's Samuelson Attacks the Myth of Management." American Productivity Center, April 1987, 6(10), pp. 1,7.

Tichy, N. and DeVanna, M.. "The Transformational Leader." *Training and Development Journal,* July, 1986, pp. 27-32.

U.S. Department of Labor, Bureau of Labor Statistics, Employment Projections for 1985, March, 1984.

Yankelovich, D., *New Rules: Searching for Self-Fulfillment in a World Turned Upside Down.* (Toronto: Bantam Books, 1981).

Afterward Comments

Michael Sheppeck

As we progress through the 1990s, the development of leaders and the evolution of systematic processes for their identification and growth remain a continuing need in U.S. organizations. Those individuals making HR decisions increasingly realize that leadership development and other HR practices must take place in the context of an organization's business environment, competitive strategy, structure, and production/service process. This alignment constitutes the next phase in the evolution of strategic HR management. Gone are the days when a training management could serve as an organization's sole means of leadership development.

Each manager must be deeply involved in both the organization's long-term strategy and in personal growth relative to the organization's needs. This requires development via experiential means, not straight classroom training. It requires the systematic shaping of the manager's capabilities and mindset via a cohesive system of HR practices: identification, orientation, coaching, appraisal, reward, stretch assignments, and broad career development. In other words, both the individual manager and the organization must take an active role in the manager's development.

This article utilizes the experience of a Fortune 100 company to illustrate how the issues identified above might be blended into a systematic leadership development process for the 1990s and beyond. In this organization the shift is clearly being made from a paradigm of management development to a process of leadership growth. In particular, these features of the process as critical today as when it was initiated, form the foundation of this approach to leadership development. First, multiple interconnected components create a leadership development system that reinforces the strategic direction of the organization. Single events like one-week classroom programs or weekend retreats cannot by themselves produce the capability and mindset shaping required for leadership development today. This article shows how multiple reinforcing activities produce a continuous movement toward leadership and maturation for those involved in the process.

Second, as suggested by several research programs, experience constitutes the most powerful influence on an individual's growth as a leader. The act of performing provides the forum for the double-loop learning so vital to maturation as a leader. Again the article describes several contemporary approaches for active learning in leadership.

Finally, the intense involvement of both the individual manager and the senior management team is vital to the manager's continuous growth. Removing the management development program for the HR function and creating a leadership development process that actively involves individual managers and the senior management team is a necessary feature of successful leader development in the future.

The lessons learned by this organization are as vibrant today as they were in the 1980s. They continue to emphasize the identification and growth of tomorrow's leaders must start today and requires intense and focused energy to ensure that the appropriate capabilities and mindset become a part of every manager's repertoire.

INTERNAL ADVANCED MANAGEMENT PROGRAMS FOR EXECUTIVE DEVELOPMENT: A SURVEY AND CASE STUDY

Matt M. Starcevich, Ph.D. and J. Arnold Sykes

The strengths and limitations of university management development programs are examined in view of the trend for companies to supplement them with internal educational efforts. One such company, Phillips Petroleum, offers an example of how an internal advanced management program can be designed and conducted. Matt M. Starcevich, Ph.D., is Director of the Center for Management and Organization Effectiveness in Bartlesville, Oklahoma. J. Arnold Sykes is Corporate Manager, Human Resources Planning and Development with Tektronix, Inc. in Beaverton, Oregon.

Companies are providing for the development of their management and executive personnel today more than ever before. One of the more definitive trends is the evolution away from reliance largely or wholly on externally-sponsored training and development programs.

A few companies, like General Electric and IBM, have a history of internal programs of a highly formalized nature. There is little published material to guide organizations considering an internal advanced management program designed to fit the unique needs of their situation. This article summarizes the approach one company has taken in developing an internal advanced management program that capitalizes on the experiences of other organizations and supplements university-sponsored programs. It also reviews the experience gained from conducting two internal programs and discusses the critical issues involved. The process used to assure commitment on the part of management, as well as the procedures

Reprinted from *Human Resource Planning*, Vol. 3, No. 3 (1980), 97-109.

used to tie the program closely to the needs of the organization, are as important as the conclusions and resulting program design.

THE NEED AND APPROACH

Phillips Petroleum, like other multi-national integrated oil companies, recruits a highly technical labor force. Formal training in business-related subjects as the technical person moves toward a general management position is limited to on-the-job experience plus short, off-the-job courses.

In 1977, because of company growth and expansion, an increased number of profit centers and an aging upper/middle management group, the company saw that in the next ten years more people would be asked to fill responsible management positions earlier in their careers with little or no formal managerial education. Each year, a limited number of upper management had participated in university programs such as the ones at Columbia, Stanford, MIT, Northwestern, and others that focused on a general management perspective. However, the large number of people who need formal management education, coupled with some notable limitations of university-sponsored programs, resulted in a thorough study on the feasibility of developing and implementing an internal advanced management program.

The research consisted of three parts: 1) an analysis of the strengths and weaknesses of university-sponsored programs; 2) a study of selected organizations that have initiated internal advanced management programs; and 3) interviews with managers in Phillips Petroleum who have attended university programs and were in a position to evaluate the management education needs of highly-rated managers in their organization. The research was initiated without any strong predisposition that an internal development program should be proposed. After analysis, a recommendation was made to the corporate executive committee that a four-week internal advanced management program would fulfill the needs of Phillips Petroleum.

UNIVERSITY-SPONSORED ADVANCED MANAGEMENT PROGRAMS

Educational programs for executives have existed for over a quarter of a century, dating from Harvard's first advanced management program in 1945. *Bricker's Directory* provides an up-to-date picture of the present 131 broad, in-residence executive management programs. Of these, Bricker identifies 26 university-sponsored programs designed for top management in medium and large companies. An analysis of the 26 programs for top level executives shows:

- Program length averages about six weeks, with a range from 4 to 14 weeks.
- The average cost for tuition, room and board is about $824 per week.

- The average number of participants is 45 with a range from 24 to 80. Average age is 42.
- The subject matter is similar to that required in an MBA degree.
- The definition of purpose shows a great deal of similarity for all programs: to broaden and expose participants to new horizons and to enlarge their outlook toward events taking place around them. Most often stressed are new methods of analysis, decision making, and strategic planning.
- The most frequent instructional methods are the case study, lecture with discussion, and small work group projects.

The following potential strengths and limitations of the university-sponsored programs appear relevant.

Potential Strengths

- Exposure to current thinking, and theory of faculty from leading business schools. New approaches and ideas can be experienced without the limitation of an individual's own organizational practices. A study of more than 6,000 participants who had attended courses in 39 universities documents that the most frequent response to the question, "What do you think happened to you as a result of attending the program?" was "The program broadened me," (Andrews, 1966).
- The opportunity to exchange views and learn about other industries' problems and solutions to problems. This exchange between participants, with the opportunity to note similarity or differences in conditions, is a strength.
- The administrative and logistical problems involved in conducting a top level program are entirely taken care of by the sponsoring university.

Potential Limitations

- Variance in faculty effectiveness, both between and within individual university programs. A complete complement of knowledgeable faculty in each subject area who can work with a mature adult audience is both critically important and difficult to achieve. Faculty effectiveness varies in these two critical criteria. The desire to use the faculty of the sponsoring university limits the use of faculty from other universities who excel in both instruction of adults and subject knowledge. With no control over faculty selection, the participant is faced with accepting the bad with the good.
- Vague definition of purpose and expected outcome for both a given subject area and overall executive program. As indicated, the mission of the university-sponsored executive program is to broaden

the perspective of participants. This makes it difficult to evaluate successful performance, and allows for greater variety in curriculum structure and subject mix. Additionally, the limited time spent on each subject area dictates that the instructor pick and choose the specific content to be covered. Academic freedom limits input or quality control over subject matter. This increases the possibility that subject areas are included based solely on the instructor's desire to teach these areas, instead of on the participant's "need to know" to improve his or her effectiveness on the job.

- The heterogeneous organization level, background and functional experience of participants necessitates that the university-sponsored program be of a very general nature. The similarity in program content across university programs raises some question as to the depth of needs analysis done by any given university. Admission standards in some cases are broad and flexible. This contributes to program content based on what is perceived to be the need of the typical executive in a program. The effectiveness of this shotgun approach varies from university to university.

- University programs cannot facilitate on-the-job reinforcement of concepts learned in the classroom. Two or three participants returning to the sponsoring organization will have only limited opportunity to create conditions where new ideas can be practiced or implemented.

- The burden is on participants to apply the concepts being discussed to their own industry situation. Cases from retail or service organizations, or consumer marketing concepts, must be translated by the participant employed in technical, process-oriented or capital-intensive industries. Although certain concepts may be universal, the translation to a different situation increases the difficulty of fully understanding their applicability. For participants from the public sector, the concepts may be interesting, but questionable in terms of their ability to be applied. Translation for the academician does not present as much an obstacle to learning as it does to the practicing manager.

- The length of a particular program is a major criterion for selection by the busy executive. The marginal gain of additional weeks is hard to correlate with the vague definition of program purpose and outcome. Good programs may be ruled out based on time considerations alone.

- The sponsoring university's practice of limiting the number of participants from the company's desire to limit the number of their participants in order not to overly influence a class, create a real problem when a large number of executives need this development experience.

- There is a limit to the number of executives who can attend reputable university-sponsored programs. The total number for any organization is proximately 50 if one assumes that two participants may attend each of the 26 programs identified by Brickers as being of equal quality and designed for top management in medium and large companies. The variance in program length and faculty quality subjects this assumption to some question Phillips places the limit at approximately 30 participants per year who would be able to receive roughly equal return in value for their investment.

THE GAP FILLED BY INTERNAL ADVANCED MANAGEMENT PROGRAMS

Several organizations have developed internal programs for their managers. General Electric's nine-week advanced management course established in 1955 was the first long-term program. Two separate four-week courses at GE for different levels of managers have replaced the original program. Few organizations have made such a commitment to internal executive education. The similarities and differences in these programs illustrate the manner in which internal advanced management programs are attempting to overcome some of the potential limitations of university programs. In 1977, Phillips Petroleum completed a detailed study of the internal education programs in the following organizations:

General Electric Company
IBM
Motorola
Shell Oil, U.S.
Marathon Oil
St. Regis Paper Company
The Federal Executive Institute

These organizations were selected as representative of the various approaches to internal advanced management programs.

Figure 1 summarizes the internal programs of these organizations. Each program has unique characteristics tailored to the needs of the organization's management. However, certain similarities are noted.

SIMILARITIES OF INTERNAL ADVANCED MANAGEMENT PROGRAMS

1. The Need For An Internal Effort

In all the organizations surveyed the internal effort seemed to result from the need to:

- Provide educational experiences for substantial numbers of employees at a rate faster than participation in regular university programs would allow.
- Make the educational experience as pragmatic as possible while providing new concepts to participants. The concepts need to be focused on the unique situations faced by a given organization.
- Have greater control over course content, curriculum design and faculty selection.
- Increase understanding of the organization and impart certain beliefs and organizational philosophies to participants.

2. Content Of The Program Or Perspective Provided

A great deal of similarity seemed to exist across the programs, as they all:

- Limited participation to upper middle-managers and other high potential individuals.
- Concentrated on skills and knowledge common to all managers; e.g., finance, accounting, economics, strategic planning, managerial style/behavior, as they relate to the unique conditions of a particular organization.
- Provided the "general management perspective" to highly functional or technically-oriented individuals who have little formal business education.
- Aimed at presenting concepts and ideas of the "nuts and bolts" of a subject area.

3. Executive Participation

Every program utilizes the key executives of an organization to provide participants with an appreciation for the organization and for the philosophy of its policy makers. Although done in slightly different ways, the use of key executives involves creating an opportunity for direct dialogue between program participants and executives. The major instructional load is carried by distinguished faculty members from various institutions across the United States. This diversity of faculty was found to be critical.

4. Relationship To University Executive Development Programs

All the organizations surveyed saw their internal effort as:

- Complementing executive programs at universities and not replacing them.
- Maintaining the positive aspects of residential "away from work" education by nationally known professors while minimizing certain weak-

nesses such as program length and lack of curriculum and faculty speaker control.

- Not excluding a person from later attending an executive development program at a university.

5. Program Duration And Design

Programs vary from two to four weeks in length, with the majority being conducted in one concentrated block of time. An interesting variation is St. Regis Paper Company's two-week program, in which each week of instruction is separated by a five-month time period. Marathon Oil's contract with Indiana University (where Indiana University handles the program administration aspects while Marathon maintains control over curriculum) is an interesting alternative. Marathon feels it has achieved the best of both internal and university programs, while minimizing the company administrative time and cost of an internal program.

6. Caveats To Consider

The following caveats were given by directors of these internal programs and are provided for those considering possible internal efforts:

- Segment your audience and set specific objectives for each audience.
- Make the first effort modest and simple enough to accomplish with perfection. Don't try to design an expansive program that will be all things to all people.
- Don't underestimate the time required, extensive work, and total cost in program design.
- Be careful about teaching methodology and philosophy. Remember, the program is being provided to adults who know best what they need. Sometimes the best teaching approach is to have them teach themselves via classroom discussion.
- Don't get into the "facilities" business initially if there is another alternative.

AN APPROACH TO DEFINING THE RELEVANT NEEDS FOR AN INTERNAL PROGRAM

Aware of the strengths and limitations of university-sponsored programs and the experiences of other organizations with internal programs, Phillips began to define their specific needs in executive education and whether these needs could best be met by an internal effort. Of equal concern was the commitment to a proposal of key executives in Phillips. To keep the program from becoming one designed by administrators, Phillips created a steering committee of four executives, one from each of

FIGURE 1
Summary of In-House Advanced Management Programs

	Emphasis/Purpose	Position of Attendees	Length & Frequency
Oil Companies —Shell Oil U.S. (32,000 employees)	3 purposes Time 1. In-depth look at Shell Oil Co. (50%) 2. How to be an effective manager (behavioral subjects) (30%) 3. Greater awareness of external forces (20%)	Upper middle managers • Those having capability of advancing to general management or higher • Also junior/senior staff personnel who need corporate overview	1 Wk. (One/Yr at 24)
—Marathon (12,000 employees)	To develop business and managerial skills similar to an MBA degree with 1/3 of the time devoted to behavioral subjects	Upper middle managers and high potential employees	2 Wks.
Other Companies —General Electric Management Development Institute (350,000+ employees)	1. Management Development Course Provide department managers with business and managerial skills	High potential department managers	4 Wks. (5/Yr.)
	2. Business Management Course Business skills for a general manager position	Top functional managers; high potential section level managers whose next step is general manager	4 Wks (4/Yr.)
—IBM (280,000 employees)	1. Advanced Management School 5 areas of concentration: • Process of decision making • Personnel management • Internal IBM environment • External social, political, legal environment • Personal development/career planning (45% external, 55% internal IBM issues)	High potential management personnel identified as executive replacements (typically out of district manager position)	3 Wks.
	2. Executive Seminar — intensive overview of current issues facing IBM executives (80% subjects external to IBM)	High potential executives	1 Wk. (2/Yr.)
	3. International Executive Program Greater understanding of internal IBM strategies and external international environment	Vice presidents, regional managers, directors, world trade executives	2 Wks.
—Motorola Executive* Institute (51,000 employees)	Graduate level management education to technically oriented executives — closely related to MBA curriculum	Senior executives	4 Wks.
—St. Regis Paper Co. (30,000 employees)	Overview some concepts and principles of management	Upper middle management	2 Wks.
—Federal Executive Institute (2.8 million Civil Service employees)	1. Heighten responsiveness to national needs and goals. 2. Increase appreciation of the totality of the government system. 3. Improve knowledge of the managerial process.	GS-16 and above for a potential of 12,000 candidates	7 Wks. (5/Yr.)

*Motorola Executive Institute not currently functioning according to latest information.

FIGURE 1
Summary of In-House Advanced Management Programs
(Continued)

Instructional Mix	Replacement For Univ. Ex. Programs	Location/Facility	Unique Characteristics (Comments)
50% provided by outside speakers 50% interaction with Shell top management	Very limited participation	Columbia Lakes Tennaco Facility, Houston, TX	—Effort has a 20-yr. history in Shell. —The effective manager topics do not stress business skill but interpersonal behavior and management style through developing information on subordinate perceptions of working environment and group behavior.
All teaching on Indiana University campus by I.U. faculty — (90%) At end of 2 wks. participants spend 3 days at home office for an overview of company operations	No — 10 people per year still attend university programs	Indiana University and Corporate Headquarters	To maintain the benefits of campus they have contracted with Indiana to develop and administer a program fit to Marathon's needs. Marathon inputs into program design, instructional mix, controls and continually evaluates performance against their needs.
90% university faculty 90% university faculty	Operations can spend budgets where they want to; a very few still attend Harvard AMP and Stanford	GE Management Inst. General Electric Campus Croton-on-Hudson, NY	These 3 programs are complemented by a host of short courses on specific subjects.
50% IBM executives 50% university faculty 50% IBM executives 50% university faculty 1 wk. at Brookings 1 wk. by IBM executives	No — 40-50 high level vice presidents or presidents of divisions per year attend university executive development programs	IBM Country Club and Management Institute Sands Point, Long Island	This effort is preceded by 3 separate one-week "Middle Management Schools" Phase I - Role of the middle manager Phase II - Developing the entrepreneurial manager Phase III - The professional Cannot attend sooner than 4 yrs. after advanced management school. Attendee mix kept at ½ nationals, ½ internationals
90% university faculty		Motorola Executive Inst. Scottsdale, AZ	Assessment by a trained psychologist takes place during the 4-wk. period.
90% university faculty		Harrison House, Glen Cove, NJ	Five months time between week one and week two.
95% FEI residential faculty 5% guest speaker		Own campus, Charlottesville, VA 95 Room Inn, 8 Acre Estate	Great deal of flexibility and option in the curriculum with emphasis on an individual's responsibility for learning and choice of courses. Emphasis on self-assessment and personal goal setting.

the three major operating groups in the company, and one from corporate planning and budgeting. The steering committee was to provide input and serve as a sounding board for ideas at each stage of the research. It was also a first-level review body prior to the presentation of the final proposal. The membership of the committee proved to be critically important in gaining acceptance of the final proposal.

Data Collection

To establish the need for formal business education and to decide on the emphasis of an internal program, interviews were held with 29 company executives. Interviewees ranged from the president and executive vice presidents to corporate department vice presidents and general managers. The executives interviewed had to meet two criteria: 1) they had attended a university-sponsored advanced management program, and 2) they had an understanding of the managerial education and functional skills needed by middle managers. The interviews required two hours or more and involved a specially designed questionnaire to discover attitudes towards management development, as well as opinions on curricula and instructors.

Of the 29 individuals interviewed, only the majority view is presented here:

Need: Eighty percent of the executives felt an internal program was needed. Approximately two-thirds of these executives felt, however, that it should supplement and not replace attendance at university advanced management programs. Even though a strong need was perceived within the company, the complementary advantages of both internal and university programs were recognized.

Mission: Again, just over 80% of the top executives felt the general purpose should be to broaden the participant's view about managerial functions. Some general comments were that the training should be:

• Conceptual, but not so general as to just skim the surface.

• Aimed at developing an understanding or appreciation of the subject matter, and not try to make experts out of the participants.

• Designed to help individuals recognize their own needs for future development.

Subjects To Be Covered: The internal programs studied had a number of different orientations. To help determine how a potential program within Phillips should be oriented, each person interviewed was asked to indicate the percentage of time which should be spent on three areas:

Average % of Time

1) Exposure to new business management ideas,
   current knowledge, concepts and information ... 70

2) Development of managerial attitudes
   and viewpoints ... 20

3) Specific professional and management skills that
   could be mastered during the program ... 10

The relatively small percentage of time placed on developing attitudes and viewpoints was usually prefaced by one of two observations: Our objective should be to broaden participant's views, not to build one viewpoint or attitude; or, The meaningful attitude and viewpoint will emerge as part of the breadth of understanding developed on the business subjects.

Under "exposure to new ideas, current knowledge, concepts and information," a number of business subjects were listed and interviewees were asked to allocate half-day segments of the time in a three-week schedule which should be spent on each. The most important subjects, in order of importance, were:

- Macro, Micro and International Economics
- Financial Management
- Individual Behavior and Human Resource Management
- Managerial Accounting
- Legal, Political and Social Environment
- Management Science Tools for Decision Making

Instructors: The majority felt that the instructional load should be carried almost exclusively by outside experts regardless of their present organizational affiliation. Executive involvement should be minimal, in the form of support, with discussions about organization direction and philosophy.

Program Length: Participants were asked to indicate what they felt an appropriate length would be for a possible internal effort. Frequencies of responses were:

Time	Respondent
2 weeks	2
3-4 weeks	15
6 weeks	2
Dependent upon final program design	6
No need for such a program	4

Location: The interviewees were unanimous that the program should be conducted away from the home office with as much seclusion and privacy as possible. This was the only issue to receive a unanimous response.

From the internal interviews, a consensus emerged as to the need and parameters of an internal program. Commitment among the steering committee and executives was high due to the effort in creating a program designed by and for line managers' needs. Knowledge of the experience of other organizations was very helpful in formulating the final program.

Program Implemented

In 1978, two four-week programs were conducted with 30 high potential middle managers in each session. This section summarizes the key elements of the actual program, the evaluation and cost factors, and the critical issues facing an organization contemplating an internal advanced management program. Significant changes were made after the first program, including certain faculty, curriculum blocks, and the resource organization coordinating the faculty for the week in Washington. There will be changes in future programs to reflect experience and learning. The following information focuses on the second four-week session.

Selection of Participants

Program participants are chosen after an evaluation of performance and future promotability. The intent is to train high potential managers at earlier points in their careers. The program is for practicing managers, with 75% coming from line operation and 25% from staff managerial positions. The internal effort complements university programs, with the possibility that a limited number of individuals will attend the internal programs and attend a top rated university program later in their career.

Program Design

Figure 2 summarizes the four-week program. There will be minor modifications in program content with time, but the following major design factors will be retained:

- Approximately 25% of the time is devoted to the external environment, with an emphasis on the government-business relationships. Both The Brookings Institution and the American Enterprise Institute, as well as the Washington Office staff of Phillips Petroleum, have been used in providing this segment. The remaining 75% of the time is spent on business management subjects, with emphasis on economics, finance, accounting, and strategic planning. Specific objectives from the interviews with executives guide the content development of each subject.

FIGURE 2
Summary of the 4-week Internal Advanced Management Program Implemented

	Sunday	Monday	Tuesday	Wednesday	Thursday	Friday	Saturday
Week 1 Classes 9:00-4:00 (unless noted)		Managerial Economics	Managerial Economics	Change and Individual Stress	Managerial Decision Making	Managerial Accounting	Managerial Accounting
	Human Rights & Corporate Policy			Discussion with Top Management			
Week 2		Financial Management	Financial Management	Future Planning & Issues	Managerial Planning & Strategy	Managerial Planning & Strategy	Marketing
	Ethics & Profits			Discussion with Top Management		Marketing	
Week 3		Implementing Strategy	Individual & Organization Behavior	Individual & Organization Behavior	Macro-economics	International Economics	Personal Estate Planning
	Consumerism & Business			Discussion with Top Management			
Week 4 (In Washington, D.C.)		Public Policy Formulation as it Involves Congress & the Presidency	Public Policy Formulation with Respect to: • Economic Issues • Growth of Regulation • Energy Issues	Public Policy Formulation in International Affairs	Congressional Dynamics	Public Influence Policy & the News Media	
	Public Policy Process			Discussion with Top Management	Executive Department Dynamics	ADJOURN	

- Sunday evening sessions are devoted to exposing participants to different and sometimes controversial subjects to stretch their understanding of individuals and interest groups with a different philosophy from that of the business community. Examples of presenters used in this fashion are Vernon Jordan, President of National Urban League; Kathleen O'Reilly, Executive Director, Consumer Federation of America; and Leonard Silk, Economist, *New York Times*.
- Wednesday events are reserved for open dialogue with two company executives. Involvement to date has included the chairman, president, all executive vice presidents and selected corporate functional department heads, such as the vice presidents of planning

and budgeting, human resources, and the treasurer. Participants formulate the agenda and questions prior to the meeting. As they respond to questions, the executives have an opportunity to express philosophy, policy, and overall direction of the management. This has been a major interest segment of both programs to date.

- Faculty are selected for their knowledge of the specific field and the ability to work with a mature audience. The ability to involve participants and build excitement and understanding about the subject area is critical. Final selection of faculty, as well as a program design, has been the prerogative of the steering committee, program coordinator, and the corporate executive committee. The latter was the initial approval body for the program and has remained very interested and involved in the program's development.
- Cases, illustrations, and class discussions are built around situations relevant to the heavy manufacturing or process industries.

Program Evaluation

Open-ended evaluation of strengths, weaknesses, value of the topic, and time allotment is obtained immediately after each instructor's session. One week after the program ends, participants are asked to evaluate the appropriateness of the time spent on each of the topic areas during the four weeks and for an overall rating of the program. More detailed evaluations are planned. However, results as reflected by present evaluations are very encouraging. The average rating by participants was 4.5 with 5 representing maximum. Future efforts will be spent on improving what is considered by management to be a highly effective program.

Between the first and second sessions, some program content and instructor changes were made to respond to stated needs of participants. An example was the need to move subjects like Managerial Accounting and Finance to time blocks earlier in the program. Participants' abilities to deal with business planning and managerial strategy were enhanced by having their professional skills sharpened in these functional areas.

Although no extensive formal evaluation process has been instituted, Phillips' management continues to review the need for the program during the annual reviews of its corporate development committee. The only change being contemplated is to reduce the number of program offerings from two per year to one, reasoning that a large amount of the organization's need has been satisfied.

Critical Issues Facing Internal Advanced Management Programs

After reviewing the experience of leading organizations in internal advanced management programs, as well as the experience of Phillips with its initial efforts, there are a number of critical issues that merit consideration by any organization contemplating a similar program.

Costs in Perspective

The most significant cost is the investment of time of a significant number of the organization's top managers for extended periods. Faculty costs and logistical and administrative expenses, although not small, should be viewed in this perspective. Realistically, all costs associated with such an effort can be expected to increase. For the program outlined here, the total cost per participant was $3,300. The exceptional faculty members will be harder to obtain because of the increasing number of organizations vying for their time in consideration of their university obligation.

Faculty Selection and Availability

The successful program will require more than just administrative coordination of faculty. As more reputable and experienced faculty become harder to secure for instructional purposes, other faculty will have to be identified and developed to work with a demanding adult audience. Individuals responsible for these programs will not only have to be sensitive to changing curriculum requirements, but also to the identification of teaching talent. Keeping faculty in harmony with participants' "need to know" is crucial.

Matching Curriculum with Specific Company Needs

A blueprint for the correct definition, proportion, and nature of subject matter for an internal advanced management program is nonexistent. Critical to the success of the program is the degree to which specific management education needs have been defined, and the degree of visible commitment to top managers. The Phillips process and experience in designing and implementing an advanced management program provides a base upon which other organizations may build. To be responsive to the changing society and environment, continuing study and attention is essential. The active involvement of management provides that catalyst for Phillips.

Organizations are looking critically at what their specific needs are in the area of management education, and making provisions to satisfy those needs internally. Individual company approaches should differ, since there is no "one best way" to train and develop managers.

Companies will use to a greater degree what has worked for them in the past and what they feel will work for them in the future. The program described here is one that has worked extremely well for Phillips Petroleum. These ideas on the research, development and implementation of the concept may be of value to others considering the expansion of their internal management education efforts.

REFERENCES

Andrews Kenneth R., "The Effectiveness of University Management Development Programs." Division of Research, Harvard Business School, Boston (1966).

Bricker, George, *Bricker's International Directory* (1979).

AFTERWARD COMMENTS

Matt M. Atarcevich, Ph.D., Co-Founder,
Center for Management and Organization Effectiveness
Arnold Sykes, VP, Alex Sheshunoff Management Services Inc.

Twelve additional years of executive development experience convinces us that, in our rapidly changing business environment, there is an even greater need for a relevant, company-specific Internal Advanced Management Program. In retrospect we should suggest program changes in three areas:

1. **A More Precise Definition of Need**

We would retain the basic interview approach but broaden the goal to the actual competencies (knowledge, skills, beliefs) a sample group of successful managers engage in to produce critical results. This model or standards of excellence for managerial performance would provide the additional guidelines for program content.

2. **Re-Orientation of the Curriculum**

The focus should shift and elevate the high potential participants from Management to Leadership Development. The following topics, although not inclusive, would emerge as critical competencies: managing cultural diversity, managing in a global marketplace, managing a highly decentralized organization, computer-based executive support systems for decision making, ethics, building teams, creating an empowered continuous improvement environment, orchestrating both a business and human approach to restructuring, and strategic planning. These would replace Managerial Finance/Accounting and the Management Science tools in the original curriculum. These topics are best covered in shorter, specific skill-related courses.

3. **Utilize Multiple Adult Learning Methodologies**

A greater emphasis would be placed on innovative "action-learning." This would include the use of outdoor experiential-based leadership and team exercises, the utilization of validated leadership feedback assessment information and individual counseling, pre and post program learning contracts between the participant and manager to serve both to focus attention and as a follow-up discussion after the program, off-shore visits to selected countries and industries that represent considerable competitive threat or possible strategic alliances, team consulting projects to be completed during or after the program that address actual business issues facing the organization, and the use of course-break-course design as opposed to a single one-time course.

The art of leadership development will always be in transition. In the past twelve years we have experienced many changes in this area and are excited by what is yet to be discovered in the future.

CRAFTING COMPETITIVENESS: TOWARD A NEW PARADIGM FOR EXECUTIVE DEVELOPMENT

Albert A. Vicere, Pennsylvania State University
Kenneth R. Graham, Allstate Insurance Company

One traditional paradigm has tended to frame executive development efforts in many organizations. This paradigm has as its focus the executive as an individual. Organizations that subscribe to this paradigm tend to give little attention to the role executive development can play in organizational development and in strategy implementation.

A few companies share a different view. For these companies, executive development is more than just a vehicle for individual development—it is a mechanism for cultivating the collective managerial talents, perspectives, and capabilities that can help propel an organization into the future. These companies are helping to create a new, more strategic paradigm for executive development.

In this paper, we discuss the challenge faced by organizations attempting to shift toward this emerging paradigm for cultivating managerial and executive talent. We draw on the experiences of five of these new-paradigm companies to examine the potential benefits that can accrue to an organization when it adopts this strategic approach to developing organizational capability and crafting ccmpetitiveness.

"We've cut to the bone and there's no fat left. We're making money, gaining market share. The problem is that we have no management depth. There are damn few of us around here anymore, and even fewer who are ready to move into our slots."

These comments—made to the authors by a middle manager from a large company that recently orchestrated a stunning turn around—articulate one of the greatest challenges facing organizations today: how to retool and reinvigorate management ranks after sustained periods of retrenchment, reorganization, and turmoil. In response to this challenge, many companies are attempting to revitalize their

Reprinted from *Human Resource Planning*, Vol. 13, No. 4 (1990), 281-295.

internal executive-development processes in an effort to help refocus the organization and enhance competitive effectiveness (Fulmer, 1988; Bolt, 1989; Ulrich, 1989; Vicere and Freeman, 1990).

For a number of those companies, breathing new life into executive-development efforts has proven a slow, difficult process. This paper discusses why this process is difficult and presents a framework to help organizations realize the full potential of executive development as a tool to facilitate organizational transformation and competitiveness.

THE CONTEXT OF THE PROBLEM

Over the years, we have conducted extensive research and worked with dozens of companies to assess executive-development needs and determine the most effective ways to address them (Graham and Vicere, 1984; Vicere, 1989; Vicere and Freeman, 1990). During that time, we began to notice a remarkable consistency across the majority of the organizations we dealt with in terms of their perceptions of how the executive-development process should operate. This pattern of perceptions was so widely used that it will be referred to in this paper as the "traditional" paradigm for executive development.

This traditional paradigm had as its focal point the executive as individual. Organizations that subscribed to this traditional paradigm tended to support a somewhat regimented executive-development process in which high-potential managers were identified at an early age and moved through a relatively standard progression of executive-development experiences that included job rotation, training, and further education. This cultivation of talent, skills, and experience was expected to lead to the achievement of senior management status by a select group of carefully nurtured individuals.

Although this traditional paradigm seemed to frame the executive-development practices of many organizations, a few companies shared a very different view. For those companies, executive development had become more than just a vehicle for individual development. Rather, it had become a mechanism for cultivating the collective managerial talents, perspectives, and capabilities that would help propel the organization into the future. The exceptional companies that shared this strategic, organization-oriented approach to executive development also were remarkably consistent with regard to their perspectives on how the process should work. So much so that in this paper their views will be referred to as the "new" paradigm for executive development.

This new paradigm has as its fundamental purpose the utilization of executive development as a force for overall organizational development—a tool to develop organizational culture, create commitment to strategic directions, promote managerial teamwork, facilitate a broader understanding of the organization, and cultivate an environment for continuous improvement and innovation.

We believe this new paradigm holds the key to using executive development as a force for organizational revitalization, transformation, and competitiveness. In this paper, we discuss why we believe this is so. We outline the challenge faced by organizations attempting to shift toward this new approach to cultivating managerial and executive talent. We draw on our own experiences—as well as the experiences of five new-paradigm companies—to examine the potential benefits that can accrue to an organization that adopts this strategic approach to developing organizational capability and crafting competitiveness.

EXAMINING THE TRADITIONAL PARADIGM FOR EXECUTIVE DEVELOPMENT

We have suggested that a traditional paradigm or mind-set has framed the executive development efforts of many organizations. As with all paradigms, this framework is rooted in a number of basic assumptions that can substantially limit thinking, particularly in an environment of change (Barker, 1985). We discuss below the traditional paradigm for executive development and its incompatibility with the demands of today's dynamic business environment.

Traditional Assumptions

In working with corporate directors of executive development, we often encounter a tendency to discuss the executive-development process in terms of candidates' ages and/or years of business experience. This has led us to conclude that, for most companies, the executive-development process can be broken down into four distinct phases as shown in Exhibit 1. Each of these phases accounts for approximately one-quarter, or ten years, of an individual's typical 40-year career span. We also have found that a consistent array of executive-development techniques seem to be associated with each of the four phases of executive development. For the most part, those techniques are employed to help confirm an individual's executive potential and to refine individual capabilities during a career phase. The executive-development process itself frequently is described as a pyramid with decreasing numbers of managers participating in the process at each phase. Movement from one phase to the next is based on the premise that an individual already has been identified and selected as a person with high potential for increased managerial responsibilities.

This somewhat Darwinian approach substantially limits the number of individuals engaged in the process of executive development at any given time. It also has an inherently *individualized* focus with little attention given to the cultivation of organizational culture and teamwork. Further discussion will help bring the problems and pitfalls of this approach to light.

EXHIBIT 1

Executive Development: "Traditional" Process

Developmental Phase	Age	Characterization	Traditional Development Activities
First—learning the ropes"	Mid 20's– early 30's	Individual contributor	• selection • initiation • further technical education • evaluation • coaching • project management • rotation—functions/divisions • supervisory experience • identitication of potential

Second— "rotational assignments"	Early 30's– early 40's	Promotable mid-career	• budget responsibility
			• manage others in larger units
			• rotational assignments across:
			  • business environments (growth, mature, etc.)
			  • line/staff units
			  • divisions
			  • functions
			  • countries/cultures
			• coaching
			• evaluation
			• limited external developmental experiences

Third— "becoming a general manager"	Early 40's– early 50's	Experienced mid-career	• move to senior functional positions • external executive education experiences • leap to general management positions • some rotation still appropriate • manager of managers—developing a CEO perspective • executive education in-depth if senior leadership potential
Fourth— "foundation for the future"	Early 50's– and beyond	Senior leader statesman	• occasional briefing sessions • external representative to society and other businesses (directorships. etc.)

The Traditional Process

Phase One of the traditional executive-development process begins when individuals are selected carefully from "good" colleges and hired into positions generally recognized as "breeding grounds" for future mangers. Most often in their twenties, these individuals are exposed to executive-development activities that included initiation into or orientation to the company, technical or specialized training, evaluation/identification of their future potential, and some exposure to top management through focused project assignments and related developmental opportunities.

Those individuals identified as "high-potential" during this first stage are then advanced to Phase Two of the process. Now in their early thirties or forties, these managers traditionally are exposed to rotational assignments, increased levels of management responsibility, and further attempts to confirm their potential. Those who emerge successfully from this stage move on the Phase Three. Now in their early forties or fifties, these managers typically are viewed as prime prospects for general management positions. Because of this, they are likely to be given increased levels of management responsibility and very likely to be involved in both internal and external executive education programs. They are groomed continually for general management responsibilities.

Those who eventually become general managers are observed for their effectiveness and perhaps exposed to additional executive education programs. If successful, they advance to Phase Four of the process and move into senior leadership positions sometime in their early fifties. At that stage of an executive's career, he or she traditionally is viewed as having "arrived" at full executive potential with little need for further executive development attention other than occasional briefings on topical issues or perhaps participation as a director of an external organization.

In a very generalized sense, this model portrays what until recently was the standard pattern of executive development across most large U.S. firms. When we analyzed this model, we concluded that many organizations had within their grasp the elements for a successful, forward-looking executive-development effort. With few notable exceptions, however, most companies made little effort to focus these elements to build overall organizational competitiveness.

This exclusive, individualistic focus was acceptable in a stable business environment. Today, due to profound environmental changes, many of the assumptions underlying this traditional viewpoint are obsolete (Walker, 1988; Kanter, 1989). The most critical of those assumptions involve anachronistic perspectives concerning the role of age in executive development, as well as similar perspectives regarding career longevity, "plateauing," and corporate "statesmanship." Let us discuss each of these notions below.

Age

In an era of decreasing numbers and layers of managers, age no longer can be considered a valid indicator of an individual's stage of executive development. Today the determining factors must be an individual's experience base and job responsibilities.

This is partially the result of downsizing and reorganization efforts that push significant amounts of management responsibility downward in organizations (Walker, 1988; Kanter, 1989). Because of this, managerial authory and autonomy are delegated to individuals at earlier career stages. These individuals are generally bright, well educated, ambitious specialists who bring high levels of technical, financial, marketing, or other types of functional expertise to their organizations. To fulfill their expanded managerial responsibilities, they must receive earlier and broader orientation to general management principles and roles than would have been necessary under the traditional approach to executive development (Modic, 1989).

For example, in 1984 a reorganization at Allstate Insurance Company eliminated the zone offices that separated each region from corporate headquarters. As a result, regional vice presidents suddenly found themselves with multifunctional responsibilities—and a direct, reporting relationship to the home office—far earlier in their careers than traditional Allstate executives. Many had been prepared for careers as functional specialists and had had little exposure to the generalist perspective required in their new roles.

This situation caused Allstate to rethink its corporate approach to executive development. The firm decided to give greater attention to promoting a general-management orientation among managers at all levels of the company. To date, these efforts have focused on building depth across the entire management team—not the kind of technical depth for which a specialist is originally hired, but *business depth*: a working knowledge of the insurance business and a vision of the entire organization as an operating entity comprised of interconnected, often interdependent, parts. Allstate's objective is not simply to use executive development to facilitate business depth within individual managers. Rather, it is to evolve a distinct form of competitive advantage in their industry by creating a well-prepared, well-informed team of managers at all levels who are committed to growing and developing an aggressive, strategically focused company.

In contrast to Allstate's situation, in organizations with fewer management levels and greater demands for specialized knowledge, some now achieve management status much later in their careers if at all. This especially is true in mature businesses or in industries that rely heavily on research, scientific, or technical expertise. After long periods spent as individual contributors, professionals with a high level of technical or functional specialization may lack the organizational and/or business exposure necessary for management (Guttridge, 1988; Kanter, 1989; Miles, 1989).

In this era of specialization, multifunctional project teams, rotational assignments, and coaching are crucial to help potential managers develop an early appreciation of the business as a whole and a network of contacts throughout the firm. Without this exposure, the broad-based, team-oriented perspective required in today's network- and project-oriented organizations is difficult, if not impossible, to cultivate (Walker, 1988; Miles, 1989; Kanter, 1989).

For example, General Electric (GE) encourages their research and technical experts to develop ideas and then market them throughout the company. As a result, the *Wall Street Journal* reported, "GE is turning around the equation of U.S. business. Instead of pushing marketers to come up with ideas and then asking scientists to make them work, the company gives researchers wide berth to imagine and invent—and then shop the invention around GE's divisions" (Naj, 1990). This form of cross-pollination helps GE blend the expertise of its managers and technologists to more effectively manage the transfer of technology from laboratory to market—a critical success factor for competitiveness in the 90s (Prahalad and Hamel, 1990).

Longevity

Traditional approaches to executive development were based on the notion that an individual's formal education prior to employment would provide him or her with an adequate base for a 40-year career within an organization. Today, however, restructuring efforts, coupled with continuous environmental and technological change, contribute to rapid and job obsolescence among managers at all levels. Kenneth Labich (1989) in a recent *Fortune* article stated, "It is the worst of times for middle managers . . . either jobs are vanishing in mergers, takeovers, and restructuring, or management vogues are radically altering their traditional roles."

These profound changes require that executive-development efforts begin to focus as much on renewal and recommitment across the entire management hierarchy as they do on the identification and development of high-potential management talent (Moskal and Rohan, 1988). For example, executive development efforts at Xerox have been cited as a core element of that organization's revitalization process. Because CEO David Kearns and executive resource planners at the company realized that career obsolescence or "plateauing" among executives could quickly lead to an inability to survive in a highly competitive, technologically sophisticated marketplace, Xerox mounted a major executive development effort that included strong emphasis on executive updating and revitalization. That effort is credited with being a key catalyst for the culture change that has taken place within the company and helped to reposition Xerox as a world-class competitor (Bolt, 1985; 1989).

Similarly, IBM and GE long have understood the role of executive development in organizational development and culture building. Their expansive commitment to executive development is testimony to the strategic importance each organization attaches to the process (Braham, 1987; Tichy, 1989; Ulrich, 1989; Noel and Charan, 1988). The *mission statement* for GE's Crotonville (executive-development) operation underscores the critical role executive development plays in the company:

"[Crotonville's mission is t]o leverage GE's global competitiveness as an instrument of cultural change, by improving business acumen, leadership abilities and organizational effectiveness of General Electric professionals."

Noel Tichy, a former director at Crotonville, refers to the operation as "a staging ground for corporate revolution" (Tichy, 1989). He credits GE's executive-development efforts with being a major force for positive evolution and change throughout the company. He also emphasizes the critical importance of GE Chairman Jack Welch's commitment to making the process a force for competitiveness. Ulrich (1989) noted that to fully utilize executive development as a tool to facilitate competitiveness, "top managers, particularly the CEO, are involved.... [It requires] top management ownership, visibility and commitment." As demonstrated by Xerox and GE, when top management assumes this form of ownership for building the executive talent base, executive development often becomes a major catalyst for ongoing organizational revitalization and development.

"Plateaued" Managers

The quotation that opened this article reflects a major problem in today's competitive business environment: many organizations facing a lack of "bench strength." Due to reorganization and rightsizing efforts, they simply don't have ready replacements available to fill vacated management positions. That fact has challenged the notion that executive-development efforts should focus primarily on candidates for senior management. Finding and developing tomorrow's CEO clearly is important, but that person will need a team of competent, dedicated managers in middle- and upper-middle-level positions to bring strategic visions to reality (Kelley, 1988).

Today, managers that fall out of the running for senior management slots (this includes most members of the management team) must remain part of the executive-development process. Without the luxury of excess layers of management and the resulting stockpiles of management talent, today's organizations must work to keep all their managers—"high potential" or otherwise—committed and involved. They also must learn to cultivate the abilities of these managers to serve as coaches, conveying the lessons learned from their experience to newly developing managers within the company (McCall, 1988). As GE Chairman Jack Welch says, "As for middle managers, they can be the stronghold of the organization. But their jobs have to be redefined. They have to see their roles as a combination of teacher, cheerleader, and liberator, not controller" (Tichy and Charan, 1989).

Coaching as part of the executive-development process traditionally has received lip service but little else in most organizations (Evered and Selman, 1989). This is unfortunate because many plateaued middle managers have a wealth of experience and the interpersonal skills that would enable them to be outstanding coaches and mentors. William Tack (1986), a Massachusetts-based management counselor, noted, "Older and wiser cultures, less caught up in technology and a fast pace, foster, venerate, and utilize the wisdom born of experience, and while they flourish we flounder."

Executive-development planners today must acknowledge that plateaued managers have options (Kaye, 1989). They can play a key role in the organization's future development. They can improve and enhance the job they currently hold. They can act as intellectual resources for those senior managers who develop and implement policies and strategies. They can serve as instructors, coaches, mentors, and role models for technical specialists and newer managers. They also can function as external scanners for environmental trends, opportunities, and challenges that are identified more easily by seasoned managers than by novice managers. These benefits can occur only if these individuals are encouraged to maintain their vigor and intensity. Horizontal moves, rotational assignments, and other developmental experiences must continue for these managers. The value and importance of their efforts must become an acknowledged part of the corporate culture. Without renewed experiences, the potential for boredom, withdrawal, and disaffection is great (Evered and Selman, 1989; Labich, 1989).

This focus on the continuous, ongoing development of managers at all levels in a core element of what is being termed a "learning organization" (de Geus, 1988; Stata, 1989). Kiechel (1990) described the learning organization as a company that has fostered an ingrained capacity to change—an ability to anticipate, embrace, and capitalize on events and opportunities in the business environment.

Nonaka (1988) has called this built-in capacity: "middle-up-down management." He holds that middle managers working in multifunctional teams are best positioned to integrate information from top managers and line workers in the development of new products, processes, and perspectives. As such, he notes, it is "middle management's role to create and realize verifiable business concepts for the creative solution of contradictions and gaps between the ideal and the actual." As an example, in a case discussion of the highly successful Honda Motor Company (a company with a distinct middle-up-down culture) Nonaka showed the kind of competitive leverage that can be gained when executive-development efforts adopt this middle-focused perspectives toward developing strategic and competitive effectiveness.

The "Statesman" Role

One of the most dramatic shifts taking place in executive development is based on the need for today's organizations to change their view of the corporate "statesman" role. Traditionally, that role was the provce of senior officers. For the most part, in management only the top ɔmen and men in the organization were expected to deal with the public, interface with the political environment, facilitate joint-venture relationships, plan on a global basis, or explain corporate policies and directions to subordinates. No longer. In leaner, flatter, more flexible, globally competitive organizations, the role of statesperson begins as soon as the management stripes are correct (Kanter, 1989). Failure to cultivate an understanding of that role early in an individual's managerial career can leave a company dangerously vulnerable to external influences. As Raymond Miles (1989), Dean of the Business School at the University of California at Berkeley, noted: "In the newer, flatter, and leaner firms, management jobs are fewer, more demanding and, for the most part, more satisfying.... [I]nstead of being in charge of a division or department, the top executive of production, design or supply components is a general manager running a complete business itself. His or her staff must also share a broader vision."

Traditional approaches to executive development leave the tasks of developing and communicating corporate missions, goals, and visions to senior officers. In a highly competitive environment characterized by growing reliance on the network or project organizational form, these skills must be developed throughout the organization. Driving this strategic focus down to lower levels of the organization requires greater emphasis on communication and team-building efforts during executive development (MacQueen and Vicere, 1987; Ulrich, 1989).

As a result, the skills-oriented training programs that were the backbone of internal management-education and development efforts at Phases 1 and 2 of the traditional model now must be supplemented by policy-focused executive-development efforts geared to facilitating strategic and cultural changes within the organization that formerly were reserved for managers at Phases 3 and 4 in the traditional model. Company-specific executive-education programs fast are becoming a core element of organizational efforts to facilitate this change (Braham, 1987; Ulrich, 1989; Tichy, 1989, Vicere and Freeman, 1990).

For example, Allstate determined that in order to quickly and effectively implement their reorganization and facilitate competitiveness, managers at all levels must be actively involved in policy-level discussions of corporate objectives and directions. Through an ongoing series of internal executive-education programs, Allstate managers, directors, and officers discuss not only the firm's current policies, but also the strategic "why"s behind the policies. These programs help open channels of communication within Allstate, thereby facilitating management's understanding and commitment to key policy decisions and organizational changes.

Similarly, in 1976 the U.S. Congress enacted legislation to form the Consolidated Rail Corporation (Conrail), a company comprised of a number of bankrupt railroads serving in the Northeast and Midwest sections of the country. Early on, Conrail senior management realized that the key to the company's viability was to move away from a traditional railroad culture toward a new, strategic vision of a market-driven transportation company.

One effort to enact this vision involved establishing a middle-management development program (MacQueen and Vicere, 1987). The purpose of this two-week general management program, developed in conjunction with the College of Business Administration at Pennsylvania State University, was to enhance the management capabilities of participants by strengthening their abilities to work as a team to understand, communicate, and implement this new, marketing-oriented strategy. The positive contribution of this effort to Conrail's impressive record of performance improvement is reflected in the following comment from a past program participant: "Now I can more knowledgeably talk about why our corporate structure has changed with time.... I can build into my conversations an 'advertisement' for the importance of a market orientation for Conrail."

THE CHALLENGE OF THE FUTURE

As executive-development practitioners attempt to deal with the challenge of building competitiveness, many find that no matter how hard they work to "fix" their old system, it never seems to be in synch with environmental demands. Effective executive development in today's business environment requires a major shift in thinking—a movement away from mid-career development for a few high-potential people toward ongoing talent planning for a vital team of managers at all levels of the organization. As more and more organizations come to this realization, a new paradigm for executive development begins to emerge.

In this new paradigm, executive development is recognized as a *process of organizational development,* not just a prescribed series of activities and programs targeted to specific individuals. Practitioners of this new paradigm seek to blend coordinated work experiences and various forms of education and training in an effort to build management depth and competitiveness across an entire organization. Executive-development efforts become more than just techniques to prepare individual managers for increased responsibilities. Rather, they are used to cultivate the managerial capabilities and teamwork that will drive an organization's *overall* performance and competitiveness (Bolt, 1989; Tichy, 1989).

Adapting to the New Paradigm

To move toward this new paradigm, a company's executive-development process must flow logically from the strategic intent of the firm and its business units (Hamel and Prahalad, 1989; Prahalad and Hamel, 1990). The focus of the process should be identifying and developing those managerial talents the company needs to achieve its long-term strategic objectives.

This process should help ensure that managers at all levels have an understanding of the strategic directions of the company and an in-depth understanding of current and future market demands. Specific executive-development efforts should be built around this market-oriented focus, coupling it with a strong element of competitive analysis, to help managers at *all* levels understand the respective strengths and weaknesses of the firm and what it will take to build competitive advantage in the marketplace (Bolt, 1985; 1989). This notion of competitiveness then must be translated into a focus on the organization itself—the systems, relationships, structures, goals, and processes that will facilitate and maintain a competitive advantage (Tichy, 1989; Ulrich, 1989).

As the examples discussed in this paper show, an executive-development process built around such a strategic focus can help create and refine the values of an organization in support of its strategic directions (Ulrich, 1989). Through its access to managers at all levels, the executive-development system can be a key communications vehicle used to inform managers about strategic directions, explain to them why these directions are being pursued, and update them on organizational and business-unit progress. Through these efforts, executive development can build commitment to strategic directions and generate support for necessary changes or adjustments in business practice (MacQueen and Vicere, 1987; Tichy, 1989). Finally, a strategic executive-development process also can act as a "conscience" for the organization, encouraging managers to continually evaluate programs, policies, and directions to ensure their consistency and focus (Tichy and Charan, 1989). Equipped with this strategy/culture/consistency focus, an organization engaged in strategic executive development is positioned to build both competitive advantage and management depth in pursuit of organizational excellence.

The Emerging Process

The basic operational requirements of this new approach to executive education are listed in Exhibit 2. Individually, each element is far from a new idea. Together, however, they form the core elements of an executive-development process that can help foster overall organizational development and a renewed sense of competitiveness. These elements are grounded in the experiences of organizations like GE, IBM, Xerox, Conrail, and Allstate—organizations that have learned how to harness the potential of executive development to build a competitive advantage.

EXHIBIT 2
Executive Development: Today's Requirements

Executive-Development Activities

For all managers, throughout their careers	• Early and ongoing cross-functional and project assignments • Early and ongoing executive education in interpersonal skills and strategic management • Early and ongoing coaching and mentoring • Early and ongoing opportunities for external executive education • Early, ongoing, and regular performance appraisals and feedback • Early, ongoing, and frequent briefings on the organization and its levels of performance • Opportunities to serve as coaches/mentors
For advancing managers	• Bottom-line responsibility • Guided experiences in global and statesman roles • Opportunities for positions of increased scope and responsibility

For all managers, throughout their careers, the requirements for a strategically focused executive-development process include:

- early and ongoing cross-functional and project assignments designed to build business depth

- early and ongoing executive education and training in interpersonal skills and strategic management, coupled with opportunities to coach and mentor that are designed to cultivate and hone management capabilities

- early and ongoing opportunities for external executive education designed to refresh perspectives and challenge basic operating assumptions (Drucker, 1989)

- early, ongoing, and regular performance appraisals and feedback, coupled with regular briefings on the organization and its culture and strategy designed to facilitate communications, commitment, and organizational development

- opportunities as coach/mentor to teach others about the organization and its business

All of these activities help maintain the open, broad-based management perspective necessary for competitiveness in today's business environment (Kanter, 1989; Ulrich, 1989).

Executive development must compare to include techniques for identifying high-potential managers (Kotter, 1988) and for providing them with bottom-line responsibilities, guided experiences in global and statesperson roles, and opportunities for assignments of increasing scope and responsibility that lead to multi-functional, general management positions. However, an organization that continues to focus only on this traditional segment of the executive-development population is likely to find it increasingly difficult to facilitate the organizational flexibility and teamwork required in today's competitive environment (Walker, 1988; Kanter, 1989; Modic, 1989).

EXECUTIVE DEVELOPMENT AS A COMPETITIVE FORCE

The traditional paradigm for executive development helped organizations produce a small, elite group of individuals who could be slotted into senior executive positions. Unfortunately, in today's world such a process produces a flat, fluid organization vulnerable to environmental pressures. An organization today must work to build a team of committed, competent managers working together to meet the challenges of an intensely competitive environment. Hambrick (1987) noted that strategy researchers and consultants have searched for years to discover tools and techniques to improve corporate performance. However: "[management] team qualities are the essential foundation for a strategic process within the firm. The amounts of open-mindedness, perseverance, communication skills, and other key characteristics that exist within the team clearly set the limits for how well the team—and, in turn, the firm—can operate" (p. 89).

The emerging perspectives on executive development described in this paper can help create within organizations a foundation for teamwork and competitiveness. By developing a broader and deeper understanding of the organization through coordinated work experiences; by cultivating critical talents and skills through education and training efforts; by building commitment to corporate directions and values through company-specific educational programs and related assignments; by promoting organization-wide interaction and communication through managed developmental activities like project teams, taskforces, and internal seminars; and by challenging and reinvigorating managers through external executive education and development experiences that provide exposure to different cultures, companies, and environments, executive development can help to create a force for corporate transformation, growth, and competitiveness (Vicere, 1989).

This type of executive-development effort requires a clear investment of time, energy, and involvement on the part of senior managers and executive-development professionals (Bolt, 1989; Ulrich, 1989), but the benefits far outweigh the costs. Schein (1961) some time ago noted that management development was a process of influence for growth, change, and development. At a time when adaptability, flexibility, and speed are vital to an organization's competitiveness, a strategically managed executive-development process offers organizations a powerful mechanism for influencing and enhancing organizational effectiveness. The examples cited in this paper from companies like IBM, GE, Xerox, Conrail, and Allstate testify to the efficacy of this notion.

CONCLUSION

A new, emerging paradigm for executive development is on the horizon. In this new paradigm, executive development is moving far beyond its traditional role as an appendage of succession-planning efforts. Rather, executive development is becoming a tool to build the experience base of all managers across the many functions and business units of the organization. It adds perspective to these experiences through carefully targeted education, training, and performance feedback efforts. It provides opportunities for managers to apply this refined perspective to their jobs through coordinated career opportunities of expanded scope and responsibility. And it helps cultivate the organizational vision and values that focus the energy, and build the commitment, of the management team. As these objectives are met, the executive-development process becomes not only a vehicle for individual growth, but a facilitator of talent, commitment, teamwork, and competitive advantage (Bolt 1989; Tichy, 1989; Ulrich, 1989).

As executive-development practitioners step back from the traditional process and analyze their function, many may conclude that there must be a better way to cultivate executive talent. We hope the ideas in this paper will help focus efforts toward further defining and operationalizing this new paradigm. By overcoming preoccupations with individual development, age, and tenure as driving forces in executive development; by redefining notions of career longevity, plateauing, and statesmanship; by refining views on how to cultivate executive talent and teamwork; and by viewing executive development as a key tool for implementing strategy, executive development can move beyond a process that benefits only a few individual managers toward a process that helps drive the flexibility, commitment, and competitiveness of the entire organization.

REFERENCES

Barker, J.A., *Discovering the Future: The Business of Paradigms* (St. Paul, MN: ILI Press, 1985).

Bolt, J.F., *Executive Development: A Strategy for Corporate Competitiveness* (New York: Harper and Row, 1989).

Bolt, J.F., "Tailer Executive Development to Strategy," *Harvard Business Review*, November/December 1987, pp. 168-176.

Braham, J., "Cultivating Tomorrow's Execs: How Do GE and IBM Grow All That Talent?," *Industry Week*, July 27, 1987, pp. 34-38.

de Gues, A.P., "Planning As Learning," *Harvard Business Review*, March/April 1988, pp. 70-74.

Drucker, P., "Managing the Post Business Society," *Fortune*, July 3, 1989, pp. 70-71.

Evered, R. and Selman, J.C., "Coaching and the Art of Management," *Organizational Dynamics*, Autumn 1989, pp. 16-32.

Fulmer, R.M.. "Corporate Management Development and Education: The State of the Art," *Journal of Management Development*, 7(2), 1988, pp. 57-68.

Graham, K.R. and Vicere, A.A., "BEOC (Big Executives on Campus)," *Training and Development Journal*, June 1984, pp. 28-30.

Guttridge, T.G. (1988), "The HRPD Profession: A Vision of Tomorrow," *Human Resource Planning*, 11(2), 1988, pp. 109-124.

Hambrick, D.C., "The Top Management Team: Key to Strategic Success," *California Management Review*, Fall 1987, pp. 88-108.

Hamel, G. and Prahalad, C.K., "Strategic Intent," *Harvard business Review*, May/June, pp. 63-76.

Kanter, R., *When Giants Learn to Dance* (New York: Simon & Schuster, 1989).

Kaye, B., "Are Plateaued Performers Productive?" *Personnel Journal*, August 1989, pp. 57-65.

Keichel III, W., "The Organization That Learns," *Fortune*, March 12, 1990, pp. 133-136.

Kelley, R.E., "In Praise of Followers," *Harvard Business Review*, November/December 1988, pp. 142-148.

Kotter, J.P., *The Leadership Factor.* (New York: Free Press, 1988).

Labich, K. (1989), "Making Over Middle Managers," *Fortune*, May 8, 1989, pp. 58-64.

MacQueen, C. and Vicere, A.A., "Conrail's Management Program: On Track toward the Company Vision," *Personnel*, December 1987, pp. 10-14.

McCall, M., "Developing Executives through Work Experiences," *Human Resource Planning*, 11(1), 1988, pp. 1-11.

Miles, R., "Adapting to Technology and Competition: A New Industrial Relations System for the 21st Century," *California Management Review*, Winter 1989, pp. 9-28.

Modic, S.J., "Redefining a Successful Career," *Industry Week*, April 18 1989, pp. 28-29.

Moskal, B.S. and Rohan, T.M., "A Much Tougher Line Faces Line Managers," *Industry Week*, November 18, 1988, pp. 14-15.

Naj, A.K., "GE's Latest Invention: A Way to Move Ideas from Lab to Market," *Wall Street Journal*, June 14, 1990, p. 1.

Noel, J.L. and Charan, R., "Leadership Development at GE's Crotonville," *Human Resource Mangement.* 27(4), 1988. pp. 433-447.

Nonaka, I., "Toward Middle-Up-Down Management: Accelerating Information Creation," *Sloan Management Review*, Spring 1988, pp. 9-18.

Prahalad, C.K. and Hamel, G., "The Core Competence of the Corporation," *Harvard Business Review*, May/June 1990, pp. 79-91.

Schein, E.H., "Management Development As a Process of Influence,"

Industrial Management Review, May 1961, pp. 59-77.

State, R., "Organizational Learning-The Key to Management Innovation," *Sloan Management Review,* Spring 1989, pp. 63-74.

Tack, W., "Don't Ignore Seasoned Managers—The Case for Management Cycling," *Sloan Management Review,* Summer 1986, pp. 63-70.

Tichy, N.M., "GE's Crotonville: A Staging Ground for Corporate Revolution," *Academy of Mangement Executive*, 3(2), 1989, pp. 99-106.

Tichy, N.M. and Charan, R., "Speed, Simplicity and Self Confidence: An Interview with Jack Welch," *Harvard Business Review*, September/October 1989, pp. 112-120.

Ulrich, D., "Executive Development for Competitiveness." In A.A. Vicere (ed.), *Executive Education: Process, Practice and Evaluation.* (Princeton: Peterson's, 1989).

Vicere, A.A., *Executive Education: Process, Practice, and Evaluation.* (Princeton: Peterson's, 1989).

Vicere, A.A. and Freeman, V. T., "Executive Education in Major Corporations: An International Study," *Journal of Management Development*, 9(1) 1990, pp. 5-16.

Walker, J.W., "Managing Human Resources in Flat, Lean and Flexible Organizations," *Human Resource Planning*, 11(2), 1988, pp. 125-132.

AFTERWARD COMMENTS

Albert A. Vicere
Associate Dean for Executive Education
The Smeal College of Business Administration
The Pennsylvania State University

When Ken Graham and I wrote, "Crafting Competitiveness: Toward a New Paradigm for Executive Development," we envisioned a sea change with regard to practices and strategies for executive development. What we may have underestimated was the speed with which this sea change would occur. The framework of the new paradigm has become much clearer in the period since the original article was written. I have tried to capture more of the essence of the new paradigm in Table 1 (Vicere, 1991), the core elements of which are discussed below.

TABLE 1
New Paradigm For Executive Development

	OLD	NEW
WHO	FEW	MANY - ALL
WHAT	"CHECK MARKS"	LIFELONG DEVELOPMENT
WHERE	CLASSROOM	• WORKPLACE • CLASSROOM • THE WORLD
WHEN	INFREQUENT	ONGOING
HOW	PROGRAMS	PROCESS
WHY	"RITES OF PASSAGE	COMPETITIVENESS

ELEMENTS OF CHANGE

Who?

In the traditional paradigm, executive development efforts were reserved for an elite few who had been identified as having high potential for executive positions. This process helped the organization create a small pool of executives form which future leaders could be drawn. In the new paradigm, executive development is a more all-inclusive process, involving managers at all levels of the organization in the process of continuous learning and culture development.

What?

Traditionally, the executive development process often was viewed as a series of "checkmarks" on a manager's record indicating that he or she had completed a predetermined rite of passage into the next level of management. The new paradigm views executive development as a lifelong process through which managers at all levels of the organization are continuously involved in an ongoing process of training, education, experiential assignments, team building, and enculturation. This process is used to help facilitate strategy implementation and the development of organizational values and capabilities.

Where?

The new paradigm has moved away from the classroom as the main venue for executive development, and instead focuses on experiences and action learning approaches. Action learning goes beyond the case study approach to involve mangers in the facilitated solution of real-life organizational problems on a real-time basis. This form of development combines the power of learning from experience with the lessons of the classroom.

When?

In the traditional paradigm, executive development experiences were few and far between. In the new paradigm, executive development is used as a competitive weapon to build teams, develop networks, and implement strategies. For this reason, executive development is managed as an ongoing part of the strategy implementation process.

How?

Traditional executive development efforts tended to be discrete, uncoordinated efforts that included classroom experiences, rotational assignments, and, if the manager was lucky, some formal performance feedback. The new paradigm seeks to formalize these efforts into an ongoing process of individual and organizational development, a process driven by a supportive infrastructure of human resource management practices in selection, development, reward, and appraisal systems.

Why?

The old paradigm viewed executive development more as a rite of passage—stripes earned for achievement and service. The new paradigm views executive development as a competitive force, a force for defining, building, and maintaining competitive capabilities in a complex, global environment.

THE NEXT WAVE

Continued analysis of new paradigm practices suggests a growing focus on the establishment of what might be called "flexible educational systems" for executive development in a highly dynamic environment (Vicere, 1992). What are flexible educational systems? The are new paradigm systems that seek to blend work experiences, classroom activities, and action learning opportunities into an ongoing, real-time system for sustaining organizational vitality. Furthermore, they are development systems that seem to be tightly woven into the fabric of the HR management system of the company—the selection, development, reward, and appraisal processes that shape the organization's culture and influence its competitiveness.

The further definition and development of flexible educational systems could well be the next wave in the evolution of the new paradigm for executive development. It is a challenge that requires us to rethink the meaning of executive development in a changing world.

In order to begin the rethinking process in your organization, you might wish to ask yourself the following questions:

- Does your company recognize executive development as a competitive capability that assists in the development, implementation, and revitalization of the organizational strategy?
- Does your company view executive developments as a tool for creating a talent pool of leaders at all levels of the organization?
- Does your company make executive development part of a consistent HR strategy that blends the processes of recruitment, selection, development, reward, and appraisal into an integrated system for talent pool management?
- Does your company utilize the real-time solving of real-life business problems as part of your executive development process?
- Does your company view executive development as a tool for both individual and organizational development?

When you can answer "yes" to all of the above questions you're on your way to building a flexible educational system for executive development, a system firmly rooted in the new paradigm for crafting competitiveness in a changing world.

REFERENCES

Vicere, A. A., (1991). The changing paradigm for executive development. *The Journal of Management Development.* 10 (3), pp. 44-47.

Vicere, A. A., (1992). The challenge of flexible educational systems. *The Bricker Bulletin on Executive Education.* XI (3), p. 17.

SUCCESSION PLANNING

Almost forty years ago, succession planning was described as a means to assure a supply of qualified managers for the future. Mahler observed in 1981 that the methodology of management succession planning had become static—there was not one significant breakthrough in the preceding decade. Today, over 13 years after Mahler's statement, there may be new insights into the theories underlying succession planning, but here are few innovations in actual company practice. Given today's highly competitive and volatile business climate and the increasing complexity and scope of management positions, successful succession planning has become a strategic imperative to the long-term survival of organizations.

A flow of qualified managers through the ranks of an organization can enhance its competitive and strategic advantage. Likewise, unresponsive, non-strategic succession planning can cause a deficit in leadership capabilities when business needs change rapidly, resulting in adverse effects on the business. Mahler attributes some large companies' losses to their lack of qualified top management in a changing business environment. Their succession planning system failed to produce leadership that could respond and adapt to redirection.

While the value of succession planning seems to be widely accepted in theory, problems arise in implementation. In their article, Walker and Armes discuss the application of management succession planning in diversified companies. To be effective, they note, it must be tailored to satisfy the changing requirements of the business as they are reflected in the long-range strategy. Indeed this best practice of closely linking succession planning with business goals and objectives echoes throughout all the articles and current Afterwards. Walker and Armes describe management succession and development as a process of strategic importance, enabling companies to build needed leadership capability.

Several authors link succession planning and experiential learning, that is, using a continuous process of learning embedded into work assignments to shape future leaders. Walker and Armes believe that development of leadership talent occurs primarily through on-the-job experiences. They emphasize varied job assignments as important factors in career progression and leadership development. Similarly, Mahler stresses the importance of cross-functional moves incorporated into the succession planning as a way to develop and advance entrepreneurial leaders.

Vetter argues that the latest approaches to succession planning are not as effective as concentrating on mastering the basics and adopting an approach that fits the realities of your particular business and management team. His Afterward Comments reaffirms a need to master the basics of succession planning, yet he suggests the application of new technologies and techniques for accomplishing this task. For example, tools such as assessment inventories engage senior management and the targeted high potential managers in making planning decisions. This is desirable, Vetter suggests, because employees are critical of succession planning techniques that do not provide payoffs for their own careers. High potential managers given the opportunity to better manage their own careers and the job assignments and developmental opportunities to get ahead have an enhanced overall commitment to the organization.

Today there is growing recognition that organizations cannot simply rely on executive recruitment or other *ad hoc* solutions to fill leadership gaps created by a changing business environment. Companies must adopt coherent, integrated succession planning strategies to meet their leadership needs. The following articles discuss best practices in the area of succession planning, and, perhaps more importantly, provide some guidance on how these might be implemented.

MONITORING THE FLOW OF MANAGERIAL TALENT: CREATING AND USING A MODEL

Paul J. Gordon and Paul H. Meredith

Managing the managerial resource for any enterprise can be a matter of strategic significance, yet problematical as an area for research and practice. The authors have created a model that executives might use to monitor the flow of managerial talent, including women and minorities. They put the model to use with executive help by conducting a survey of 743 managers in four state agencies. Paul Gordon is a Professor of Management and Chairman of Administrative and Behavioral Studies at the Indiana University Graduate School of Business. Paul Meredith is an Assistant Professor of Management at the Georgia Southern College School of Business.

A flow of qualified managers through the ranks of an organization can enhance competitive and strategic advantages for the future. In addition, equal opportunity for women and minorities cannot stop at the entry levels. Provision for mobility (upward, lateral and otherwise) must be included. Further, to speak of mobility requires some way of planning and monitoring movements through time. Static reporting alone is not enough.

Defining the Problem

The problem as we initially defined it was to create a model that executives not trained in human resource planning might adopt or adapt as their own in planning and monitoring the flow of managerial resources, including women and minorities. We recognized that published materials of a prescriptive character were generally not supported by empirical re-

Reprinted from *Human Resource Planning*, Vol. 5, No. 2 (1982), 69-82.

With the assistance of Mitchell S. Novit, Indiana University; Mary D.R. Meredith, Georgia Southern College; and a special project grant from the Indiana Office of Occupational Development.

search. Also, those active in this area were generally reluctant to reveal publicly the substance, and sometimes the method, of their work.

The term "model" can be troublesome. In using it, we were thinking of a demonstration project, one that would provide an illustration for practitioner guidance and also meet some relevant research standard. We meant to include clues on the theoretical streams behind the study, the conceptualization of what data might be relevant, the tools to collect data, the ways of analyzing data, and the whole process of seeing the project to completion. To achieve the desired end-product, one for executives to use. we tried the model with a stratified sample population to see what the practitioner response to its use might be.

We also perceived as part of the problem the relative dearth of shared experience in this situation. Few journals include in their published reports the early pangs of getting started, and few of the vanguard companies and agencies are in a position to make their real experience publicly available. Insight into the experience involved was considered as important as any methods or findings that might be shared. It is not that such experiences are unique. but that they seldom get published.

The Three Basic Questions

The object of this whole exercise was to create the model, to try it, and to comment on its use. In fact, three questions triggered our work and provide the central headings for the balance of this report:

1. Can we create a model that practitioners who are not specialists in human and managerial resource planning can put to use in monitoring the flow of talent generally, and women and minorities in particular, through managerial ranks?
2. What illustrative findings might be generated when practitioners put the model to use—in this case in a stratified sample of 743 managers in four state agencies?
3. What useful learning, generalizations, conditions, inferences, transferability, insights, might be shared and discussed beyond the sample as a result of this venture?

A Public Sector Stratified Sample

In order to proceed, we needed access, insight and candor. We also wanted to build-in sufficient diversity so that we might subsequently remark on the uses and limits of the approach taken. This meant units of enterprises with differing missions, professional and non-professional components, technologies, and job structures. It also meant greater variations in personnel systems than might characterize a manufacturing, retailing, or banking enterprise. There were those who warned us that success in devising a method to cut across policy level appointments, federally funded appointments, veterans' preference, civil service and patronage would be unlikely. Yet the public sector choice assured access to public records if internal cooperation could be secured.

CREATING THE MODEL

Creating the model was the most difficult part of the whole project because it involved the greatest uncertainty. Generally, the first part of any research is likely to be more nebulous than later stages. Practicing executives and researchers have long recognized that decision processes, executive or scientific, are not so tidy as step-by-step handbooks and published reports might suggest.

Defining a "Problem"

In the final analysis, "problems" have no built-in empirical referents. They are thought to exist as they are perceived, or as they are defined by some kind of consensus. There is no certain route to correct identification that will lead to tractable solutions. There is no way to spare people the debilitating feeling that somehow, something that is possibly evident to others, is escaping them. It takes a creative act to shape a problem definition to fit certain limits.

The process of discovering the limits, shaping and reshaping the definition through a series of incremental corrections, sometimes refining and sometimes starting over, has been generally recognized as one aspect of decision making. But this is not always described as a predictable aspect of getting some kinds of research started. In fact, we failed more than once and had to go round and round to get theoretical, empirical or practical reference points on which to build. Actually, we were well into the project before we had any basis for confidence that the approach taken might be feasible.

Reconstruction to Assist Exposition

With the benefit of hindsight, Figure 1 provides a kind of reconstructed logic to assist in telling how the basic building blocks of the model were inductively derived. The only parts that we considered as part of a possible model were Phase I on planning and Phase II on monitoring. The experience was less sequential and linear than Figure 1 and the following might suggest.

The policy problem of assuring an adequate flow of managerial talent with due representation of women and minorities was the motivating concern of the public agencies. We assumed that our problem was that of adapting theory or method from other settings to fit the needs of state and local agencies. We expected to cite from the literature either theory, method or findings to establish a base for our work. Even though the literature has grown since, there was a paucity of published material grounded in experience when we began.

FIGURE 1
The Evolution of a Model[1]

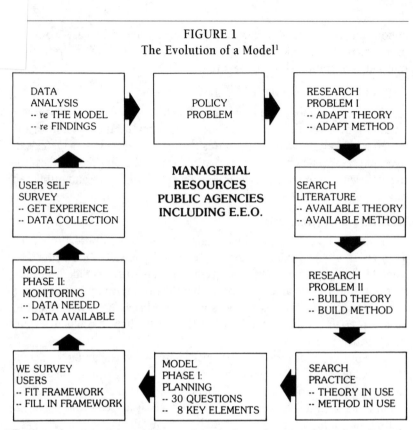

* The above schematic is not *the* model. It is intended to supplement the text in explaining the *evolution* of a model.

Therefore, we had to rethink the whole thing, redefine the problem, and find an alternative way to build theory and method. Contrasted with the idea of building on published work which would have been more deductive, the radical mid-course correction was more inductive. We resolved to take the more risky course of discovering in practice and combining techniques that might provide components for our model. We redirected our effort, and lined up a number of public and private enterprises and knowledgeable individuals to discover theory and method in use. From this experience, we derived what we now consider stronger theoretical justification, and method more closely aligned to EEO reporting requirements than we found in the literature. The advantage of the latter was a minimum of redundancy.

We then generated *Phase I*—The Planning Component (see Figure 2). In fact, we conducted no research with this instrument because some of

1 The above schematic is not *the* model. It is intended to supplement the text in explaining the *evolution* of a model.

the data suggested were not available. Collaboration at this point with public executives, however, helped us to learn the state of practice among the varied agencies. Also, subject to testing, we are persuaded that the eight major elements provide a logic structure for others with concern and data for planning. Survey work with potential users to learn the framework within which they operated led to the stratified sample selected.

FIGURE 2
The Phase 1: Planning Component
8 Major Elements[2]

1. **ABOUT THE AGENCY** - A brief history of the agency, its principal officers, its mission, its strategy, its size, location, functions, etc.

2. **ORGANIZATIONAL STRUCTURE** - The formal organization structure, manning tables, ordinary channels of advancement and mobility, alternate tracks and combinations, etc.

3. **FORECASTING DEMAND** - External and internal premises and indicators used in forecasting the future direction, priorities, size, shape and needs of the agency, the lead times, the relation to budgets, the specifics of how this is done, etc.

4. **DEVELOPING SUPPLY** - Internal and external sources of supply, relevant labor pool, experience with existing sources, developing sources of managerial capacity, relevant criteria for assuring representation of women and minorities getting into the pool, nurturing other than conventional sources, etc.

5. **ANALYZING GAPS** - Identifying differences between demand and supply, ways of recognizing coming shortages or overages and their consequences, generating inferences concerning diagnosis and remedial actions, etc.

6. **AUTHORIZATIONS** - The institutionalized arrangements, channels and controls related to authorizing that positions be started, continued or ended, their bearing for developing managerial cadres and women and minorities in the mix; variations for merit and non-merit, etc.

7. **QUALIFICATIONS** - Provisions related to developing job specifications, rating performance, rating potential and their bearing for developing managerial career structures including opportunity for women and minorities.

2 The logic structure intended above is not sacred. The first four points might lead up to critical analysis throughout and especially at point 5 with several avenues of corrective action suggested thereafter. The points might provide the framework for detailed questionnaire schedules.

8. **POLICIES** - The way the personnel aspect of the agency is now set up to operate, policies on all the foregoing and other related aspects of employment, training, advancement, counseling and so on, ease of obtaining and processing related data.

After this, we generated *Phase II*—the Monitoring Component (see Figure 3). Whereas the planning instrument called for qualitative and verbal responses, this called for quantitative data. The next step was the user self-survey. We had two concerns at this stage: (1) whether executives would use the monitoring instrument in the form presented, and (2) whether its use would result in data readily subject to the analysis contemplated with findings of sufficient significance to illustrate the potentials of the whole approach. The final step was analysis of the data collected by the agencies.

FIGURE 3
The Phase ll: Monitoring Component
Originally Two Pages[3]

YOUR NAME: _____

YOU REPORT TO:

Social Security Number				
1. Age				
2. Sex				
3. Race				
4. Education (years)				
5. Years Employed by Government (position)				
6. Employee Job Class Code				
7A. Salary step				
B. Salary (Bi-Weekly)				
8. Months in Current Employee Job Class				
9. Prior Employee Job Class				
10. Estimated Highest Potential Position Person Can Attain				
11. Estimated Next Position				
12. Estimated Months Until Qualified for Next Promotion				
13. Current Performance 1-5				

---

3 The original of the above had two pages which we omit to save space. The above was to be completed for the current employees. The reverse was to be completed for employees no longer under the manager's control. For the latter, points 8 through 13 were couched in past tense. A point 14 provided for recording "reason no longer under your control." Use of symbols other than Social Security number was optional and effective. Detailed instructions to aid respondents were provided.

Existing Practices

The published references at the close of this article are those that we now recommend to anyone who might initiate or proceed with this kind of work. As noted, however, we really proceeded by building in reverse. The early field visits to public and private enterprises were to complement the literature search and to see practice in operation.

At AT&T, corporate strategic planning provided a guide to the need for managerial resources and the use of the managerial assessment center. At Indiana Bell, we were shown a human resource information system at the operating company level with the forms and documentation to maintain it. At EXXON, the corporate staff was concerned with a global and lateral tracking of future executives. EXXON U.S.A maintained a computerized personnel information system for the domestic operation. Prudential was engaged in personnel planning, career planning and documenting the transferability of managerial capacities across functions. I.B.M. maintained corporate strategic planning plus operating plans at the division level. Managerial demand, supply gaps and ratios were monitored.

The Office of Personnel Management's Bureau of Executive Manpower was using experimental approaches, including subjective probability. The Equal Employment Opportunity Commission Research Unit was concerned with structural blocks to opportunity, including those represented in organizational and civil service procedures. The Department of Labor had a program designed to recruit women for executive positions. Finally, the District of Columbia Personnel Division showed a Markov model for human resource planning that had been tried in a preliminary way in at least one agency. Subsequent steps awaited subsequent funding.

The kinds of questions that we asked state agencies were those now reflected in our Phase 11: Planning Component. This line of inquiry was intended to learn about the agencies that might host the study, their history, structure, practices, the kinds of data that might be available and the form in which they might be available. It seemed practical to work with existing systems rather than to expect great cooperation and subsequent adoption by imposing totally new ones that might be foreign to existing requirements.

The timing of the state effort along this line was compatible with ours. The state had recently completed a system of job classification and job code numbering and was moving in the direction of a fully integrated and computerized personnel information system. What we wanted, state officials also wanted. At that point, however, systematic information to complete our planning component was simply not available. Some officials in specific agencies indicated no real planning, but were living from budget to budget following meetings of the state legislature. Others indicated long-term lobbying with legislative subcommittees but could not provide evidence of systematic planning. These preliminaries suggested the possible utility of the planning guide that we had devised but we had no way to proceed with it. So we went ahead with the monitoring component, recognizing its possible immediate utility and recognizing that later interest in planning might follow.

Using The Model

The findings that follow are intended to be illustrative of what the monitoring instrument yielded, but are in no way conclusive. They are based on 743 managers and potential managers in four state agencies which were chosen on the basis of diversity. The diversities intended were political, patronage, federally funded, merit, highly professionalized, relatively skilled, unionized and veterans' preference categories. We ended up without the last two. Also, in one agency a major professional component was omitted due to competing survey demands. Other criteria were met including diversities in age, sex, race, education, pay and so on. There was no provision for the handicapped. Inclusion of this category would be relatively easy.

The Use of the Term "Manager"

The term "manager" was used broadly to include executive, managerial, supervisory, professional, semi-professional and technical categories that might provide sources for filling managerial positions. This was consistent with the practice of the agencies and the terms of reference for executives gathering data. Imposing other definitions would have been inconsistent with that experience and our orientation to discovery, opportunity and mobility.

The Data Analysis

The data were analyzed in three ways. Current demographic characteristics were cross-tabulated by age, sex, race, education, months in position, pay, managerial level, agency and so on. Position (job code) changes for a one-year period were tracked by cross-tabulating beginning stocks and flows with subsequent job codes or separations. (Data for longer than a year might be advisable, but this was all relatively new for the agencies involved and older data were increasingly difficult to secure.) Possible feeder source positions for filling higher ones were discovered through cross-tabulating: (1) on the basis of jobs currently held; (2) on the basis of superior forecast of incumbent's next job; and (3) on the basis of superior forecast of highest job potential. The tracking of job movements and the sourcing of feeder positions for higher ones with breakdowns by age, sex, race, agency, etc. suggested the possibility of teasing out potentially significant patterns.

Table 1 shows the *general characteristics* of the sample, the demographic distribution of managers among the four agencies. Agency 1 was a long-established line agency with a number of professional components, mostly civil service and the greatest number of managerial positions. Agency 2 was a staff agency that had enjoyed recent growth and included a relatively large proportion of younger people. Agency 3 was included especially because it was a long-established line agency with a patronage personnel system. Agency 4 was a long-established line agency from which a sizeable professional component that included women was omitted because of competing survey activity going on at the same time.

Table 2 tabulates by agencies (column headings) the experience of *females compared to males* and *blacks compared to whites* on the basis of age. years of education (row headings) and so on. For example, females and blacks were younger on the average than males and whites with three exceptions. Females and blacks were employed longer except for women in the "younger' agency. Pay for females and blacks was lower across the board except for Agency 4 which was also the one in which a major block of women was not included in the data collection.

TABLE 1
General Characteristics
Sample Size

	Agency 1	Agency 2	Agency 3	Agency 4	Row Totals
Agency	500	53	66	124	743
Male	398	20	36	46	500
Female	102	24	30	78	234
Missing Observations	0	9	0	0	9
White	463	41	63	57	624
Black	7	4	3	67	81
Other	25	1	0	0	26
Missing Observations	5	7	0	0	12

TABLE 2
General Characteristics
Females and Blacks

	Agency 1		Agency 2		Agency 3		Agency 4	
	F:M	B:W	F:M	B:W	F:M	B:W	F:M	B:W
Age	.2 higher	5 lower	4 lower	5.7 lower	6.3 lower	4.3 higher	1.5 lower	5.8 higher
Years of Education	.4 lower	.6 higher	1.1 lower	2.3 lower	.6 lower	4.4 lower	1.2 higher	1.8 lower
Years Employed	.7 higher	.7 higher	1.9 lower	5.5 higher	.4 higher	7.9 higher	2 higher	4.2 higher
Pay Bi-weekly	74 lower	96 lower	155 lower	22 lower	58 lower	53 lower	10 lower	5 higher
Months in Position	24 higher	equal	6 lower	3 lower	14 lower	30 higher	2 higher	7 higher
Performance Rating	.2 lower	4 lower	.2 lower	.1 lower	.3 lower	.2 higher	.4 higher	.5 lower
Sample Size	102/398	7/463	24/20	4/41	30/36	3/63	78/46	67/57

TABLE 3
Tracking Job Movements
Changes Based On One Year

Classification	Present Job Code	Probability of New Job Code								
Male Female	2010	64035	70014 61.9	70024 4.7	70025 4.7	70034 4.7	71073 4.7	72023	72044 9.5	72094 9.5
		5.8						35.2	58.8	
Male	3091	13073 9.0	13083 45.4	S13085 18.1	W13083 9.0	W13223 9.0	309150 9.0			
Male	3100	13072 10.0	13361 10.0	S13065 10.0	S13084 20.0	S13085 20.0	S13333 10.0	S13334 10.0	310052 10.0	
White Black	200	201 85.8	7001 14.2	9002 100						
White Black	201	6403 3.0	7001 38.3	7002 5.8	7003 25.0	7107 25.0	7202 17.6	7204 25.0 32.3	7209 25.0 3.0	
White	310	1307 4.1	1308 4.1	1333 54.1	1336 4.1	S1306 4.1	S1308 16.6	S1333 8.3	31005 4.1	
White Asian Am.	311	1308 12.5	2006 70.8	E2006 8.3 100.0	S2006 8.3					
White Black Asian Am.	1306	1306 34.7 40.0	3303 8.6 20.0	3423 4.3	3424 20.0	S1306 4.3	W1306 8.6	10 22.0 100.0	41 4.0	43 13.0	51 20.0

Table 3 illustrates the cross-tabulation designed to *track job movements* for one year for males and females, whites and blacks, from one job code to others. For example, male and female incumbents of job code 2010 followed different tracks thereafter. The figures under the subsequent job code numbers tell what percentage of the people who moved from job code 2010 moved into subsequent job code numbers. These percentages for one year might suggest future probabilities if extended data were available. Also, 100% of the white incumbents who moved from job code 200 moved into job code 9002 (an executive job code), whereas 100% of the black incumbents moved into job codes 201 and 7001.

TABLE 4
Sources for Higher Positions
Based on Present Positions

Classification	Higher Code	Probable Source Job Codes					
Agency 4	0280	0260 50.0					Direct Hire 50.0
Agency 1	12023	2940 12.5	2950 37.6	2951 18.7	12024 25.0		Direct Hire 6.2
	13083	2091 3.7	3080 7.4	3090 59.3	3091 22.2	3108 3.7	3112 3.7
	13084	3113 50.0					Direct Hire 50.0
Agency 2	31133	0660 20.0	0670 40.0	31134 20.0	S31125 20.0		
	31134	21055 20.0	31135 80.0				
	31135	T64666 50.0					Direct Hire 50.0
	34113	33014	60024				Direct Hire 100.0
Agency 1 Agency 2 Agency 3		33.3	20.0				66.7 80.0
Agency 1	E00005	15010 20.0	31031 20.0	34111 20.0			Direct Hire 40.0
Agency 1	S13085	2091 33.3	3091 33.3	3100 33.3			
Agency 3	S60026	60024 8.3					Direct Hire 91.7
Male	E00005	15010 20.0	31031 20.0	34111 20.0			Direct Hire 40.0
Male Female	S13015	1301 100.0	13013 100.0				
Male Female	S60026	60024 16.7					Direct Hire 83.3 100.0
Male	13062	3030 19.1	3040 14.2	13062 4.7	13063 28.6	13064 9.5	Direct Hire 23.9
Male Female	13063	3030 14.2	3040 7.1	13063 14.2	13064 7.1		57.4 100.0
Male Female	31133	0660 100.0	0670 50.0	31134 25.0	S31125 25.0		

Table 4 illustrates the cross-tabulation designed to identify lower job code sources for higher rated positions. For example, based on the past experience of one year, openings in higher rated job code 0280 might be filled from lower rated job code 0260 or from direct hiring of new people into Agency 4. Higher job code 13083, in contrast, might be filled from any of six lower rated job code numbers in the much larger Agency 1.

Survey Findings

The primary finding, of course, was that the executives used the monitoring instrument shown as Figure 3 with negligible difficulty and it yielded the data in Tables 1 through 4. The illustrative findings for this study (hypotheses for other studies) are:

1. Racial minorities, by any standard, were underrepresented in the stratified sample chosen for this study (see Table 1). We must add, however, that determination of the relevant labor pool would be important before reaching conclusions.

2. Women, by any standard, were in the aggregate less than proportionately represented at the managerial levels, and especially beyond the first level, but with variation among agencies (see Table 1). Again, determination of the relevant labor pool would be important before reaching conclusions.

3. Age appeared at no point to be a basis for systematic and negative discrimination in this sample, although it might be an organizational problem for some agencies in planning for retirements and for age distribution for the future (see Table 2, line 1).

4. Years of education beyond those necessary to qualify for entering managerial positions appeared not to be an important criterion for determining subsequent managerial career moves (see Table 2, line 2).

5. Years employed appear to equate substantially with age and years to retirement and not to serve as an important variable in explaining the data that we have analyzed (see Table 3, line 3).

6. Pay bi-weekly was lower for women and for blacks throughout the study, excepting only the case of blacks in one agency. Across the board, this finding was not systemically explained by variations in such possible independent variables as age, years of education, years employed, months in position or performance ratings (see Table 2, line 4).

7. Months in position is an item that we judge to be an important mobility measure, especially when comparing the experience of women and racial minorities with the larger population. It should also be an important measure in planning lead times for filling managerial positions at higher levels (see Table 2, line 5).

8. Performance ratings, recognized from the start to be softer as empirical referents than other items, were in all instances but one less statically significant in explaining sex and race differences than years of education, bi-weekly pay and months in position (see Table 2, line 6).

9. Separations by sex and race suggested nothing disproportionate to the rest of the study.

10. Separations cross-tabulated with performance ratings and stated reasons for leaving (not the hardest of data), suggested the possibility that a sizeable portion of the people who left by the resignation route were among the better rated people.

11. The computer program documentation was effective in tracking job movements on the basis of sex, race, agency and education.

12. The computer program document was effective in discovering source jobs for higher ones differentiating on the basis of age, sex, race, agency and so on.

13. The procedure was also possible, though the data base became leaner, when superiors were asked to look at subordinate current jobs, forecasted next jobs. and forecasted highest potential jobs.

14. Examination of superior responses in evaluating subordinate current jobs as sources, and especially in forecasting next and highest jobs, led us to generate questions about the existence and widespread knowledge of mobility and career job structures within and especially across functions and agencies.

15. Though we have been reluctant to speak of findings or conclusions for tracking job movements and for source feeder positions, the work done goes beyond what has been available and provides sufficient empirical demonstration: to merit scrutiny by agency officials and specialists; and to generate hypotheses for further research.

16. Our best information is that courts to date have not accepted as evidence statistical treatments that rely on assumptions that underlay analysis of variance. We used simple tests of significance. Our efforts to use Markov technique failed for lack of sufficient data for each discrete cell. See references to May and Heneman at the close of this article.

Learning from Experience

Throughout, we have indicated concern with theoretical anchorage, empirical base, method, practicality and so on. We can now remark on terms of reference for continued work of this kind, including sources for theoretical leverage to get started, data requirements, timing, and agency support.

Terms of Reference

The strategic decision focus that is now emerging in the literature of academics and practitioners provides a suitable theoretical housing and leverage for work on planning and monitoring the allocation of managerial resources. A major strategic concern faced by executives is that of positioning an enterprise (or any major part) for the future in light of environmental, demographic, legislative, technological, value, resource and constituency considerations, plus internal capacities. Work tied to these considerations will have an identifiable focus and significance not always accorded more fragmented social science and personnel activity.

The experience of this study suggests that availability of a sufficient personnel data bank is a prerequisite for serious analytical work. This would include as a minimum the kinds of data that we have used, preferably for a five-year period, with job code numbers and for a unit of about 500 people.

There is also the question of method, the one we have described, plus alternates. For more advanced endeavors, there are several tractable and productive analogies for developing concepts and applications. We include, for example: economic analyses of external and internal labor markets; the return-on-investment concept borrowed from finance; the accounting concept of starting with the gross figure (such as forecast demand) and working to the bottom line; classical production-inventory models and more recent "materials requirement planning" models; systems analyses generally of inputs, transformations and outputs; recent work on managerial and personnel information systems; analyses of personnel stocks and flows including Markov possibilities; and the possible addition of subjective probabilities where other probability measures cannot be established.

The fit of managerial resource and personnel planning and monitoring to state-wide and agency-wide strategic planning and budgetary cycles is probably critical Human resource planning not geared to these realities will proceed without one of its strongest justifications and will be out of phase in terms of accomplishing its objectives. These were carefully meshed in the major public and private enterprises that we visited. Any other theoretical or practical roots for this activity were further enhanced by this pragmatic linkage. Political, legislative and auditing activities in the public sector may suggest not impossibility, but longer lead times.

Any success that might result from this study had to be based on recognition that research of this nature constitutes social intervention. The respondents and the subjects were not totally unaware of this aspect. Their hopes, anxieties and interpretations constituted part of the fabric. Throughout, our stance was that our intent was supportive, not judgmental, and we tried to confirm this by our own behavior. To suggest, however, that the research had no bias would be ridiculous. We were concerned with tools for facilitating social change. The gathering and the feedback of data represent one of the ways to facilitate social change.

In the matter of change, we may have discovered structural blocks to organizational mobility that may apply to all comers, not solely women and minorities. Based on the limited data returned when we asked superiors to estimate future movement prospects for subordinates, it has occurred to us that some of the blocks may be in the heads of the raters rather than in the potential of the candidates, or in barriers inherent in the organizational charts. If true even in part, this and other better-documented findings suggest two implications. One is that of focusing on organizational blocks, real or imagined, and proceeding with clean-up and education. The other has to do with the great variety of career counseling and upward mobility reinforcements currently popular. Unless some of these are grounded in the realities that surfaced in this survey, raising expectation without regard to promising and unpromising channels might represent a tragic disservice. Executive commitment at top and middle levels is critical for doing this kind of study or yielding any results. This means commitment sufficient to sustain both the patience and the questioning involved in working through an exploratory undertaking without assurance of immediate agency or personal benefit. In no case, however, did we interpret hesitation as non-commitment to agency or public policy.

A Closing Without a Finish

All of this leads to the claim that a model has been created. When used with executive assistance, the potential to produce results has been demonstrated. Implications for policy and for continued research have been suggested. The technique is probably transferable to other settings, even though the political and cultural milieu may differ. In the final analysis, this total exposition may support three conclusions. The first is that we may have created an instrument for problem-finding more than one for problem-solving. The second is that monitoring may establish the case for planning. at least in some instances, more than the reverse. And the third is that "muddling" as part of getting on with ill-structured decisions may hold for both the executive and the researcher once the obscuring mystique of total rationality is eased.

REFERENCES

Burack, Elmer H. and Thomas G. Gutteridge. "Institutional Manpower Planning: Rhetoric versus Reality," *California Management Review.* (Spring 1978).

Burack, Elmer H. and Nicholas Mathys. "Career Ladders. Pathing and Planning: Some Neglected Basics," *Human Resources Management.* (Summer 1979).

Gould, Sam. "Characteristics of Career Planners in Upwardly Mobile Occupations," *Academy of Management Journal* (September 1979).

Grinold, Richard C. and Kneale T. Marshall. *Manpower Planning Models* (New York: North Holland, 1977).

Heneman, Herbert G. and Marcus G. Landver. "Markov Analysis in Human Resource Administration," *The Academy of Management Review.* (October 1977).

Killian, Ray A. *Human Resource Management: An ROI Approach.* (New York: American Management Association, 1976).

Levine, Charles H.(ed). *Managing Human Resources* (Beverly Hills, CA: Sage Publications, Inc., 1977).

Mahoney, Thomas and George Milkovich. "Computer Simulation: A Training Tool for Manpower Managers," *Personnel Journal* (December 1975).

May, J. Gaylord. "Statistical Methods in Measuring Discrimination," Southeastern Meeting American Institute of Decision Sciences. Jacksonville, Florida (February 1978).

Rosenbaum, James E. "Tournament Mobility: Career Patterns in a Corporation," *Administrative Science Quarterly.* (June 1979).

Smith, Catherine Begnocke. "Influence of Internal Opportunity Structure and Sex of Worker on Turnover Patterns," *Administrative Science Quarterly.* (September 1979).

Vincent, John. "Decision Analysis Forecasting for Executive Manpower Planning," U.S. Civil Service Commission Bureau of Executive Manpower. EMMTAP No. 3 (June 1974).

AFTERWARD COMMENTS

Paul J. Gordon, St. John's University
Paul H. Meredith, University of Southwestern Louisiana

Our original purpose roughly ten years ago was to create a model for tracking managerial personnel movements beyond entering positions. Equally important, it was to put the model to practical use in yielding analytical data. Further, the response of line mangers in providing the data requested was crucial. We intended a "turnkey" project that others might take over and put to their own use.

Noted at the start was the paucity of published theory, research, or methods as a base for this kind of study. For academics, impetus for establishing research agenda is thought to be found in research journals. Research problems are thought to be some gap in building an ongoing stream of knowledge or in method for such advances. Our base became the imperatives of practitioners whose problems were more likely to be some gap interfering with feasible solutions in getting work done. For practitioners faced with deadlines, it might be interesting but not essential to have explanations of underlying cause and effect relationships.

Our approach was to build on the inductive experience of practitioners then thought to be at the front edge of HR planning. We sought their method and reason for their method.

Although thoroughly enjoyable, the experience for us was also somewhat hectic. Today we would have the consolation of recognizing that we were using "grounded theory," a term that has since come into common use. In the absence of pre-existing theory, the idea is that of first examining possibly related pieces of evidence as a basis for building theory. Many of us recall that the great detective, Sherlock Holmes, was supposed to solve cases deductively. Not so! When he picked up minuscule possible clues, speculated, and ruled out some speculations, he was proceeding first inductively then deductively or mixing both.

Built inductively and with the benefit of hindsight, it may not be stretching too much to say that we had an hypothesis. It was the model, including its use, that was subject to the kind of "testing" that we did not any more elegant hypotheses. Our model was created in light of then-extant literature, prevailing practice, and the legal and juridical context of performance and its measurement.

Among the variables that we incorporated, age was more implicit than explicit. It might be explicit today, not for use in achieving discrimination, but to defend against charges of discrimination, a double-edged point to ponder carefully, with legal retirement age and pension benefits mounting as issues. The same might hold for handicaps. To include sexual preference today would be in advance of legal and judicial experience. Not for our sample but for some of the companies that we visited, affirmative action posed the issue of relevant labor pool.

Though we were and continue to be fascinated with the potential for Markov analysis (a technique for monitoring stocks and flows from one discrete state to another) in Human Resource Management, we could not pursue a serious analysis. Our survey did not yield enough data for reliably estimating annual position to position transition probabilities, essential elements in the application of Markovian methods.

What Might We Re-Emphasize for Others?

We would like to emphasize two points that can arise especially at the intersection of the "problem" agenda defined by researchers and that defined by practitioners. The points might seem commonplace for people regularly engaged in research, especially applied research, but might help those who do not yet take the uncertainties involved as par for the course.

We crystallize with the help of two declarations: (1) science as it gets reported is frequently not science as it gets done; and, (2) even for so-called "hard" sciences, (e.g., physics and chemistry), in contrast to so-called "soft" sciences (e.g., social sciences), the front edges are frequently soft.

For the first of these declarations, there may exist a misconception that "doing science" is highly rational, linear, sequential, and tidy in contrast to irrational or non-rational, non-linear, non-sequential, and messy. Reports published in scientific journals may require a logical setting forth of methods that can be followed so that others can replicate. This requirement may describe what in fact happened in some instances. It may contribute to the misconception that doing science is more totally rational than the reality.

Some of the greatest discoveries in the history of science arose, however, out of accidents. Stories such as those involved in the work on DNA are not often told. For our work, the schematic with all the arrows in the original article, telling of the steps gone through, was reconstructed logic after the fact. It was to suggest what we subsequently thought we went through or what others might have gone through under similar circumstances. It can be misleading, however, if it is taken to suggest, with the benefit of hindsight, how rational we were in processing in one-directional linear sequence.

For the second of the above declarations, the general public impression might be that physics and chemistry, for example, are "hard" sciences in contrast to social sciences and their applications which are "soft." In part and especially in day-to-day efforts, the impression may be valid. But reading the candid "insider" reports and conversations with leading physicists and chemists will confirm that the really unknown front edges of the hard sciences are also soft.

The social sciences research agenda ideally should always include efforts to improve both rigor and relevance for worldly applications but not necessarily through seeking improved status by aping physical and natural sciences and then sensing inferiority when controlled laboratory settings can only at best be simulated and then conceivably with contamination.

What Follow-up Might We Suggest?

It may be useful to use the listed findings at the close of the 1982 article as a follow-up in monitoring managerial flows today.

We continue to believe that human resources management, development, and succession will have their greatest credibility only if they are significantly tied to mission, objectives, priorities, strategies, and allocations, not as empty votes for virtue, but geared to rapidly changing technological, environmental, and global competitive advantage for the next ten years. new strategies will involve fundamental and continuing industry and enterprise restructuring, which will involve mobilities of a radically different character from those contemplated ten years ago. While human resources may increasingly be recognized as a major source of competitive advantage, investment in development will remain critical.

Finally, the model that we reported in 1982 might fit well with today's concept of Total Quality Management (TQM). To apply TQM to managing the flow of managers and professionals, we must be able to measure the process and track progress. These methods and tools provide managers with that capacity.[1]

---

[1] See Richard J. Schonberger, "Is Strategy Strategic? Impact of Total Quality Management on Strategy," *Academy of Management Executive* (August 1992) Vol. VI, No. 3, p. 83, who recommends "continually invest in human resources through cross-training (for mastery), education, job switching, and multi-year cross-career reassignments—".

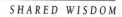

MANAGEMENT SUCCESSION PLANNING: NEW APPROACHES FOR THE 80S

Walter R. Mahler

This article identifies 11 specific improvement opportunities that are needed if management succession programs are going to meet the challenges of the 1980s. It also looks at the positive and negative conditions that now exist in the area of management succession planning as practiced at many of our large organizations. Walter R. Mahler is President of Mahler Associates, Inc, in Midland Park, New Jersey.

Two decades ago the initial systematic efforts aimed at the executive level were called executive development. As these efforts evolved, the term executive continuity became the popular title. Currently, the popular term is management succession planning. The change in terms doesn't really change the basic challenge for business and industrial organizations. When key executives step down, a talented replacement should be ready to carry on. While we may see the end result as unchanging, two changes have occurred. The task has become more difficult for many reasons. In addition, the task has become more critical. The absence of a talented replacement has become exceedingly costly. It is appropriate that we look at a new approach for the 80s to management succession planning. First let us examine how we are doing with our current efforts.

Over the last six years we have conducted two workshops a year on management succession planning. Participants prepare a thorough evaluation of the current status of their effort. The participants have come from nearly 60 different organizations and can be considered a typical cross-section of companies with a formal program. The reference to cross-section means organizations in the *Fortune Directory*.

Reprinted from *Human Resource Planning*, Vol. 4, No. 4 (1981), 221-227.

Positive Conditions

When looking at the current status of management succession planning, there are numerous positive conditions that can be identified:

1. Top managers, with a few exceptions, accept management succession as one of their major responsibilities.
2. A staff group has been established with responsibilities for succession planning. In very large organizations, the staff group will be independent of the regular human resources staff. It will likely report to the chief executive.
3. All organizations use some variation of an annual review process. It may be called annual manpower review, executive replacement planning, or management manpower planning. This process has become a habit.
4. A sizeable majority of companies regularly enroll executives in a university advanced program.
5. Almost all of the companies have an established college recruiting process for the infusion of youthful talent. The programs are sustained even during recessions.
6. Without exception, companies have an established program aimed at the accelerated development of minority groups.
7. An increasing number of companies, although not yet a majority, have an effective strategic planning process that contributes considerably to management succession planning.
8. Another positive condition, although it sounds like a negative, is the fact that a large number of chief executives are acutely dissatisfied with the results to date from their succession effort. This is reflected in frequent replacement of the staff executive in charge of the executive human resource function.

Negative Conditions

The negative conditions characteristic of management succession planning in a majority of the business and industrial organizations we have surveyed are:

1. Very few key managers are "bigger, broader, better" as a result of a formal succession program.
2. Most business and industrial organizations are quite thin on management talent in spite of the succession program.
3. Very few executives can be credited with effective coaching and development of their subordinates. Many don't even attempt it.
4. It is a rare United States company that has an effective global approach to management succession.
5. Very few of the conglomerates (of recent vintage) have an effective management succession effort.

6. Youthful candidates for executive positions often set restraints on their own careers, which complicates company succession planning.
7. Minority individuals are still found infrequently in middle management and rarely found at executive levels.
8. The quality of evaluative data for key executives is poor.
9. Most company educational programs could disappear without any apparent adverse impact. University programs can be credited with "broadening" their participants. Such programs cannot be credited with the enhancement of skills.
10. Very few "high-potential" programs really accelerate the development of younger individuals.
11. The methodology of management succession programs has been static. There has not been one significant breakthrough in the last decade.
12. Management succession staffs have a critical problem of succession within their own function. Talented individuals, faced with slow mobility, are constantly moving on. Consequently, the staff in large companies regresses towards mediocrity.

DEMANDS OF THE FUTURE

It would be much more pleasant if we could assume that the balance sheet of positive and negative conditions overstated the negatives. I don't believe it does, based on our periodic collection of anecdotal data from a large number of companies. It would seem to be a rare organization in which more than half of the negative conditions did not prevail. The balance sheet may not be completely accurate, but it is safe to conclude that present conditions tilt towards the negative.

This leads to the first demand of the 1980s: *American business and industry must get real results from their management succession programs.* They must have a truly effective management succession program. It isn't necessary to dwell on the reasons such improvement is so critical. Companies are faced with continued growth and change, with greatly increased complexity of doing business, and with painful competitive pressures, both internal and external.

The traditional alternative of going outside to bring in high-level talent will be increasingly prohibitive in the 1980s. Top-notch talent will continue to be scarce. Bringing in outsiders distorts one's compensation practices, especially when executives expect to be treated more like sport stars. An influx of outsiders also plays havoc with internal morale. The batting average on selecting outsiders remains remarkably low. It is with embarrassment that some companies fire their newly acquired, high-level talent within six months.

If the first demand is to be met, then management succession programs must provide a steady flow of needed talent. The program must permit top management to choose from several qualified internal candidates when appointing individuals to key positions. The program must also be seen as an equitable one.

This leads to the second demand: *American business and industry must set much higher standards for their management succession programs. Each company must demand a major overhaul in its current management succession system.* The overhaul needs to be made in every major component of the program. In addition, a systems approach is a necessity if a truly effective program is to be achieved. The first two demands lead us to the third, which defines the real results which must come from the major overhaul of the program. *Top management of companies must expect that executives in the program will actually enhance their managerial skills. They will change their ineffective managerial habits and they will improve their managerial abilities.*

PROGRAM PARAMETERS FOR 1980S PROGRAMS

The three previously mentioned demands lead us to define needed new approaches for management succession programs in the 1980s:

1. *Succession programs must be designed for the unique needs of a given organization.*

   Most company succession programs have evolved by copying a program from one of the leaders in the field. This pattern readily leads to the establishment of a program. But it is a sheer accident if the program meets the unique needs of a given organization. Product-oriented businesses, process-oriented businesses, service companies, governmental and educational institutions, each have completely unique requirements.

   Some companies are in a rapid growth mode: some are characterized by slow growth: some have reached a mature, commodity stage; while other companies might be declining. Each organization needs a succession program that is tailored to its unique needs. It is particularly ironic that conglomerates do so poorly with management development. The increased size and diversity of conglomerates should facilitate the development of managers. To date, the conglomerates are the biggest users of executive recruiters.

2. *Succession programs must be designed to compete with U.S. companies, Japanese companies, German companies and companies from other countries.*

   Some years ago a French journalist sounded the alarm that American management was going to dominate France in the immediate future. Recently, a television special was devoted to the question. "If Japan can, why can't we?" The special dramatized productivity and quality differences between the two countries.

The 1980s would have been a tough competitive challenge without inflation. With inflation, governmental regulations, and the steady advance of technology, a company can't slow down without losing ground. The threat to survival isn't an idle threat in the 1980s. U.S. companies must have a succession plan which produces a steady flow of the required executive talent.

3. *Different business strategies require different types of managerial abilities.* A succession program must meet the unique requirements of each basic type of organization. In addition, the succession program must have the versatility to adapt to the special needs of different business strategies.

Management succession requirements are quite different for "stars" and for "cash cows." It is a rare manager, well-suited to one strategy, who can do equally well in another strategy. This fact requires that succession programs develop managers for specific types of strategies. In addition, we must become skillful at "recycling" individuals as a business strategy changes for a given situation. We can no longer afford to scrap successful managers because they "fail" when we change the strategy for them.

4. *New methodologies must be introduced to overcome four of the negative conditions noted earlier.*

Better evaluative data is a critical need. An increasing number of companies are following the example of General Electric in making use of an accomplishment analysis methodology based on comprehensive interviews of replacement candidates and their superiors. The stress is on accomplishments as an indicator of future performance.

Better coaching is another critical need. We must increase both skill and willingness. An increasing number of companies are using our Coaching Practices Survey to stimulate willingness. In addition, they are providing skill training in conducting performance and counseling interviews. A small number of companies have proven this need can be met, but it takes a real effort.

Better results from our educational dollars is a major need. The only modern thing about management education in the last few years is a host of new edifices. Innovations are desperately needed. We need substantial investments in the "software" side, in curriculum development. We must be able to develop managerial skills and change habits for all levels of management. Periodic educational experiences are invaluable.

At IBM, every manager must receive one week of education each year. As companies get serious about periodic educational experiences, the instructional role must be placed on higher-level managers. I know of one six-week management skills program, now in its fifth year, where all instructors are high-level executives. They won't even give up this assignment.

Productive high-potential programs are a must. A few companies have found they must have not one, but three, high-potential programs: one for top functional managers, one for general managers, and one for future chief executives. Each type of program requires unique managers and a different program.

In these companies, a small number of individuals should get an accelerated opportunity to learn. The individuals should be somewhere between 27 and 33 years of age. They should get at least three diverse work assignments. Many companies have also found that hiring MBA's to be future managers is a waste of money. They quit before they have a chance to learn to manage. Many are now encouraging current employees to continue with additional education.

In summary, proven methodologies are available for these four critical needs. We must set higher standards for the management succession effort, then introduce new technology into the program.

— 5. *The succession results must be secured in every geographic area of the world for those companies operating globally.*

Many U.S. companies have been operating globally for decades. Some have exerted strenuous efforts to have qualified executives available in every geographic region. The stress is, of course, on developing managers indigenous to a country. Exxon has worked as diligently on this as any major company.

The challenge of a global approach is so complex and so frustrating one could give up. Recent U.S. governmental decisions have had tragic consequences. Most companies have a business strategy which calls for global operations. The most critical restraint to this strategy, year after year, is going to be managerial talent. It takes a real systems approach with concern for selection, development, retention, compensation policies and practices.

— 6. *The annual human resource review process must be made more productive.* The review process has been in place for a long time in most companies. In most cases, the initial process has been used year after year, without change. The review process can and should be a powerful tool. It should insure that executives:

- Think about basic questions on organization and talent.
- Have thorough discussions with their superiors.
- Arrive at specific plans of action.
- Implement the plans as scheduled.

Here are two ways to tell if you are using obsolete methodology:

- Do you use an organization chart to reflect back-ups?
- Are you looking only one year ahead, instead of five years?

We have also discovered, somewhat accidentally, that tutoring executives in their preparation for the review can upgrade the quality of the entire process.

7. *Large companies must develop and select teams rather than one executive to run the company and major sectors of the company.*

It would be amusing if it weren't so tragic that we assume one executive can run a multi-billion dollar company. It takes a team of highly talented individuals, with quite complementary skills to really run large, diversified enterprises. We need to work more at developing, evaluating and selecting teams to run major sectors and the entire enterprise.

8. *There must be a timely interaction of management succession planning and strategic business planning.*

Strategic planning has become an established process in most large companies. which leads to setting varied strategies for each business. Specific managerial abilities are required for each major strategic alternative.

For example, one large conglomerate really takes this suggestion to heart. One sector executive is noted for his ability to expand businesses, so is assigned all businesses with a high growth strategy, no matter what the technology. We need to insure that management succession planning is done to complement the strategic business plan.

9. *A collaborative planning process must reconcile organizational needs and individual executive needs.*

One top executive I know refuses to work more than four days a week (long ones). He commutes 300 miles each week. IBM once was said by employees to stand for "I've Been Moved." Not any more. Even IBM has to allow for personal values conflicting with organizational needs. We need to communicate personal preferences and restraints, as well as organizational preferences and necessities.

The planning on lateral moves and promotional moves will have to be a collaborative one in the future.

10. *The selection process must avoid predictable pitfalls.*

One classic pitfall is the "buddy syndrome." An executive screens widely but selects buddies. Another pitfall befalls the chief executive. When faced with a choice of three possible successors, the chief executive is likely to pick the least qualified one. A third pitfall occurs when a given faction endeavors to capture all appointments to key positions. The faction may be a function, such as finance, or a product group. It could also be a geographic faction. We need to work out basic policies and procedures to avoid these pitfalls in the corporate-wide selection process.

11. Management succession staffs need to be upgraded.
As the old fable says, the shoemaker's children are often in need of shoes. Most companies have had extensive experience with recruitment, development, upward mobility, and pirating of talent for the succession effort. The professionals in management succession need to apply succession planning to their own efforts.

CONCLUSION

Current management succession efforts have many positive conditions. However, any complacency is challenged by serious negative conditions. The stringent demands of the 1980s require that much higher standards be set for management succession efforts.

This article has identified 11 specific improvement opportunities needed if management succession programs are going to meet the challenge of the 80s. Fortunately, those companies that rise to the challenge will gain a significant competitive advantage.

AFTERWARD COMMENTS

Walter R. Mahler

In my 1981 article I noted that IBMers said that IBM stood for "I've been moved." In 1994 it's a different story. The IBMers now say IBM stands for "I've been mistreated." IBM failed to overcome the 12 negatives I mentioned in my article, as did GM, Sears, Westinghouse, and others. Now come the harsh realities. In the 1990s losses have run into billions. CEOs have lost their thrones. Boards have been embarrassed. Employees, by the 100,000s, have been devastated. I just completed a study of why GM, IBM, and Sears are intent on self-destruction. I didn't see the problem in 1981. I wish I had.

Here's my current explanation. General Wood of Sears, Alfred Sloan of GM, and Tom Watson, Sr. and Jr. of IBM left flourishing businesses that grew to enormous size. Ten or more years later the nature of the business changed in a significant way. The top men in the three companies had spent their entire careers in one function. In IBM the experience was in sales but limited to main-frame computers. The new CEOs were faced with the need to redefine and redirect the business. They had never done such a thing before. To put it bluntly, they couldn't do it.

They had not been developed to be entrepreneurs. We, who think of ourselves as professionals in succession planning, can't be too proud of ourselves. We just missed the boat. The 12 negative conditions were accurate but not too consequential. Giant companies are failing because top management were not broad-gauged business managers, who needed to be entrepreneurial when the basic nature of the business changed. You say we can't be expected to do the impossible; I tell you the Japanese do it. In fact, the HR function in Japanese companies do it. Their managers are routinely moved from function to function. Imagine how fortunate the Japanese general manager is to have no managers thinking and acting like our traditional functional managers. Here's an unrecognized advantage the Japanese have. It's amazing the Japanese don't know you can't make cross-functional moves and still make money.

So I would forget my nice but not too basic suggestions. Today we need to consider several imperatives.

1. We must get enthusiastic about cross-functional moves. They need to start early in the manager's career. We must create a steady stream of broad-gauged business managers coming into the top three levels of management. It will take some years before the stream appears and then becomes a source of critically need talent.
2. We must put in place an effective process to help managers to rethink, redefine, and redirect the business. This is a never-ending process. No fads please. You might ask consultants to help you design the process, but managers must do their own thinking, their own redesigning, and their own redirecting. How else will a manager develop skill and courage? The process should involve managers in their mid-thirties. In their mid-fifties some will become CEOs who know what needs to be done and can get it done. Won't it be nice to see pride restored where it belongs?
3. Let's get over our long-standing habit of relying on executive recruiters to save us from our historic ineptness. You can tell if you are making progress on the first three imperatives if each year you spend less on both management consultants and on executive recruiters.
4. Don't expect to get help from any advanced university program in solving your problem of developing entrepreneurial skills and confidence. They may help at the functional level but cross-functional moves and redefining ones business can only be done internally.
5. Do give serious consideration to splitting the chairman and the CEO positions, as GM is doing. Frankly, we can't develop the competencies needed in these two top positions in one individual, no matter how gifted. For years, Peter Drucker has been telling us it is not a one-person position. He was right. Isn't it amazing how slowly Drucker's good ideas catch on? The new chairman position puts a powerful person in a position to see that my imperatives are acted upon. The chairman will have board support.

So as I look back at my 1981 bromides I'm not very proud. Large companies didn't get the right message. Desperate situations call for basic changes. I'm optimistic that the giant company can and will change. We in HRPS have a choice. We can stand on the sidelines and wring our hands and wrinkle our brow or we can take another course on assertiveness so we can get our anxious but confused top management to work on basic problems and so, year after year. It will be a happy day when we can have a ceremony in which we give the new CEO a certificate of merit and, thus, avoid going to another farewell party.

SUCCESSION PLANNING: MASTERING THE BASICS

Eric W. Vetter

This article deals with the beginning of executive recruiting and the gradual development of succession planning. Since this is a highly visible part of HRP, it affords many opportunities for gaining credibility for the entire HRP process. Eric W. Vetter is Senior Vice President for Human Resources Development at Crocker National Bank in San Francisco.

A long-term retrospective on a human resource subject can be both interesting and informative and can help us understand the developments in the field. Looking back 30 years, we can observe that two relatively new HR activities were getting underway.

Executive recruiting was a post-World War II effort that was emerging as a real business. Indeed, the story goes that one founder of executive recruiting began his business in a Grand Central Station telephone booth with a pocket full of coins, calling prospective candidates and clients. He had moved out of the phone booth by 1954, but the new offices were not as high-toned as they are now. Executive recruiting was on the way.

Also 30 years ago, succession planning was getting underway and was being discussed in AMA and Conference Board meetings and articles. Color-coded organization charts showing backup candidates were described as the device to assure a supply of qualified managers for the future.

Now, the interesting observation is that executive recruiting is flourishing; indeed 1984 will probably be a record year for the business. But, as recruiters well know, good succession planning reduces the need for executive recruiting because candidates are available internally. Why, then, is executive recruiting flourishing when its antidote, succession planning, has been around for 30 years? Does succession planning work or is it just talk? The answer is that it can work. For success we must "master the basics" and not think that sophisticated new techniques are the answer.

Reprinted from *Human Resource Planning*, Vol. 7, No. 2 (1984), 99-104.

Let me provide a definition of succession planning so we are together. For this discussion, let's define it as the process by which the organization identifies candidates to succeed to a given position should the position become vacant during the planning horizon. If adequate backups are not identified, the process should cause a search for additional candidates and prompt development efforts for backups who are not "ready now." The process can identify a wide range of other HR problems and issues that require follow-up action such as misassignment, compensation inequities and marginal employee problems. The attention is usually directed at managers and key professionals.

The process can be quite formal and involve carefully prepared slides and color-coded charts. Or, it can be informal and involve lists of positions and managers and general discussion.

The measure of success of the activity is what happens as a consequence of the succession planning exercise. When I joined Gould a number of years ago, I found a nicely designed set of information forms in place for succession planning. Every division was reasonably reliable and on time in furnishing the information sought by the corporate HR staff. Questioning revealed, however, that the only thing that happened was to file confidential materials in a secured cabinet after a brief review by a middle manager.

The quality of the information was somewhat suspect because the Division General Managers were unsure how corporate was using the information. It was suggested that we revise the forms and talk to the divisions to obtain more information on backup candidates and high-potential managers.

The problem we had was not the quality of the information but rather a process that did not put the information to use. The solution was to organize review sessions for the CEO on the succession planning information, with an emphasis on correcting problems and developing key personnel.

Too often, however, the approach is to seek out the newest and finest techniques because the current formula isn't working. What are some of the state-of-the-arts approaches suggested as the solution to succession problems or as a way to enhance a process that isn't working?

One "modern" approach is to link succession planning to the strategy of the business. The logic is that if the business strategy is understood, the organization structure needed to implement the strategy can be defined. Then we are able to plan for candidates for new positions as well as for possible vacancies in existing positions. Because the strategy defines where we are taking our business enterprise, we need to define the human resources requirements for the strategy to succeed.

Equally as important, the business strategy can help us understand the nature of the talent we will need to fill future positions and vacancies.

What is the knowledge and experience managers should have? What skills should they have? What personal attributes will be important to success? A number of HR activities can be guided by this information; especially the identification of backups, their development needs and their utilization over time.

At this point it is important to observe that succession planning is basically a sub-element in the overall human resource planning effort. In HR planning the view is basically on macro issues; both problems and policies. Where will we be deploying our workforce? How many scarce engineers or scientists will we need and how will we obtain them? What type of corporate culture is desired?

These macro concerns are in contrast to the micro HR factors dealt with in succession planning. Who can replace Brown as the VP, Marketing, in the XYZ division? How do we internally develop generalist candidates for the top R&D position when we only need specialists to head up the labs? Can we cross-train Smith, a division controller, in both marketing and operations in order to be a backup candidate for the Division General Manager's job? Micro problems can add up to macro efforts such as identifying five potential General Managers for special development.

At this point we must ask just how much help is knowing the business strategy in dealing with Brown, Smith and the R&D situation? Unfortunately, it isn't too helpful. Succession planning problems are micro in nature while the business strategy is macro.

To be of direct help a business strategy would have to be highly polished, honed and tuned. Most strategies are not so finely detailed. Strategy formulation is a difficult analytical task and the strategic view of the business is always fragile because it is based on assumptions that are highly uncertain.

Let me illustrate. Several years ago in one division at Gould the five-year strategy was for growth via diversification. We were the supplier of a major component in a consumer durable sold nationally through a large mass merchandiser. The strategy was to use this high-volume core business as the economic base to do product and market diversification.

Capital budgets and staffing plans were tied to the strategy which all agreed was well conceived. Unfortunately, the mass merchandiser made the decision to change its marketing emphasis and sent the word that the product was being discontinued. Suddenly 30% of this capital intensive business was gone with only a 60-day notice. The strategy quickly changed from growth via diversification to one of reestablishing a core business. The staffing growth was curtailed and although marketing capability remained an important aspect for the future its focus and configuration needed to change.

For all businesses the future is uncertain. Oil embargoes, takeovers and mergers, acquisitions and divestitures, new competitors, high interest rates, product failures and technological breakthroughs are just some of the unforeseeable variables that can severely impact an otherwise good strategy.

Added to these factors is the recognition that in most instances a futuristic strategy will contain some significant departures from the past. It is not a business-as-usual view of things. It typically involves a break—a discontinuity. Certainly, every strategy has a risk element associated with it. Strategies that involve discontinuity have a high risk factor.

The details of a strategy, therefore, are not of special concern. The broad thrusts of how we must manage in the future are of concern. The fundamental issue in succession planning involves the individual competencies of managers. We may want more broadly experienced managers at the top in the future. We may feel that technological competence or marketing understanding will be more needed in the future. The strategic issue in succession planning is the type of manager we should be developing and bringing through the organization no matter what our business. The time tested managerial and leadership qualities of success are the factors that will determine whether our business will be a winner or a loser and not the strategic sophistication we incorporate into the succession plan.

A second state-of-the-art practice often discussed is to have an integrated information system aimed at the managerial and professional workforce. This kind of system can produce a wide variety of timely information in a very accurate manner. It provides information on performance, potential, managerial skills, career interests, work history, salary progression, language ability, education, key accomplishments, and similar items.

The premise is that in our succession planning this information will greatly enhance and enrich the process and the discussions. We will know in detail the managers under discussion and we won't be prone to err in judgment because critical data are lacking. Further, with this information we can use linear programming techniques, Markov chains and stochastic processes to study the stocks and flows of human resources throughout the organization. If you build an integrated and computerized information system, it is a reasonable step to move to the advanced state-of-the-art activity of mathematical modeling. The hardware is available, the software is available, and the prices are not all bad. "So. Why not? Let's go for it."

The reality is that what we really want in succession planning is qualitative first-hand information that does not lend itself to computer application. We want judgmental information from qualified observers on our managers. What are the managerial attributes of incumbents and backup candidates? How would they function in a different scenario? Can they grow a business or are they maintenance managers? What is their potential? What are their development needs? These are standard questions.

This information is subjective and we want it from people who are both keen observers of talent as well as successful leaders of enterprise.

We do not need information that has been sanitized, compressed, or coded because it has to get into the computer. If our managers, our senior managers, don't know the players well enough—either the incumbents or the backup candidates—then the information challenge is to engineer events so that the senior managers come to know the managers; not to give them computer printouts or similar material. Needed is a process that causes key managers, backups, and other critical human resources to become known by the CEO, the President, and other officers so they have personal first-hand information on the human resources who are vital to the success of the business today and tomorrow.

A popular subject, especially in the literature, is the third state-of-the-art approach: development of managers through organizational movement. This involves moving people across major organizational lines; not within a division but across division or group boundaries. In some organizations this is a stated major effort of succession planning. The object is to develop well rounded generalists to meet the business demands of the future. With the whole organization as a training ground, we can develop managerial career paths and career progression rates that provide a broad set of experiences. Positions such as product manager, financial analyst, and plant manager are usually regarded as good developmental positions, especially for high-potential managers.

The reality for most organizations today is that even filling current key vacancies from across the organization is difficult. The bench is pretty weak and moving people for development is not as easy as before. Further, American business slimmed down during the recession and the ongoing economic pressures are such that business is still eliminating many of the developmental positions. The assistant plant manager developmental position is disappearing as is the developmental district sales manager position. Companies that study costs are taking these kinds of jobs out of their organizations.

We also should note that there are few rewards for the manager who plays the developmental transfer game—even in good times. Most managers want to receive good talent. But, if we have an equal swap—lose a good person, get a good person—in bad times or in good times, we interrupt the momentum of the business and we have to train the new person. When the objective is purely developmental, and when it doesn't fit the needs of the business unit, the move is less than popular with the importing manager. The bonuses go to the profit makers much more often than to the people developers. Most firms do not have the long-term view of their business where the emphasis is on both of these abilities.

If the state-of-the-art approaches are not the answer, where should we direct our attention? I propose that we "master the basics." In most endeavors success goes to those who concentrate their energy on the fundamentals. In succession planning this means having clearly in mind a conceptual approach that fits the realities of the business and the management team.

A common malady that befalls the staff planner and analyst is to come to understand a situation in great depth. This understanding leads to solutions that can deal with the nuisances and complexities that become apparent with deep understanding. The contingencies are planned against. Over time the overall effort becomes complex and burdensome and fails to solve the problems for which the exercise was originally intended.

This leads to the first basic, that of perfecting the art of doing the doable. If cross-organizational moves do not make business sense we don't push such moves. The development process we design may be rather plain vanilla. It may be like what was described in the AMA and Concerned Board articles of the 1950s. But it should produce results. It aims at a 75% success factor against the objectives that are established.

The second basic is to design an information system that provides all of the relevant information in an easy to use and to manipulate form. The system should avoid information overload. It should not blur the attention of the users of the data. All that is needed for any organization unit are three forms that present standardized data in an easy-to-understand format.

One form is a human resource inventory that displays the organization: who are the incumbents?, what is their potential?, what is their performance?, what is their salary? You've seen these—they've been around a long time. The second form is a roster of the positions, the incumbents, the people who are "ready now" and those who will be ready in two or three years. The third form shows the development needs of the incumbents, the key backups, high potentials and other critical resources. Identifying just one relevant development need for each person for the coming period is probably all that is necessary. This approach will enable us to increase the probability that it will be achieved. Too often a laundry list of development needs is formulated and then little happens because the combined needs are overwhelming.

The third basic in succession planning is to cause review sessions to take place with the organization head presenting the HR situation to the next level or two of management and the appropriate HR managers. The necessary time is available; the clock is not the governor of the event. Interruptions are avoided. The discussion is open, thorough and provocative. The evaluations of the manager are challenged. The utilization of managers, especially the best managers, is of major concern as is the adequacy of staffing and the backup situation for key positions.

A fourth basic is that each review session results in specific outcomes that must be completed during the next 12 months by an accountable manager. Without action step outcomes, the sessions will come to be regarded as busy work and not part of the mainstream activity of the business. From each session we formulate 10 to 15 actions to include promotion, transfer, replacement, development, salary review and counselling. Putting these action steps into a written form that is updated quarterly for progress information is simple, easy and basic. Without the written hard copy document and the quarterly update, the action steps easily fade into the background as more immediately pressing actions take over the attention of the managers.

Fifth, emphasis in the identification of backup candidates is on those managers who will serve the organization well as role models. Most development takes place on the job. Therefore, we must be concerned with what our future teachers (i.e., those we identify as backups) will be modeling. Good role models set high standards, they hire quality people. they make tough decisions, they energize an organization, they build tone and pride, and they do a lot of other things often in subtle ways. I suspect that these managers are responsibility seekers who bring a lot of their intelligence, energy, positiveness and personal decency to their work.

We need to ask two basic questions regarding role models. If a backup succeeds to a job, what behavior will be modeled? We do not ask that question often enough. The second question is, what behavior do we want modeled? These two questions should provoke serious discussion about the direction we want our organization to go. Deciding who to groom and who to promote are important strategic decisions in human resource management. These people will run our business and send the signals to the organization on how to manage. And, they will do the selection and promotion of the next generation of managers who will become teachers to the rest of the organization.

In conclusion, let me observe that CEOs, Division Presidents and even SVPs of Human Resources have been known to seek "quick fixes" to problems. Often the glamour and promise of a scheme is appealing because it is a substitute for digging into a problem to learn what is going on and then working hard to achieve a sound solution.

Succession planning rests on intelligence, diligence, and insight. The computer, mathematics, cross-organizational movement of managers, and the overall business strategy have little to do with it. The task is to design a process that works. The high-potential, low-probability solution is worthless because our task is too important. The objective is not to put the executive recruiters out of business per se, but rather to help assure the survival and prosperity of our business.

Most CEOs want to know that the key positions in their organization are well staffed, that managers of promise are being developed and are not seeking careers elsewhere, and that each division has the human resources needed to "win." The challenge in succession planning is to cause these desires to become realities.

AFTERWARD COMMENTS

Eric Vetter

"As time goes by—things change."

"As time goes by—things stay the same."

Which is it?

In succession planning perhaps the saying should be: "as time goes by—things change in how we deal with the basics." That captures my views in the original article.

Basic succession planning challenges persist. Fortunately we have better technology to meet the challenges. And, good or bad, human judgement regarding performance and potential remains an imperative in succession planning.

Two basics stand out more clearly than ever. First, it is essential to have superior information on the capabilities of our key personnel and a strong commitment to develop these individuals. We need solid judgments—on how our key personnel are performing, why they are doing well or not so well, and a sound estimate of their future potential.

Second, we must know what will be important in future staffing considerations. In virtually all organizations this will mean more highly talented personnel whose value added contribution is greater than the average employee today. This translates into highly technically trained employees, adaptive individuals who can continue to make significant value-added contributions, and managers who excel in a total quality environment, a scarce resource environment, and a global environment.

AN INCIDENT OF FAULTY JUDGMENT

Let me relate an incident involving a division president. Every year Walt beat the plan for all of the important divisional financial and operating objectives. He generally achieved his bonus maximum. In Succession Planning he was regarded highly for current job performance and for his potential to run a larger division.

Information, however, began to reach me in HR from recent MBA-hires in Walt's division that they wanted reassignment. Then the long service division controller asked to be reassigned. Then the long service division controller asked to be reassigned. The group president at this point decided to find out if his top performing division had serious moral and organization problems.

Inquiry led to learning that Walt had evolved into a "driver" style manager to maintain his record of ever-improving business results. He was not concerned about "dead bodies." Far from being a leader he had become a liability. The divisional financial results were masking morale, motivation, and related organizational problems. When coaching and reassignment failed, Walt was released.

Obviously, the succession planning process was not working. Why? Simple enough. "Making plan" was the dominant criteria used to access performance and potential. Important processes of management were ignored. And, Walt's leadership ability was ignored.

In this company, the failure of the succession planning process resulted in bad staffing of a key position. The consequences? The cost to the organization of poor staffing is hard to determine. We can safely assume it is always significant. Unfortunately, bad staffing is recognized after the damage is done.

How can we improve our personnel judgments in succession planning? Several approaches are worth consideration. They involve new applications of ever improving technology.

ASSESSMENT INVENTORY: A VALUABLE TOOL

The first approach involves identifying assessment criteria that focus on the core managerial and leadership competencies needed today and foreseen for the future. These criteria are converted into a written inventory to help the manager think about his or her personnel and how they are achieving results.

It is not a test or measurement predication instrument with arithmetic results, norms, and comparisons. The criteria are kept current to meet evolving needs. Involvement of senior management in developing the criteria is important from the perspectives of relevancy, acceptance, and ownership.

The inventory is shared with the employee in the same manner as a performance appraisal. This discussion should include a self-assessment by the employee. The discussion results in a mutually agreed-upon development plan focused on current and future managerial and leadership needs. The sharing of results helps resolve perceptual differences between the employee and the manger. Overall results from the inventory can guide macro development efforts that are directed at factors important to the success of the organization.

The inventory fits the management style and culture of the organiza tion. It covers the knowledge, critical tasks, essential skills, and impor tant personal attributes and beliefs needed in the leader and the manager roles. The inventory also deals with the important strategic thrusts of the organization.

TRAINING MANAGERS IN ASSESSMENT TECHNIQUES

Related to this approach is the use of outside professionals to enhance internal succession planning judgments. The measurement instruments of the psychologist can help provide insights on the behavioral tendencies and style of managers.

Further, the outside professional consultant who comes to know our organization can bring politically neutral and objective views to the talent assessment. The professional is able to ask direct and sensitive questions that push us to a better understanding of our personnel.

The professionals are of major value when we use them to teach us how to better assess talent. They can help us identify the criteria we should assess against; they can help us identify the information we should collect on how our managers behave; they can teach how to ask pertinent and insightful questions about our talent; they can help us better understand the meaning of behaviors.

The importance of performance and potential assessments cannot be over-estimated. Assessment technology has existed for years. It keeps improving with time. When the experts teach us their techniques we can greatly improve our internal assessments.

LEARNING CAPABILITY—IMPORTANT POTENTIAL

A dimension of individual capability of increasing importance to future success involves learning capability and adaptability. The High Learner (High L) gains competency at an accelerated pace. We bet on High L's because they quickly and successfully assume increasing levels of responsibility.

High L's are highly motivated to seek and assume challenges that require developing new competencies. The High L debriefs his or her experiences with focus on why events behave as they do and what can be learned form the experience.

Complimenting these qualities are good general intelligence, a thirst for challenge, and a desire for action (decisive and sound decisions that keep events moving at a good pace).

Several weeks ago, I spent a week at an executive seminar with a rising executive who is now a successful CEO. As we flew home Roger asked a basic question "What did we learn this week?"

During the conversation I learned that Roger constantly asked this question of others. It provided the framework for him to better understand his objectives and to learn what others had gained from participation in the same events. It was especially important in his assessment of subordinates. It was how he learned how subordinates assimilated business experiences into insights on how to better manage their businesses.

IDENTIFYING FUTURE CRITICAL POSITIONS

The challenge of relating the business strategy to critical positions offers more promise today than ten years ago because our business strategies are better focused. In succession planning we must know how the organization expects to "win" in the future. This involves identifying our current core business competencies and what we will need in the future. We then translate core competencies into critical positions and critical skills. These are the positions that require major succession planning attention.

For example, in selling to retail outlets we now combine optical scanners, earth satellites, central computers, modems, and PC's to help route personnel decide how to stock a store. This is how it works. Daily sales data on company and competitor products are determined at checkout counters and fed to satellites that relay the information to company computers. Here the data are processed by decision models employing artificial intelligence developed by marketing software gurus. The AI models factor the market data into shelf-stocking guidelines for route personnel on a store-by-store basis. This information is fed first thing in the morning to a PC in the delivery truck.

The technology is costly but effective. Succession planning should assure that the human talent is available to sustain and enhance what has been a core technology involving superior decision making.

HELLO CAREER MANAGEMENT, GOODBYE CAREER PLANS AND PATHS

On reflection, it is quite apparent that another basic was not discussed in my 1984 article. This involves helping employees with career advancement. It merits significant attention today.

Employees are critical of succession planning that does not provide a payoff for their own careers. We hear comments such as: "What good is succession planning?" "Nobody I know can see how it makes any difference." "Why bother?" "What we need is real career planning and career paths."

Employees want the organization to be more involved in helping them "get ahead." The pressure for career guidance is rising because of continuous organizational and technological changes on jobs at all levels throughout the organization.

The stable organization with life-long employees is gone. The world of work is a threatening and dangerous environment for many people. Employees want to know what it takes to get ahead and they want the organization to provide the necessary training and job assignments.

Rapid changes in job content, job progression, and organization structure make it impossible to provide the structure and the guidance employees seek. We know that career plans and paths quickly become obsolete. These efforts become a negative with employees who do their share only to find the organization changes the job skill requirements and the career ladders and paths. In spite of our good intentions and sophisticated software, we cannot maintain reliable job skill and career information because of constant technological and organization changes.

PERSONAL CAREER MANAGEMENT

The organization can address the situation by developing a Personal Career Management (PCM) approach. Succession planning should not be viewed by employees as the system that deals with their career needs. PCM supports succession planning as a sub-system that provides the resources to enable employees to better manage their careers. It eschews career plans, ladders, and paths. It involves four elements:

1. Like earlier self-sufficiency efforts, PCM requires forceful communication to employees that "getting ahead" will grow as a challenge. It must drive the message that the key to career success is strong personal commitment to learning.

   Employees must understand that brainpower, skill, motivation and hard work are more important than ever. They must know that because the precise skills needed tomorrow cannot be predicted, it is imperative that they become good at learning. And, that they must acquire knowledge, skills, and attributes that can serve as foundation for success in a wide variety of job settings. These can be thought of as generic value-added abilities.

   Problem solving, influencing and persuasion, communication skills (of all kinds), and teamwork quickly come to mind as talents with application and life-long utility.

2. PCM provides aptitude and personality testing to foster self-understanding of talents and interests. A "great place to work" will have a PCM center staffed with professionals (internal or contract). The professional helps employees assess their talents and abilities and helps them formulate career plans int he context of life plans.

3. PCM helps employees become life-long learners. It teaches them to review what is happening in their lives, to identify what they are learning, and to debrief important experiences in order to accumulate "lessons learned."

PCM encourages attendance in extension courses that build mental muscle. In this regard it encourages enrollment in hard subject matters such as computer science, mathematics, chemistry, foreign languages, and statistics.

It encourages obtaining educational diplomas while making clear how the diploma will relate to opportunities. PCM fosters company-sponsored courses in many disciplines including vocational, technical, and administrative, as well as management and general degree courses.

4. PCM provides forums where successful employees from various levels and disciplines talk informally and answer questions regarding their careers and share their thoughts on what it takes to get ahead.

Co-workers are especially credible information sources. Their real experiences put truth into PCM observations such as: current performance leads to future opportunity; taking risk and seizing the moment is important; develop a mentor relationship with an insightful and trusted person; and you must never stop learning.

NO SHORTAGE OF CHALLENGE

The fundamentals remain vital to succession planning. As we move forward, the imperative is that we adapt new or existing technologies to deal with the basics. The winning organization learns and adapts because its human talent is distinguished by its superior ability to learn and adapt. In succession planning as in athletics, education, or general business success goes to those who master the basics.

IMPLEMENTING MANAGEMENT SUCCESSION PLANNING IN DIVERSIFIED COMPANIES

James W. Walker and Robert Armes

Companies have used replacement charts, management appraisals, and management education programs for decades. But today, diversified companies need more powerful, strategy-oriented processes to ensure that needed managerial talent is being developed. Successful implementation of succession planning usually requires shifts in management policy regarding managerial careers as well as commitment of time and resources to the process. The authors are with the management consulting firm of Towers, Perrin, Forster & Crosby.

T here is wide agreement on the importance of management development and the related planning activities necessary to make management development effective. A survey of practices in 167 companies conducted by The Conference Board in 1964 concluded:

Developing managerial competence occurs on the job. Recognizing this, many firms mold the work experiences of their managers by paying attention to sound organization planning, coaching by superiors, and the use of special assignments as a means for getting tasks done. Performance appraisal is used to stimulate and encourage managers to develop. Off-the-job methods are used to supplement the growth that occurs at work (Wikstrom, 1964).

Other publications have stressed that the process of developing managerial talent is a line responsibility, a long-range process, dependent upon the organizational climate and management style in a company, and dependent upon the initiative and effort of the individuals involved (Mahler, 1973; Ostrowski, 1968; English and Marchione, 1977; Desatnick, 1970; and Kellogg, 1977).

Reprinted from *Human Resource Planning*, Vol. 2, No. 3 (1979), 123-133.

There seems to have been little new thinking about management succession and development planning and even less innovation in actual company practices in this area. Planning for necessary on-the-job development experiences has largely occurred informally, or has been aided by "backup" or "replacement" charting techniques. The view of management development in many companies has not changed from the view stated in 1930 by the President of Standard Oil (New Jersey) in a letter to his company's top operating executives:

> The position of a corporation is measured not only by its assets, but also by its management, so that making provision for continuous efficient management is just as necessary as conserving assets. Therefore, every executive or head of a department should be continuously reviewing the abilities of his personnel and training them for positions of higher responsibility.
>
> The head of a company or a department may have been so intent upon his work that he has neglected, or has been reluctant, to delegate real authority to his subordinates. The result has been that on certain occasions when executive positions have had to be filled, trained and tested executive material has not been available.
>
> No executive can be said to have done his full duty unless and until he has made available for promotion to his position a man or men capable of assuming and administering his office (Habbe, 1950).

The responsibility for developing successors certainly rests with operating managers and development certainly occurs principally through on-the-job experience. However, the increasing complexity and scope of company organizations and of executive positions call for a more comprehensive process of planning for managerial succession and development. This article discusses the needs for a broader, future-oriented approach to management succession planning and requirements for its effective implementation in diversified businesses.

A Changing Context

Developing your own replacement may be an adequate answer to the management development question in a small, single-product, single-location business. This approach may even work, for a time, in a larger, multi-divisional or multi-location organization where each unit is charged with meeting its own managerial staffing needs. Even today, such large, diversified companies as Textron, ITT, United Technologies and Beatrice Foods have minimal corporate-wide coordination of management development activities. Where a philosophy of management calls for decentralized business autonomy, decentralized management development and succession may be appropriate.

In recent years, however, many large, diversified companies have identified a need to integrate their varied management development efforts and to project needs farther into the future. The development of backups for particular positions has yielded to the development of pools of more broadly-experienced and tested managers. Key executive positions go to individuals who have had experience in managing different functions and different product areas. In many cases, those key individuals advance who have been tested under fire by multiple managers, usually in an accelerated career path.

The pressures swell from various sources, most commonly, however, from a perceived shortage of managerial talent. Companies feel that their managers have been stretched by growing job demands and have been promoted rapidly, sometimes without an adequate cadre of additional talent moving up behind them. In many instances, growth has been achieved through acquisitions, where the acquired companies suffered from thin management ranks.

Another source of pressure is competition, including a rising quality of management performance in key competitor companies. Many banks, for example, became interested in the broadening and strengthening of their officer ranks when their competitors aggressively moved into previously secure markets and into new banking technologies. The intensive attention given managerial development in Citicorp, for example, is frequently cited as a factor contributing to its leadership position in banking. Conversely, oil companies and utilities tended to neglect management development until recently, in part due to a lack of competitive pressure or strains from within.

Competition for high-talent personnel itself is another source of pressure. A limited availability of engineering and scientific talent, particularly talent with potential for managerial careers, has impelled many companies to recast their management succession planning processes. Greater career expectations among high-potentials, high turnover (in the face of constrained compensation opportunities), and more vocal demands for responsibility and accelerated careers all are cited as characteristic of today's younger work force. Affirmative action programs, mandated by compliance agreements or by court-approved settlements of suits, have also drawn management attention and resources to management succession and development.

In the 1980s, a final source of pressure is likely to be acute: the need to maintain a lean organization while achieving strategic business objectives that are more difficult to attain. The cost-effectiveness of management staffing is increasingly subject to scrutiny. With slower economic

\d company) growth and with inflation beating on profit margins, com-
˛...ﬁes are reexamining their management staffing requirements, with the
view of having fewer, but better, managers. Merely grooming successors
does not address the need to change patterns of management staffing, quan-
titatively or qualitatively.

THE PROCESS OF SUCCESSION PLANNING

As illustrated in Figure 1, the management succession planning process involves matching projected supply of managerial talent with projected demands for talent. Implied is a need to interpret the strategic business plans of an organization and to project future organizational structure and staffing requirements, rather than succeeding existing managers.
Also implied is a pooling of candidates, individuals who might advance to
various positions, rather than pinpointing successors for specific positions.
Finally, the "bottom line" identified is developmental action—actually doing something to enhance the availability of needed talent.

FIGURE 1
Elements of Management Succession Planning

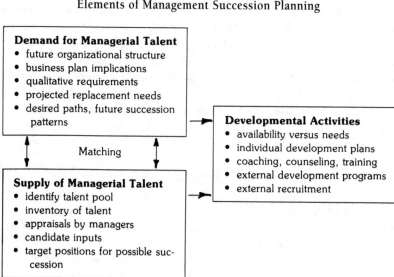

Three fundamental questions need to be considered:
1. Do we adequately know what our changing needs are or will be?
2. Do we know our people (high-potential managers) adequately?
3. Are we taking adequate actions now to meet our future needs?

These questions, which may be answered informally in small organizations, require a more comprehensive planning process in large, diversified businesses.

An understanding of future needs requires a management sense of evolving organizational identity and purpose. Management styles and capabilities must shift to accommodate new acquisitions and new qualities of a large and diverse business. Above all, management must decide whether its future senior managers should have experience in the different parts of the business, rather than single product or single technology experience.

Knowledge of the calibre of the talent available calls for more than individual manager's subjective appraisals. More objective yardsticks of "general manager potential" require testing of individuals on different assignments under different managers. Too often we see in individuals what we want to see (often reflections of ourselves) rather than what we ought to see in developing managers for the future. This suggests a limitation of relying on executives as mentors for promising individuals on a one-to-one basis.

Candidates should be made visible to senior management through a variety of challenging business assignments. Individuals should be held accountable for performance on each job and promotions should go to those who have successfully performed in different business environments and thus have developed a broad view of the corporation's strategy. Of course, this means that company policy must encourage innovative management assignments, careful tracking of performance, and the adoption of a "fall-back option" for individuals who take the risk and fail. High-talent individuals who follow this track are thus "corporate" talent, beyond the ownership of particular units. Implicit is a commitment to an investment in the development of these employees and the "forcing" of developmental assignments even where short-term, local business needs might dictate deferral of developmental activities.

OBSTACLES TO SUCCESSION PLANNING

The problems of management succession planning are not usually ones of concept. The kind of process outlined here reads like motherhood and is widely acknowledged as desirable. The problems typically lie in translating concepts into practice. Implementation is the key concern. The frustration of trying to develop managers *in practice* was highlighted by Theodore Alfred in a *Harvard Business Review* article over a decade ago:

> Most corporate practices make it possible for managers to hoard good people to the detriment of the total organization....Most corporate practices make it possible for a manager to promote from within his own department or from among his own acquaintances without considering others in the organization....An individual's opportunity to

be considered for other jobs in the organization depends far too much on his present supervisor's opinions and knowledge (Alfred, 1967).

To establish a broad management succession planning and development process, it is necessary for management to adopt a philosophy and to introduce the mechanisms necessary to effect change.

Figure 2 presents a series of shifts necessary for effective implementation of a succession planning process. Shifts in management approach are called for in defining managerial and staff responsibilities, in appraising individual potential and development needs, in managing career progression, and in planning development activities. Such shifts are particularly important as a company moves toward operating as a multiple product, multiple function, decentralized business. Geographic dispersion, rapid growth, international activities and acquisitions with different management approaches all complicate succession and development planning.

It seems that the required shifts in approach conflict with fundamental management attitudes, perhaps aspects of human nature itself. The shift calls for a coordinated approach, whereas a diverse business prides itself on its autonomy of management and the flexibility that accompanies autonomy. Immediate business needs command immediate attention, and talent, like any resource, is applied where it is needed to achieve results. Candidates may be reassigned, relocated, or held in a position to satisfy operating needs. Where operations are lean and margins thin, there may be little staffing slack for development activities; the highest-potential individuals may be those least easily spared for training or developmental assignments.

It is common, too, for managers to rely on personal knowledge and judgment in succession planning. Criteria frequently reflect the qualities and career paths of the managers themselves, or qualities the managers themselves would like to see in their proteges (a sort of Pygmalion theme in management development). An MBA degree or a technical background may be over- or under-rated. Sex, religion, race, age, and social relationships may bias assessments and thus actual succession and development plans. Aggressive individuals are sometimes quelled; candidates may advance who are no threat to the status quo and who will not leave. Those who leave are rationalized as "not so great, anyway."

Employees, too, may compound the effects of these obstacles. An increasing prevalence of dual careers, reluctance to relocate, and concern for the quality of life add to constraints on effective succession planning. Many talented candidates simply do not wish to pursue management careers if the toll on their personal lives is too high.

FIGURE 2
Necessary Shifts In Approach

Responsibility

Groom backup for your position ⟶ Develop pool of broadly qualified candidates

Decentralized development planning—each unit's responsibility ⟶ Centralized control over actual actions affecting key positions and candidates

Extensive staff activity in succession planning, with line input and reviews ⟶ Line responsibility with staff input and assistance

Appraisals

Subjective, informal appraisal or third party assessments (e.g., psychologist) ⟶ Systematic criterion-related appraisal by more than one manager

Criteria for appraisal subjective, often personality-oriented ⟶ Criteria defined by activities to be performed in the future

A select few have management potential and are developed as "high potentials" ⟶ Potential is widespread; screening should be wide and flexible. Don't zero in.

Career employment—tolerate marginal performer, reward service ⟶ Terminate or retrain marginal employees; unblock positions needed to develop managerial talent

Controlled, confidential system ⟶ Inputs from individuals, open discussions of actions, but no "promises"

Career Progression

Technical competence primary indicator of managerial potential ⟶ Abilities to manage in different functions, ability to learn quickly and to anticipate and manage change are keys

Progression up a function ladder is primary management path ⟶ Zig-zag (diamond pattern) progression across functions is primary path

Cross-functional moves after proven as managerial candidates late in careers ⟶ Cross-functional assignments early in career as soon as identified as possible managerial candidates

Development Activities

Training programs, executive development programs, seminars primary development activity ⟶ Sequential job assignments provide primary development experience, supplemented by specific programs

Staff for current needs, develop managers through performance demands ⟶ Allow slack in staffing to permit developmental assignments

Take advantage of vacancies to promote candidates ⟶ Create assignments for development purposes (e.g., exchanges, planned chain reactions)

Promote from within when qualified candidates; otherwise, recruit externally ⟶ Promote candidates when 70% qualified; recruit primarily inexperienced talent at entry level

Overcoming the Obstacles: A Case

The problems of implementing succession planning are overcome by adapting the management process to accommodate the necessary approach. Senior management, working through a strong decentralized line management organization, can bring about the shifts in management attitudes and practices called for. Staff and external consulting support provide assistance in implementing the changes.

AMC is a diversified manufacturer of industrial machinery with sales of $560 million. (AMC is a fictitious case, representing a synthesis of actual company characteristics.) The Power Systems Division, the major operating division of the company, represents the original company, American Machinery Company, which was founded in 1871. The company had pioneered the production of steam power units for agricultural and stationary industrial applications. In this century, the company has grown through introduction of new products developed by its industrial equipment division and through acquisitions. A major growth step occurred in 1959 when the company merged with a food processing equipment company, now representing a third operating division. Expansion has been dramatic during the past two decades, as the company has applied its engineering capabilities to energy recovery, pollution control, and industrial water conditioning.

The company operates 52 manufacturing facilities at 44 locations in the United States, Canada, and Europe. Operations are managed through six primary divisions, following product lines. The diversity of products, the number of locations, and the sheer size and rapid growth of the company necessitated a divisional structure with a central corporate management.

Since 1974, when George Sherman became President, the role of corporate management direction and controls has increased. A planning and budgeting process was installed in 1976 and staff functions for marketing, international, personnel, and operations effectiveness have been established.

Management Development Needs:

The character of management in AMC stems from the traditions of American Machinery. The company had always rewarded loyalty and service among its employees. Terminations were rare and there was little pressure for moving people across locations. Executives tended to be older, highly experienced individuals who had worked their way up the ladder over twenty or thirty years. Candidates for management vacancies were identified largely by personal knowledge, as the stronger performers were well known to the senior executives.

With the strains of growth and acquisitions, this approach seemed to break down. "People used to know everyone, but we don't anymore," observed one manager. Further, the supply of capable managers to fill new positions and take on greater responsibilities was felt by top management to be very thin. As a rule, the company had promoted from within, but in the past few years, Sherman felt the need to bring in some executives from other companies, notably the Vice Presidents for marketing and international. "We need to keep abreast of the latest techniques available if we are to take advantage of our opportunities for growth," he said.

A major obstacle to management development on a corporate-wide basis was the diversity of management styles across the company. The Power Systems Division, which had not changed appreciably over the years, continued to emphasize technical competencies and on-the-job development. Food Equipment had a different style, reflecting the strong marketing orientation of its business. This division had applied management by objectives in all aspects of its activities prior to the merger, reflecting management's concern for aggressive product marketing. The other four divisions, formed as ventures or acquired as small companies, lacked any formal management development systems. The executives felt they did not have the time or resources to give this area attention, even though they agreed it was highly desirable for the long term.

In a meeting of all the general managers, Sherman expressed concern that AMC needed to do a better job of identifying and developing its high potential employees. "Somebody really has to take responsibility to know these people, follow them, make judgements on them, and help them get the experiences they need to move ahead," he said. During the next five years, he observed, the corporation would need 300 managers for new positions and replacements for those retiring and leaving for other reasons. "We talk a good game in management development," he said, "but we frankly lack follow through."

Actions Taken:

Sherman then appointed an AMC Management Succession Committee, comprised of five of the general managers and chaired by himself. Over a six-month period, the Committee reviewed the company's practices, policies, and needs, with the assistance of external consultants.

Among the findings and conclusions discussed by the committee were the following:

- Individuals targeted for general management positions should have experience in at least two divisions and should have experience in marketing as well as manufacturing or engineering.
- The smaller divisions cannot reasonably be expected to develop talent for the larger divisions; nor should they be expected to select individuals for their own key positions solely from within their businesses.

- Greater exchange of talent between Food Equipment and Power Systems would be desirable, to bring fresh perspective and skills to each, as well as to broaden high-talent individuals.
- While there may be specific training needs that could be met by designing special programs within AMC, there appears no need for an extensive management education effort. The company's emphasis should continue to be on job-related experience, supplemented with external programs where candidates may mix with executives from other companies and industries.
- Many managers are not attuned to counseling with employees or even doing formal appraisals. To make management development effective, objectives and accountabilities should be built into the business planning process.
- Managers often fill jobs from within the divisions simply because they don't know other candidates; similarly, individuals don't know of career opportunities in other divisions.
- Needs for managerial talent in the growth areas will not be met by internal development. To the extent possible, younger talent should be hired into the established divisions and then transferred to the new areas as demands arise. This may require adding some developmental "slack" for these divisions and forced opening of some vacancies by terminations and retirement inducements.

It was clear early on in the discussions that there could not be a single succession planning process and inventory in AMC. Rather, the decentralized management approach called for each division to prepare development plans for its own high-talent employees and meet its own staffing needs. From the key functional manager level upward, however, the positions and candidates for these positions should be considered an AMC concern. There were 32 key management positions in this group, with obviously 32 incumbents. Additionally, an estimated 100 individuals (1% of the salaried work force) were considered possible management candidates for these key positions. This became the scope of the corporate process. An additional group approximately this size would be examined within each division. Development plans for individual candidates would be reviewed by the committee in an annual "Management Depth Review," identifying individuals available for developmental assignments across divisional lines.

It was also felt that the requirements of positions needed to be defined with a view to changing roles. "What are we developing people for?" It was agreed that pro forma position descriptions ("position profiles") should be developed for the key corporate positions as guides for identifying and developing candidates. The process could then be applied in a similar manner to key positions within each division. To help identify possible developmental assignments or alternative career paths across divisional and functional lines, career paths would be identified. A grid would indicate the exempt position titles by level across the organization, with supporting definition of the basic content and requirements of the positions.

None of these actions is unusual or profound. But together they provided AMC with a foundation for building a corporate-wide succession planning process. The strategy introduced new thinking and actions without undermining the strong decentralization characterizing AMC. The personnel staff roles remained consultative and supportive, without a centralization of the development process. The use of the committee allowed changes to be introduced through collaboration. The process created an awareness that AMC senior management expected the divisions to formalize their management succession and development activities and to draw them into some type of corporate process.

COMPLICATIONS

The larger the corporation, the more complex the design and administration of a process. As a corporation exceeds the billion dollar revenue mark, operating divisions may themselves be multidivisional. Thus, at each level of organization, succession planning needs to be integrated, providing developmental opportunities and managerial staffing plans to meet the needs. It has been this feature of bridging diverse businesses that has been the hallmark of development and succession planning processes in such highly regarded corporations as General Electric, Procter and Gamble, General Motors, Exxon, DuPont, and AT&T.

Finding the right balance between decentralized and centralized management practices is important as a company grows. Also, while large corporations have the benefit of a large talent pool to draw from and varied developmental opportunities to offer candidates, they may also face the greatest obstacles in maintaining a flow of talent to meet future needs. The businesses that need that talent most may not have it available; other businesses may suffer the elephantine problem of overstaffing, both with talented individuals and with plateaued performers. *Trying to optimize management staffing on a corporate wide basis involves both decentralized and centralized succession and development planning.*

The complication of the plateaued performer is particularly noteworthy today because of impending pressures on staffing levels and because of new protections given employees age 40 and over against employment discrimination relating to age. Forced early retirements, terminations to reduce staff, and even forced retirements at age 65 without adequate individual justification are now patently proscribed by federal and state laws. Thus, executives who have peaked and are blocking developmental career paths may have every right to stay on until age 70 if they wish (or later, depending on their retirement income and state law) (Walker and Lazer, 1978).

It may be, however, that organizational "deadwood" may be an overlooked energy resource. Management succession planning should include reassessment of individuals passed over for promotion or transfer, with the view of renewing their careers. Awareness of career planning, "the end of mandatory retirement," and of the deleterious effects of prospective inflation on retirement incomes have prompted many to seek new, challenging career shifts. In other cases, executives blocking development paths have accepted lateral or downward assignments in order to continue their careers. Companies facing a shortfall of capable managers and technical personnel have found this a valuable alternative to external recruiting in a tight labor market .

And there is the complication of slow growth. It is certainly easier and more fun to plan careers in a growth environment. Growth provides accelerated promotion opportunities, increased challenge, and pay increases. It also allows management to overlook shortcomings in individual capabilities and performance. But even when growth levels off, the pressures on performance and on selective placement of the most capable individuals become great. Progression opportunities slow down, the work force ages, and turnover declines. Stagnation becomes a risk that concerns management and succession planning becomes a tool for building vitality in the management organization.

Finally, succession planning is complicated when a diversified company lacks meaningful strategic planning. To be effective, management development and succession should be tailored to satisfy the changing requirements of the business, as reflected in long-range strategies. Where business plans are essentially short-range operating plans, few clues are given as to future needs. Supply data can be generated by establishing an inventory, introducing management appraisals, and formulating individual development plans. But the demand factor can only come from management plans and projected organizational needs.

A list of management conditions identified by a major commercial bank as necessary for implementing their management succession program is presented as Exhibit One. The conditions clearly point to the responsibilities of operating managers for the success of the program.

> **EXHIBIT ONE**
> **Necessary Conditions for Implementing Succession Planning**
>
> 1. **Assume corporate-level responsibility** for all assignments affecting key "corporate" positions and also developmental assignments of individuals identified as "corporate" management talent. Needs of particular departments may yield to corporate needs.
> 2. **Project future managerial requirements** 5–10 years ahead, both in qualitative and quantitative terms, as guides for appraising possible candidates and identifying developmental needs.
> 3. **Take time to appraise** individual candidates thoroughly and objectively and to coach them personally in their career development. Also, be willing to make difficult judgments which affect certain individuals adversely.
> 4. **Commit resources** (time and money) for the development of individuals; take risks to stretch and test individuals on developmental assignments. Long-term needs must take priority over short-term needs while sustaining requisite performance levels.
> 5. **Rely on staff** or consulting resources in the maintenance of the process while retaining direct involvement and responsibility for planning developmental activities. This may require providing additional staff resources.

CONCLUSIONS

This article proposes that management succession planning can be effectively implemented in diversified companies. The objective may be defined as a formal, systematic, corporate-wide process that will ensure that candidates are being effectively developed for key managerial positions five to ten years in the future.

The obstacles to succession planning lie in the implementation process. Significant shifts in management attitude and practice are needed to make succession planning effective on a corporate-wide basis. Additionally, implementation strategies need to build upon the strengths of decentralized organization while providing centralized guidance, coordination, and resources.

REFERENCES

Alfred, Theodore M, "Checkers or Choice in Manpower Management," *Harvard Business Review.* (January–February 1967). 157–168.

Desatnick, Robert L. *A Concise Guide to Management Development*, (New

York: AMACOM. 1970).

English, John and Anthony R. Marchione, "Nine Steps in Management Development." *Business Horizons.* (June 1977). 88–94.

Habbe, Stephen, *Company Programs of Executive Development.* Studies in Personnel Policy No. 107, (New York: National Industrial Conference Board, 1950).

Kellogg, Marion S., "Executive Development." in D. Yoder and H. Heneman (eds.), *ASPA Handbook of Personnel and Industrial Relations.* (Washington, D C.: Bureau of National Affairs, 1979).

Mahler, Walter F. and William F. Wrightnour, *Executive Continuity,* (Homewood, Illinois: Dow-Jones Irwin. 1973).

Ostrowski, Paul S., "Prerequisites for Effective Succession," *Management of Personnel Quarterly.* (Spring 1968) 10–16.

Walker, James W. and Harriet L. Lazer, *The End of Mandatory Retirement Implications for Management.* (New York: John Wiley and Sons, 1978).

Wikstrom, Walter S. *Developing Managerial Competence: Changing Concepts and Emerging Practices.* Studies in Personnel Policy No 189. (New York: The Conference Board, 1964).

AFTERWARD COMMENTS

James W. Walker, The Walker Group
Robert Armes, Towers Perrin

I s the process described in the article an applicable "best practice" for today and the future? When we wrote this article, companies were divisionalizing and decentralizing, requiring management succession and development planning to adapt and become more flexible and more focused on diverse business unit situations and requirements. This trend has accelerated, as companies seek to be market, focused, flatter, leaner, and high-performing.

Accordingly we are seeing an emphasis on management succession and development as a process of strategic importance—enabling a company to build needed leadership capability. It sets the pace and the standard for developing managers and employees at all other levels.

In the article we called for focus on changing needs, in both quantitative and qualitative terms. As companies perceive future requirements for executive leadership to be changing, this aspect of the process is receiving increased attention. Requirements may be specific to executive positions, types of positions (e.g., Regional VP), or to the company (e.g., AMC Manager of the Future profile). While some excellent leadership competency models have been developed by researchers and consultants over the years, these are not a substitute for company-specific competencies. In our view, best practices are applied when managers identify the relevant competency requirements before conducting individual assessment and development planning. In many companies, succession review meetings address requirements prior to any discussion of the talent.

Appraisal

We also called for executives to take time to appraise individual candidates thoroughly and objectively, and targeted the use of appraisals by multiple managers as necessary. Today, managers are often evaluated in part on how effectively they appraise and develop talent in their organizations. While managers in some companies see the process as required exercise, more are seeing it as a serious responsibility.

The use of 360 degree evaluation techniques is becoming more common (see, for example, the special double issue of *Human Resource Management* on this subject edited by Walter Tornow, Volume 32, Nos. 2 and 3, 1993.) While the primary benefit of multiple rater feedback is for performance improvement and development planning, multiple rater appraisals are also important as the basis for succession decisions. As executive selection decisions become more critical for businesses, techniques to improve quality, relevance, and objectivity of competency assessment will be used more intensely.

It is interesting to reflect that we have come a long way from the prevailing appraisal practices of the 1970s. Then, managers often rated candidates based on traits or personal characteristics; they rated potential and promotability in terms of how many levels a person may progress within five or ten years (and considered them qualities inherent in individuals). Current job performance appraisal was co-mingled with longer-term evaluations. We have largely changed the mindset of evaluation—today, potential is considered the capacity to learn at an accelerated rate. Our focus on development enables managers to tap and challenge this potential.

Job Assignments

In our article, we emphasized varied job assignments as important for career progression and managerial development. Today, position vacancies are widely considered to be the most valuable developmental resource available; succession planning needs to enable management to select the individuals for assignments who will benefit most from the developmental experience. The costs of relocation and job learning are high and need to be managed as development investments.

This focus is particularly important for international assignments, which provide valuable global perspective and operational management experience (and frequently profit and loss responsibility). According to a 1992 study, the most aggressive company practices intensely manage international assignments as part of succession and development plans (Tom Bechet, *International Executive Development Practices of Benchmark Survey Participants*, The Walker Group, Phoenix).

In relation to filling vacancies with development in mind, companies are also *creating* vacancies in some more planned way. Managerial assignments that key developmental position are too valuable to be filled by individuals who are "peaked and parked." By more carefully and aggressively evaluating potential and performance, individuals in management positions are identified who need to be redeployed, retrained, or moved out of the company.

The focus of succession planning has rapidly shifted away from merely identifying replacements for key position replacements towards development. As a result, companies are seeking to build talent pools—groups of individuals who are continually learning and developing as candidates for alternative future assignments. This was a new idea in the 1970s and was slow to be accepted because it challenged the established notion of "replacement planning." Flexibility is becoming vital as organizational and management staffing needs become increasingly fluid.

In some companies, we are seeing this flexibility extended to include managers who are external candidates (still working in other companies). In a fast-changing, diversified company environment, it may be practical and necessary to build a boundary-less talent pool rather than to try to develop all talent from within.

In summary, the trends we cited in 1979 are accentuated by today's urgent need for broadly experienced managers who can thrive in rapidly changing, divisionalized organizations.

Editors' Afterward

Assess your reaction to the fundamental practices that seemed to account for the success of this field, particularly those highlighted by this book. We have tried to capture in panel judgments, qualitative analysis techniques, and authors' opinion the practices that might be helpful for the twenty first century. The practices identified, integration, experiential learning, and commitment, seem straightforward enough. Perhaps too straightforward. Perhaps these strategic practices were too easy to identify and really consist of the *old rules* that best apply in our traditional, hierarchical, homeostatic organizations. Will these rules work in post-modern organizations characterized by an organic metaphor, where change is irreversible, structure fluid, and management strategies both global and local, integrated and inconsistent?

We do not know. We advise practitioners to adopt an experimental attitude. We sought to identify wisdom: distilled experience as a guide to future action and satisfactory implementation. We encourage you to use this wisdom as an adjunct to your own.

ALSO AVAILABLE FROM
THE HUMAN RESOURCE PLANNING SOCIETY

THE HRPS BEST PRACTICES SERIES

This series is designed to provide HR practitioners with valuable concepts, approaches, methods, and applications in subject areas of interest. Each book is developed by a team of editors who specialize in the subject area and presents what they have determined to be the "best practices" on important HR issues.

HUMAN RESOURCE FORECASTING AND MODELING

Editors: Dan Ward, Thomas P. Bechet, and Robert Tripp

A collection of proven techniques, models, and processes that have immediate applicability as a solid foundation in today's best practices and will also serve as a solid foundation for the next generation of workforce analysis and planning breakthroughs. Topics include: (1) concepts of modeling, (2) major types of models, (3) determinging workforce numbers, and (4) workforce diversity.

Price: $32 Current Member Price: $25

MANAGING STRATEGIC AND CULTURAL CHANGE IN ORGANIZATIONS

Editor: Craig Eric Schneier

This book examines what makes certain companies succeed in their transformations, while others struggle; the type of changes companies are attempting to make; and how they are making change happen. The three primary areas of focus are: (1) the leader's role in successful change efforts, (2) change approaches that work, and (3) companies' successful change experiences.

CORPORATE SPONSOR FORUM PROCEEDINGS

HR's ROLE IN BUSINESS EFFECTIVENESS . . . DIFFERENT ROADS TO A COMMON DESTINATION

Proceedings of the 1993 Corporate Sponsor Forum

These proceedings contain the following presentations: "Organizing HR Around Business Imperatives," Mark Bieler, Bankers Trust Company; HR at Ben & Jerry's . . . Principles, Practices and Lessons," David Barash, Ben & Jerry's Homemade, Inc.; "Business Performance Improvement—A Human Resource Perspective," Peter Mercer, Allied-Signal, Inc.; "Marriott

Corporation Case Study," Richard Bell-Irving, Leslie K. Cappetta, and Shonda D. Johnson, Marriott Hotels, Resort and Suites; "Crossfire Panel: The Future of the HR Function," James W. Fredrickson, University of Texas and Reuben Larson, Reuben A. Larson and Associates; "Cutting Edge and Beyond," Randall P. White, Center for Creative Leadership; Morgan McCall, University of Southern California; and, Jerry McAdams, Martiz Inc.

Price: $32 Current Member Price: $25

CHANGE AS THE STATUS QUO: IMPLICATIONS FOR HR PROFESSIONALS
Proceedings of the 1992 Corporate Sponsor Forum
This publication provides innovative ideas, insights and case studies on how organizations are dealing with today's constantly changing business environment. Included are: "IBM Workforce Solutions: The Changing Role of HR" by William J. Colucci, President, Workforce Solutions; "Motorola University: A Competitive Advantage" by Kenneth H. Hansen, Director, Educational Design Services, Motorola University; "Continuous Change: Converting to a Performance-Driven Corporate Culture" by Judith M. Bardwick, Management Consultant; and "Facing Change" by Felicia Zimmerman, Management Consultant.

Price: $32 Current Member Price: $25

DELIVERING THE FUTURE ORGANIZATION: KEY LEVERS FOR SUCCESS
Proceedings of the 1991 Corporate Sponsor Forum
These proceedings contain presentations from two leading academicians: Michael Beer, Harvard Business School, on "Critical Path to Corporate Renewal: Developing Human Resources While Focusing on the Business," and David Ulrich, University of Michigan, on "The Changing Expectations of HR: Anticipating HR in the Future." It also includes four case studies from top managers at key organizations: Deborah Smith, VP/Human Resources and Personnel Services, Xerox Corporation, "Quality—Managing the Human Resource Factor in the Pursuit of the Baldrige Award"; Walter Trosin, VP/Human Resources, Merck & Co., Inc., "Techniques for Producing Innovations in Technical Functions"; James Wessel, VP/Human Resources, Becton Dickinson, "Strategic HR Management at the Executive Level"; and Teri Teat, VP/Personnel Resources, American Airlines, "Using Leadership for Competitive Advantage."

Price: $32 Current Member Price: $25

OTHER HRPS PUBLICATIONS

ACHIEVING ORGANIZATIONAL SUCCESS THROUGH INNOVATIVE HUMAN RESOURCE STRATEGIES

Proceedings of the 1993 Research Symposium
This two-volume set contains 23 papers in six sections: Volume 1: (1) Emerging Organizations—five papers address various aspects of "the shape of things to come" (2) Managing Diversity—four papers on understanding and managing diversity (3) Building Competitive Advantage—three articles which address how HR can partner with management and the workforce to make the company perform better; Volume 2: (3) Building Competitive Advantage—two papers; (4) Quality and Customer Service—four papers describe efforts to do things better in regard to quality and customer service; (5) Managing the HR Function—this section features three articles dealing with the adoption of HR planning, benchmarking and HR's role in downsizings; and (6) Global HR Management—two articles which look at "HR going global" and Japanese/America experiences.

Two-volume set: $64 Current Member Price: $50

HUMAN RESOURCE PLANNING—SOLUTIONS TO KEY BUSINESS ISSUES

Edited by David M. Schweiger and Klaus Papenfuss.
Published by Gabler Publishing.
Contains selected readings from the journal on management practices required for business success. This book is a response to the social, legal, and economic changes of the past decade that have made employees increasingly important to the success of their organizations, but have also made them more complex to manage. Intended for executives who want to manage their employees more effectively, contains material on the human resource function in transition, strategic human resource planning, mergers and acquisitions, performance appraisal and performance management, compensation, succession planning and executive development, and strategic responses to changing work and family issues.

Price: $52 Current Member Price: $36

QUARTERLY JOURNAL

HUMAN RESOURCE PLANNING

Contains current theory, research, and practice in strategic human resource management. Focuses on the HR practices that contribute to the achievement of organizational effectiveness. At least one special issue a year focuses on a single key topic such as "Balancing Worklife and Family," "Globalization," "Executive Resource Planning and Development," or "Service Quality and Organizational Effectiveness." Back issues are available.

1994 Subscription rates (Volume 17): $80 Domestic, $94 Canada (and International)

Discount available for multiple subscriptions to same address (5+ issues)

TO ORDER PUBLICATIONS,
OR FOR MORE INFORMATION,
CALL OR FAX HRPS AT:
212/490-6387
(FAX) 212/682-6851